INTRODUCTORY COMPUTER SCIENCE

COMPUTER SCIENCE PRESS

Alfred V. Aho, Columbia University; Jeffrey D. Ullman, Stanford University
Foundations of Computer Science: Pascal Edition
Foundations of Computer Science: C Edition

Michael J. Clancy, University of California at Berkeley
Marcia C. Linn, University of California at Berkeley
Designing Pascal Solutions: A Case Study Approach
Designing Pascal Solutions: Case Studies Using Data Structures

A. K. Dewdney, University of Western Ontario
The New Turing Omnibus: 66 Excursions in Computer Science
Introductory Computer Science: Bits of Theory, Bytes of Practice

Robert Floyd, Stanford University; Richard Beigel, Yale University
The Language of Machines: An Introduction to Computability and Formal Languages

Michael R. Garey, Bell Laboratories; David S. Johnson, Bell Laboratories
Computers and Intractability: A Guide to the Theory of NP-Completeness

Judith L. Gersting, University of Hawaii at Hilo
Mathematical Structures for Computer Science, Third Edition
Visual Basic™ Programming: A Laboratory Approach

Ellis Horowitz, University of Southern California; Sartaj Sahni, University of Florida
Fundamentals of Data Structures in Pascal, Fourth Edition

Ellis Horowitz, University of Southern California; Sartaj Sahni, University of Florida;
Susan Anderson-Freed, Illinois Wesleyan University
Fundamentals of Data Structures in C

Ellis Horowitz, University of Southern California; Sartaj Sahni, University of Florida;
Dinesh Mehta, University of Tennessee Space Institute
Fundamentals of Data Structures in C++

Ellis Horowitz, University of Southern California; Sartaj Sahni, University of Florida;
Sanguthevar Rajasekaran, University of Florida
Computer Algorithms

Thomas W. Parsons, Hofstra University
Introduction to Compiler Construction

Gregory J. E. Rawlins, Indiana University
Compared to What? An Introduction to the Analysis of Algorithms

Wei-Min Shen, Microelectronics and Computer Technology Corporation
Autonomous Learning from the Environment

James A. Storer, Brandeis University
Data Compression: Methods and Theory

Steven Tanimoto, University of Washington
Elements of Artificial Intelligence Using Common Lisp, Second Edition

Kim W. Tracy, AT&T Bell Laboratories; Peter Bouthoorn, Gröningen University
Object-Oriented Artificial Intelligence Using C++

Jeffrey D. Ullman, Stanford University
Principles of Database and Knowledge-Base Systems, Vol I: Classical Database Systems
Principles of Database and Knowledge-Base Systems, Vol II: The New Technologies

INTRODUCTORY COMPUTER SCIENCE

Bits of Theory, Bytes of Practice

A. K. Dewdney

The University of Western Ontario

Computer Science Press
An imprint of W. H. Freeman and Company
New York

This book is dedicated to Florence Ecclestone (née Donner), who was as good as aunts get.

Library of Congress Cataloging-in-Publication Data

Dewdney, A. K.

Introductory computer science : bits of theory, bytes of practice / A. K. Dewdney

p. cm.

Includes index.

ISBN 0-7167-8286-3

1. Computer science. I. Title.

QA76.D447 1996

004—dc20 95-52602

CIP

Printed in the United States of America

The fish graphic on page 105 is Image FISH13©1992 by Mike Miller, created using POV-Ray ray tracer. Used with permission of POV-Team.

Design and production by Editorial Services of New England

Computer Science Press
An imprint of W. H. Freeman and Company
41 Madison Avenue, New York, NY 10010
Houndmills, Basingstoke RG21 6XS, England

Contents

Preface

TO THE INSTRUCTOR

Today millions of computers silently shuffle cascades of electrons behind their grey or black facades. And today's students, whatever their major, will increasingly rely on these marvelous machines. Will they understand computers? Will they be prepared for future developments?

I wrote this textbook because I believe that every student needs an introduction to the basic ideas of computer science. Every student deserves to enjoy it, too. Unfortunately, introductory textbooks short-change students by teaching only programming. Computer science majors recover from this treatment in the semesters that follow the freshman year, but non-majors are stranded on this beach. By now there are millions out there who believe that computer science is programming! This simple fact has surely damaged public understanding of the computer revolution. After all, some of those nonmajors ended up with the media. How often do you hear the phrase "computer science" misused as public television runs rampant through "cyberspace"?

This lamentable state of affairs must change, and this book provides a gentle nudge in that direction.

Where Are We Going?

This book has three broad aims. First, students should come to appreciate the power of computer science as an indispensable background for understanding today's computer-dominated world. Here, in the world of all possible programs and all possible machines, I begin with a particular computer in Chapter 1 and awaken the program sleeping within it. The distinction between hardware and software is the first of many crucial ideas that will clarify computer science for the nonmajor.

Second, a student is cheated by any course that attempts to teach "computer literacy" without a real taste of programming. I have chosen Turbo Pascal as the course language because it is the most popular Pascal around, while Pascal itself continues to enjoy high currency in universities. It has a clean, simple structure that makes teaching it to undergraduates a joy.

Finally, students need all the help they can get in what might well be their only exposure to the science of computing and the art of programming. I have organized every chapter around a project that starts with a problem to be solved, moves on to an algorithm to be designed, then presents a program to be written and tested. This approach permits time to talk to the student, weaving new programming ideas and computer science concepts into the fabric of each project as we go. This approach is demonstrably superior to the traditional, concept-example-concept-example approach. Students are far more likely to care about and remember concepts as parts of a meaningful story (the project) than as isolated program fragments that by themselves go nowhere.

Features

Projects Each chapter of *Introductory Computer Science* begins with a project—and never lets it go. As the chapter's ideas and programs develop, that project continues to unfold, almost like a story. Whether to write a simple tutorial program for children learning arithmetic or to write a program that encodes secret messages, the project provides a focus for the student to absorb certain new programming ideas. This approach naturally illustrates the usefulness of these ideas not by means of artificial and isolated examples, but by the organic process of solving a problem that the student has learned to care about. The project teaches not only new programming ideas but also knowledge from computer science and, inevitably, a few key mathematical ideas that lie at the very foundation of computing and much else in this high-tech world.

Graphics *Introductory Computer Science* enlivens the learning experience of nonmajors still further by stressing computer graphics, something still rare in introductory texts. Graphic software makes the operation of a program visible in a way that number-spewing programs cannot match. Here, students see investments grow in vertical bars of color or watch a simulation of an Internet server backing up with red messages.

Boxes Students who turn aside from the reading adventure of any chapter may rest in the shade of a box. Some boxes provide additional details of the Turbo Pascal language. Other boxes explain knowledge brought in from the outside world to make a particular program work. Still other boxes take the student aside to explain puzzling peculiarities, such as why programmers think they are programs.

Explorations Each chapter of *Introductory Computer Science* comes equipped, at the end, with Explorations. They begin with simple questions that test the student's understanding of the most basic programming and computer science concepts introduced in the chapter. Further explorations then lead into the programming project developed in the chapter. Students may be asked to modify the program in a simple way, then run it and report on the results of the modification. In subsequent questions, students may be asked to analyze a similar program, to change an entire section of the program, or even write a whole new program that solves a similar problem. Interspersed with these programming explorations are questions that probe the student's ability to think abstractly about bits, bytes, numbers, simple data structures, and other key concepts from computer science.

Organization of the Book

The book begins with an imagined journey in the computer itself, finding within its hardware memory a sleeping program called Chaos that can be awakened with the press of a key. On examining the program we begin, almost without realizing it, to learn some Turbo Pascal. In my experience, the nonmajor is intellectually robust enough to appreciate a simple working Turbo Pascal program even before he or she has a complete knowledge of the language constructs involved. Students get off to a running start.

The next three chapters offer a more standard presentation. Nevertheless, new programming concepts are used immediately—and not in trivial examples. Each project is designed to engage students' attention from the beginning of the chapter until the end. By the time students get to Chapters 5, 6, and 7, they are merrily designing elevators, piling up data in histograms, and even simulating an Internet server! As they go, they have simultaneously learned about conditional statements and Boolean expressions (the elevator), three types of loop (the histogram project), and functions and procedures (the server simulation).

In subsequent chapters students write an encryption program, conduct a race between two programs, and finish with sorting and editing files. In these chapters they learn about characters and text files (encryption), algorithmic analysis and complexity (the program race), and record data types (sorting a file).

The motivational approach, rushing as it does to the climax of a finished program, must sometimes omit key details of various Turbo Pascal statements that, although not relevant to the project in hand, may be important in other projects of the student's own undertaking. For this reason, I have also included an appendix—called the Turbo Pascal Advisory—that contains some additional language details.

Supplementary Materials

This book is accompanied by an *Instructor's Manual* and an *Instructor's Disk* containing programs and relevant files.

The *Instructor's Manual* provides guidance on teaching from this book, including solutions to Explorations and special pointers to topics with which nonmajors often have difficulty. The pointers are embedded in a lecture-by-lecture schedule for instructors who prefer a moderate pace—the pace at which I myself teach the course. Instructors with special requirements may prefer to set their own pace, even choosing to skip a chapter or two. For these teachers I include a collection of additional projects at intermediate up to advanced levels. Why not write your own chapter based on one of these projects?

The *Instructor's Disk* contains Turbo Pascal source code for every program that appears in the book (except for fragments and extremely short examples). It begins with a helpful "read me" feature followed by a menu that permits access to individual items. You may readily compile any or all of the programs into executable form suitable for your particular educational computing environment. Although you will find it convenient to have these programs available for downloading or for disk entry, I think it is advisable, especially in the early stages, for students to type in their programs. The *Instructor's Disk* also contains the relevant files for the programs that appear in the later chapters.

TO THE STUDENT

If you drop a computer from the top of a tall building, it will fall to the ground with a horrendous crash and abruptly cease to work. This book is about computers, programs, and computer science. I have just illustrated the very important distinction between the first two. You can drop computer hardware from a tall building (or have David Letterman do it), but you can't drop a program from a tall building. It doesn't even make any sense.

If the new machine has a soul, it is the program. Without a program in it, the computer is nothing more than an expensive paperweight. Without a program, a computer could not keep track of aircraft in the crucial task of air traffic control. Without a program, a computer could not enable munchkins to play Zapping Zork.

In the pages ahead you will appreciate this distinction as never before. You will understand computer hardware not in excruciating detail but in general view, enough to appreciate that programs run on computers one step at a time, for example.

Once you understand thought patterns like these, you will also come to appreciate the incredible power of computer science. Computer science is a set of ideas that fit not only the hardware and software you will see in the pages ahead but all possible machines and programs, even ones that aliens might invent! That possibility alone ought to keep you on the edge of your seat.

I would be immodest if I said that you're lucky to have this book for your course. Instead, I will say that you would be lucky to have a book like this one. Yours is the first generation with a chance to avoid being short-changed by pure programming textbooks. To see what I mean, sneak a glance at To the Instructor.

ACKNOWLEDGMENTS

I wish to thank those most directly involved in this project, starting with John Haber. With monumental patience and the keen editorial eye that distinguishes all Freeman editors, John has guided *Introductory Computer Science* through the valley of readers, the mountains of drafts, and on to the plains of production. Marching at his side, Penelope Hull has hacked her own share of verbose underbrush and kept the author honest, as to both content and schedule.

Special mention must go to Burton Gabriel, who conceived of this project before going on to better things, to publisher Richard Bonacci, who had the wisdom and patience to see the project through, and to the thoughful reviewers who kept the book on solid pedagogical rails: John H. Avila, San Jose State University; Aija Downing, University of Western Ontario; Ed C. Epp, University of Portland; Ann R. Ford, University of Michigan; Brian Harvey, University of California, Berkeley; Jeff Jenness, Arkansas State University; Margaret Johnson, Stanford University; Daniel T. Joyce, Villanova University; Kenneth G. Krauss, Northampton Community College; Stephen P. Leach, Florida State University; Craig Partridge, Stanford University; and Dale Shaffer, Lander University.

1 A Program Called Chaos

Hardware Meets Software

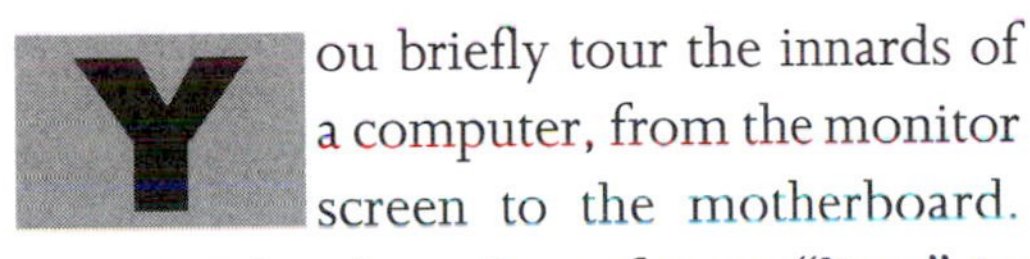

You briefly tour the innards of a computer, from the monitor screen to the motherboard. Your route through the hardware reveals where the software "lives" in the computer, namely, in the computer's memory chips. The distinction between hardware and software is crucial to those discovering computers and programming for the first time. It is the key component in any reasonable definition of computer literacy.

You learn that computer hardware is structured in a way that makes understanding it unnecessary in the programming process. At the same time, hardware has its fascinations for some people.

You discover that the home of software is in the memory chips, and you encounter software in the form of a Pascal program that is stored there. This program illustrates some key concepts of Pascal, a programming language. This program can be understood readily, even by a beginner. At the end of the chapter, numerous "explorations" allow you to tinker with the program and to test yourself on some of the other concepts introduced in what follows.

It's a bit of an oversimplification, but you could say that hardware is material and software is, well, ethereal.

Inside the Computer

It's late, and you sit in front of the computer, staring, almost hypnotized, at the screen. You wonder what goes on behind it. You know that computers are very complicated. But, actually, a computer is merely a collection of simpler parts.

The screen by itself is easy to understand. It not only looks like a television screen, it *is* one. But this screen doesn't show a television program. It shows computer *programs* in action. These carefully constructed series of statements bring the hardware to life. On the screen you may see

1. the *name* of a program, as in a menu or a directory, for example
2. the *listing* of a computer program, that is, a list of the instructions that make up the program
3. (most exciting) the *output* of a program. Output consists of the numbers, text, or graphics produced by a program as it tackles the problem that it was written to solve.

Anything is possible—almost literally—when you run a computer program. It all depends on the program—the software!

software = programs

This is the very first lesson in computing, the one essential fact that makes almost everything that follows much easier to understand. The physical computer, the *hardware*, houses *software*, or programs. The computer does nothing; the programs do everything. Am I being unfair to the hardware? The physical computer, after all, *executes* the programs. (This doesn't mean the hardware kills the programs.) The hardware carries out a program's instructions to the letter. In this sense, the software is the boss and the hardware the worker.

A Program Called *Chaos*

Consider again the most obvious part of the computer's hardware, the one you look at most often—the screen. Suppose you have called up a computer directory listing on the screen. There before you, etched in light, are the names of several programs. One of the programs catches your eye. *Chaos*. It sounds like a game. You find yourself pressing the keys that take you into the Turbo Pascal programming system. The program *Chaos* is written in a specific language called Turbo Pascal, the language used throughout this book. The Turbo Pascal programming system, whether based on DOS or Windows, gives you the option of running this or any other Turbo Pascal program listed in the directory.

You type in the name of the program and press the button that brings the listing of *Chaos* to the screen. In a twinkling, the listing appears in front of you. It's written in Turbo Pascal, of course, but at the moment it might as well be in Sanskrit. You find that you can run a program by selecting the RUN option on the screen. The screen then goes blank. The program is running. A message appears:

```
Enter a number between 0 and 1.
```

To "enter" something in the computer, you press the appropriate keys for the thing being entered, whether a name or a number. Then you press the ENTER key. You decide that "a number between 0 and 1" must be a decimal number, such as 0.5 or 0.8224761628. A computer doesn't normally recognize fractional numbers like 4/9, even though fractions also happen to represent (for humans) numbers between 0 and 1. Tentatively, you enter 0.5, having no idea what will happen next. The instant your finger presses the ENTER key, zzz-i-p, the game of chaos is over. The program called *Chaos* has printed ten numbers on the screen below the number you typed.

Output of the Program Called *Chaos*

```
Enter a number between 0 and 1.
0.5
0.9750
0.0951
0.3355
0.8695
0.4426
0.9622
0.1420
0.4751
0.9726
0.1040
```

This is chaos? Yes. You will discover later in the chapter that *chaos* is a word that physicists use to describe certain physical systems that have unpredictable behavior. At the moment, the significance of chaos lies solely in furnishing just one example of a computer program among millions. This particular program happens to be so simple that you can understand it after receiving only a brief explanation of how it works.

In the meantime, all you see are the ten numbers that the program has generated. How did it do this? Being too tired to think about it anymore, you turn off the computer. Time to get some sleep.

A Journey Behind the Screen

While you're sleeping, you might as well dream about something useful. So let me take you on a quick tour of some computer hardware. It won't be exactly the same computer that you just turned off because (a) I don't know what kind of computer you happen to be using and (b) the dream computer has been simplified in ways that make it easier to understand. I call the dream computer the Simplex 2000. You begin moving slowly toward the letters on the screen, toward the E of "Enter." You are about to embark on a short journey into the heart of the computer. There you will discover something about the difference between hardware and software.

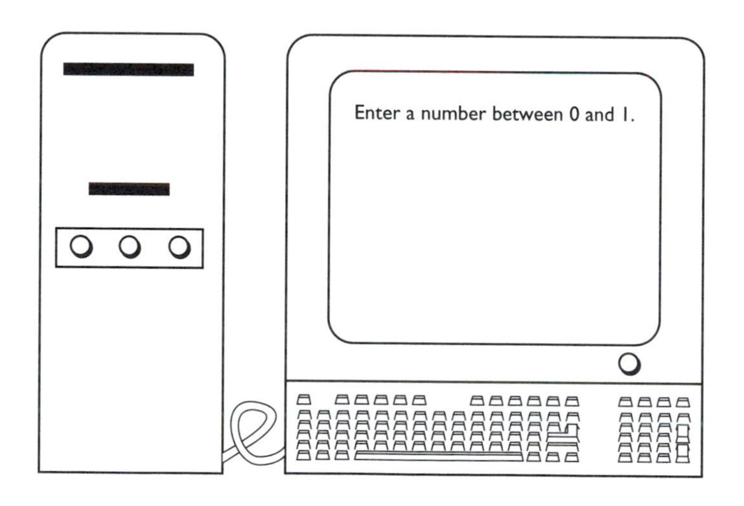
Enter a number between 0 and 1.

The Simplex 2000

The screen is hardware. It's made of a physical material—glass—that is coated on one side (the inside) with a phosphor compound that lights up when electrons strike it. The E, created by the impact of electrons on phosphor, must arise, somehow, from the software called *Chaos*. Let's follow the E back to its source.

As you approach the screen, the E looms and dissolves into a collection of huge dots as you pass right through the glass of the screen as though it weren't there. In doing so, you also pass through the phosphor that coats the back of the glass. The dots all came from an electron gun at the back of the screen. You follow the E-shaped beam of electrons to the back of the picture tube, where some wire coils surround a short cylindrical object, the electron gun itself. One of the wires that enters the gun, the control wire, carries all the information. The other two wires cause the electron beam to sweep across the screen many times a second. But the control wire carries a signal that turns the gun on and off thousands of times every second. It creates the E by turning the gun on just long enough, as the beam sweeps swiftly past, to paint each little dot on the screen. It creates all the other letters in the message by the same method.

For some people, this is a dream of wonder; for others, it's an electronic nightmare. Remarkably, both kinds of people can be equally effective programmers and equally able to understand basic computer science.

The letter E as a dot matrix

Chips and Real Estate

The journey to the source of the message continues backward along the electron gun's control wire, into the heart of the Simplex 2000. You follow the wire along a cable that leads out the back of the monitor and down into the back of the gray box beside it, where several circuit boards carry other essential hardware. The circuit boards resemble alien cities. Miniature silver highways run here and there between resistors, capacitors, and mysterious black "chips" that now, to your miniature eyes, resemble buildings. You encounter two boards on your electronic journey, the video board and the motherboard.

On the video board, the wire you follow enters one of the chips, the one generating the signals that produce the message on your screen. In this chip, the message consists of *bits*, that is, on-signals and off-signals. Although you have become very small, you are not small enough to notice the electronic signal-bits that zip along the metallic highway below your feet.

The video board is not the ultimate source of the software (the *Chaos* program) that you are trying to track down, however. After all, the characters that the computer displays on the screen only pass through this chip on their way to the screen. So you follow another wire that leads from the video board to another board, the most important one in the Simplex 2000 computer—the motherboard. This hardware houses the real action.

Technical Terms

Any technical term that is not italicized need not be remembered. It's like the place name of a town that you pass through on your way to a more important destination. Italicized terms, both here and in later chapters, are important. You should eventually understand what they mean. You don't necessarily have to remember them now because you'll meet them again, later in this book. If you can't remember what a certain term means, merely look it up in the index at the back of the book. The number of every page on which the term appears is listed in the index, and the number for the page that contains the most useful description or definition of the term is printed in boldface type. You can turn to that page whenever you need to rediscover the meaning of a term.

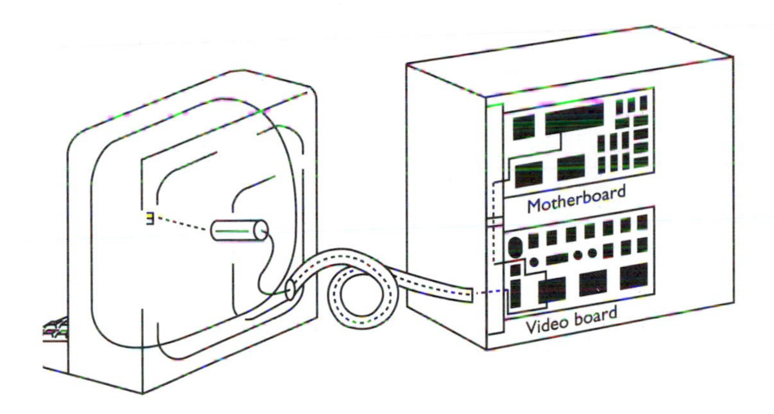

The path that leads to the program

As you can see in the accompanying illustration, the motherboard resembles an industrial park more than a city. It is packed with large black chips, all interconnected by those ubiquitous metallic roads. The two most important kinds of chips on the motherboard are memory chips and the microprocessor. The road you are following takes you to one of the memory chips. Here, concealed inside the chip's plastic casing is another "city" that looks even stranger than the first one. Hardly wider or thicker than a large postage stamp, it nevertheless contains a vast territory in the eyes of the chip designers. They refer to this tiny silicon city as "real estate." On it, they have laid out an enormous pattern of pathways and junctions in silicon, polysilicon, and aluminum. The portion displayed in the illustration on the next page occupies an area so small that it would easily fit inside the period at the end of this sentence.

The pathways and junctions amount to millions of transistors, the basic functional units of the computer. Each transistor happens to be in one of two states referred to as "off" or "on." More abstractly, you can also refer to these states as 0 and 1. You will see why, presently.

The Source of the Code

The transistors that make up the computer's memory contain the 0's and 1's that represent all the information that a computer stores or processes. You can't tell by looking at the illustration, but the transistors form natural groupings in which the 0's and 1's amount to a single piece of information, such as an alphabetic character. Thus, if you had the patience

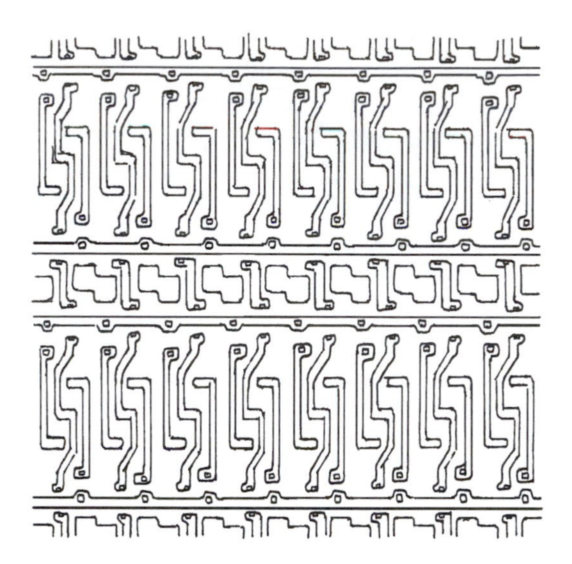

A small part of a memory chip

and the knowledge, you could reconstruct the information carried in memory by assembling the 0's and 1's into alphabetic and numeric characters.

Luckily, this is a dream, where such things can happen, as if by magic. Suppose the characters lurking in this portion of memory have been reconstituted, and you can read the memory as a series of lines, each containing a line of the program called *Chaos*. You can even see the E of "Enter" in the fifth line from the top of the program. This line is the origin of the E on the screen. Hardware at last gives way to software.

The *Chaos* Program

```
PROGRAM Chaos;
VAR Xvar: REAL;
VAR Count: INTEGER;
BEGIN
WRITELN('Enter a number between 0 and 1.');
READLN(Xvar);
FOR Count := 1 TO 10 DO
   BEGIN
   Xvar := 3.9*Xvar*(1-Xvar);
```

```
    WRITELN(Xvar:6:4);
    END;
END.
```

This program, written in the computer language Turbo Pascal, is said to be in *source code*. Another version of the program, called the *executable code*, is the one that actually *runs*. In other words, the computer obeys the instructions in the executable version of the program, but it does no harm to pretend that a program in source code runs. In fact, most programmers talk about "running" their source code program as if the executable version didn't even exist.

If the *Chaos* program were to run right after you saw it on the screen, it would display the following message:

```
Enter a number between 0 and 1.
```

At that point, the microprocessor chip has just executed the statement on the fifth line of the *Chaos* program but is waiting to execute the statement on the sixth line:

```
READLN (Xvar);
```

Something is holding the computer up. You'll see why by the time my explanation of the program reaches line 6.

The *Chaos* program, like any other program, consists of *statements*. For present purposes, I shall describe these as separate lines of the program, each a miniature task that the computer must execute, or carry out. Taken together, and performed in the right order, these small tasks become one large task that is greater than the sum of its parts.

Inside the Program

The programmer who wrote the *Chaos* program wanted to illustrate the physical process called chaos (see the box on page 16) by simulating it with a computer program. To explain the program, I will go through it, one statement at a time. I will explain what each statement means and how it works in the context of the program. This will be your first introduction to Turbo Pascal. In later chapters, you will encounter these statements again and deepen your knowledge of how they work.

The *Chaos* program is typical of Turbo Pascal programs in the way in which its sections are organized. First comes a *header* (the word PROGRAM and the name of the program), followed by a *declaration section* in which the program declares its variables:

```
PROGRAM Chaos;          } header
VAR Xvar: REAL;         }
VAR Count: INTEGER;     }  declaration section
```

The declaration section of a Turbo Pascal program tells the computer the names it will use. Such names include not only the name of the program (*Chaos*), but the names of the variables (*Xvar* and *Count*). You may recall from math courses that a variable is just any quantity that varies. You could consider your own age to be a variable, for example. Once a year, this variable increases by 1.

Following the declaration section, the next (and final) section of the *Chaos* program is called the *main body*. In any Pascal program, the main body always begins with the Turbo Pascal word BEGIN and ends, logically enough, with the Pascal word END, followed by a period.

```
BEGIN
WRITELN ('Enter a number between 0 and 1.');
READLN (Xvar);
FOR Count := 1 TO 10 DO
   BEGIN
   Xvar := 3.9*Xvar*(1-Xvar);
   WRITELN(Xvar:6:4);
   END;
END.
```

The main body of the *Chaos* program is not exactly transparent to untutored eyes, so let's take it apart further. The first part could be called a *prompt* because here the program tells the user that some input is expected. The program prompts the user for a number.

```
WRITELN ('Enter a number between 0 and 1.');
READLN (Xvar);
```

Conventional Thinking

In presenting Turbo Pascal programs, I use several helpful conventions. Although nothing in the Turbo Pascal language requires this, I shall use capital letters for words that belong to the Pascal language and mixed uppercase and lowercase letters for names that a programmer has selected for use in a program. The person who wrote the *Chaos* program, for example, used the Turbo Pascal words PROGRAM, VAR, REAL, and INTEGER in the declaration section. He also used words of his own devising: *Chaos*, *Xvar*, and *Count*. This convention makes programs very easy to read, because you can see at a glance which words are Turbo Pascal words and which were selected by a programmer.

Another convention that makes programs easy to read calls for the indentation of certain statements. Some statements in Turbo Pascal contain other statements within them. Such compound statements can be confusing to read, so programmers frequently indent the contained statements. The FOR-statement in the *Chaos* program, for example, is a statement that contains two other statements, sandwiched between the Turbo Pascal words BEGIN and END. This part of the program is indented.

Turbo Pascal programs would run just as well if these conventions were not used, but they would not be as easy to read or understand.

The first statement, containing the word WRITELN, sends a message (within the parentheses) to the screen.

```
Enter a number between 0 and 1.
```

Whenever the computer executes a WRITELN statement with a message inside its parentheses, the computer prints that message on the screen.

The next statement contains the Turbo Pascal word READLN followed by the variable name *Xvar* inside parentheses. Whenever the computer executes a READLN statement, it must wait until the user of the program enters the required data, in this case, a number between 0 and 1. As soon as the user enters this data, the computer stores it in memory under the name *Xvar*. So, when the *Chaos* program runs, the computer pauses at the READLN statement and waits. It will wait until someone enters the required data or turns the computer off. If neither of these events occurs, it will wait until the universe ends.

So far, the program has informed the computer about its own name and the names of its variables. Then it has prompted the user to enter a number that the program needs. Now the program is ready for the final phase of its execution, as specified by its third and final part, called a loop:

```
FOR Count := 1 TO 10 DO
   BEGIN
   Xvar := 3.9*Xvar*(1-Xvar);
   WRITELN(Xvar:6:4);
   END;
```

This loop introduces you to a very important feature of Turbo Pascal programming—or any other kind of programming, for that matter. A *loop* is a statement that enables a certain computation to be repeated over and over again. Your life is full of loops. For example, when you unpack books from a box, you might well employ a loop of sorts. You take a book out of the box and place it on the shelf. Then you take another book out of the box and place it on the shelf. Then you take another book . . . . You will even find some loops specified on commercial products. A tube of Head and Shoulders® shampoo, for example, contains the following instructions:

Rinse, lather, repeat.

Being a computer scientist, I once took these instructions too literally. I rinsed my hair, then lathered it. The tube said to "repeat," so I went to the beginning of the instructions. I rinsed my hair, then lathered it. The tube said to "repeat," so I. . . .

The third part of the *Chaos* program body is called a loop because the computer will cycle through these statements, over and over again, until the program causes it to stop (a most important requirement). This particular loop is called a *FOR-loop* because it contains the Turbo Pascal word FOR. Like all FOR-loops, it consists of a loop control part and a loop body.

I can "translate" the loop control into an equivalent statement in English:

> "For each value of the variable *Count*, starting at 1 and ending at 10, execute each of the following statements once."

Just as the *Chaos* program itself has a body, enclosed by the BEGIN–END pair of Pascal words, so FOR-loops may have a body that is also enclosed by a BEGIN–END pair. Between the BEGIN and the END of the *Chaos* FOR-loop are just two statements:

```
Xvar := 3.9*Xvar*(1-Xvar);
WRITELN(Xvar:6:4);
```

According to my translation, this body of two statements will be executed once for each value of the variable called *Count*, from 1 to 10. The effect would be exactly the same if this section of the program simply consisted of these two statements repeated ten times:

```
Xvar := 3.9*Xvar*(1-Xvar);
WRITELN(Xvar:6:4);
Xvar := 3.9*Xvar*(1-Xvar);
WRITELN(Xvar:6:4);
Xvar := 3.9*Xvar*(1-Xvar);
WRITELN(Xvar:6:4);
Xvar := 3.9*Xvar*(1-Xvar);
WRITELN(Xvar:6:4);
Xvar := 3.9*Xvar*(1-Xvar);
WRITELN(Xvar:6:4);
Xvar := 3.9*Xvar*(1-Xvar);
WRITELN(Xvar:6:4);
Xvar := 3.9*Xvar*(1-Xvar);
WRITELN(Xvar:6:4);
Xvar := 3.9*Xvar*(1-Xvar);
WRITELN(Xvar:6:4);
Xvar := 3.9*Xvar*(1-Xvar);
WRITELN(Xvar:6:4);
Xvar := 3.9*Xvar*(1-Xvar);
WRITELN(Xvar:6:4);
```

You can see why loops are handy! They obviously save the programmer a lot of writing time. In any case, only one unanalyzed thing remains in the *Chaos* program, namely, the two statements themselves:

```
Xvar := 3.9*Xvar*(1-Xvar);
WRITELN(Xvar:6:4);
```

The first statement in the loop is called an *assignment statement*, because it assigns a value to the variable that appears on the left-hand side of the := symbol—called the *assignment operator*. How does it arrive at such a value? On the right-hand side of the := symbol, you will usually find a formula of some kind that the computer must evaluate. The assignment statement in the *Chaos* program, for example, has the following formula, or *expression*, to the right of the := symbol:

```
3.9*Xvar*(1-Xvar)
```

This expression is pretty easy to understand once you know that the asterisk (*) means "multiply." The minus sign (-) means "subtract," as you might suspect. So now you could work out the value of this expression yourself if someone gave you a value for *Xvar* to substitute into the expression.

Every variable that is stored in any computer's memory has a value at all times, once the variable has received its first value. When the computer executes the READLN statement, *Xvar* receives its first meaningful value—whatever the user decides to type in.

Let's return to your dream. Suppose you type in a value, say, 0.5. The computer can now get on with its business of executing the program. As soon as it has the value 0.5 safely tucked away in memory under the variable name *Xvar*, the computer begins to execute the loop. It does this by setting the variable *Count* equal to 1, then goes on to execute the first of the two statements inside the loop body, namely, the assignment statement.

The expression to the right of the := symbol contains the variable *Xvar*, so the computer looks up the stored value of this variable and finds 0.5. It then substitutes the value 0.5 for both occurrences of *Xvar* in the expression. Effectively, this substitution yields the following calculation for the computer to make. As I mentioned earlier, you could easily do this calculation yourself as follows:

```
  3.9*0.5*(1-0.5)
= 3.9*0.5*(0.5)
= 3.9*0.25
= 0.975
```

The computer can evaluate this formula much faster than you or I can, of course, but it arrives at the same answer. It completes the execution of the assignment statement by assigning the resulting number, 0.975, to the variable *Xvar*. In other words, it stores this new value for the variable *Xvar* under the name *Xvar* in its memory.

The second statement inside the FOR-loop happens to be another WRITELN, something you already know a little about. In executing this statement, the computer sends the number 0.975 to the computer screen (see the display on page 3.) Actually, the computer displays the number as 0.9750, an extra 0 having been added. The reason for this is close at hand. Within the WRITELN statement, the variable *Xvar* is followed by a curious set of colons and numbers, namely, :6:4. This is called *formatted output*. It means that six spaces are allocated to the displayed value of *Xvar*, four of them for decimal digits, the other two for the decimal point and one whole-number digit. The computer added an extra zero to the answer in order to conform to this format.

The FOR-loop causes the computer to execute the two statements inside the loop body ten times each. But each time it executes the statements anew—that is, for each *iteration*, as programmers say—the computer has a new value for the variable *Xvar*. For example, when it executes the statements for the second time, the variable *Xvar* stored in its memory has the value 0.975. Because of the new value of *Xvar*, the effective formula is now

```
  3.9*0.975*(1-0.975)
= 3.9*0.975*(0.025)
= 3.9*0.0244
= 0.0951
```

This result is the very next number that the Simplex 2000 computer displays on its screen as it executes the FOR-loop.

Over and over again, the computer, under the direction of the FOR-loop, iterates the loop body until the FOR-loop tells the computer to stop. Each time the computer produces a new value for *Xvar*, it substitutes that value into the formula for the next iteration.

Chaos

The program presented in this chapter mimics the physical phenomenon known to physicists and mathematicians as chaos. This phenomenon, thanks to public television, is widely misunderstood. It does not mean that a physical system behaves wildly; rather, a chaotic system merely acts in a manner that is hard to predict, even with a computer. Let me illustrate this point.

The formula in the *Chaos* program is one of many possible chaotic formulas. This particular formula describes the behavior of a particular unstable electronic circuit. It also describes an idealized population of animals, some predators, others prey. If the variable *Xvar* (see the program) represents the number of predators that live in a given area, then each time the formula is evaluated and a new value assigned to *Xvar*, some simulated time has passed and you get a new population level for the predators.

```
Xvar := 3.9*Xvar*(1-Xvar)
```

When a computer calculates the formula over and over again, each time assigning a new value to *Xvar*, a sequence of numbers results. If you start with a value of 0.5 for *Xvar*, you get the sequence of numbers listed earlier. Compare those values (listed in the middle column below) with the values that result from the starting value of 0.51 for X (the right-hand column):

	***Starting value of* X:**	
Iteration	**0.50**	**0.51**
1	0.9750	0.9746
2	0.0951	0.0965
3	0.3355	0.3401
4	0.8695	0.8752
5	0.4426	0.4259
6	0.9622	0.9536

Iteration	0.50	0.51
7	0.1420	0.1726
8	0.4751	0.5570
9	0.9726	0.9623
10	0.1040	0.1414
11	0.3634	0.4734
12	0.9023	0.9722
13	0.3439	0.1052
14	0.8799	0.3672

Although the starting values of 0.50 and 0.51 do not differ by very much, it doesn't take very long for the two sets of numbers to begin differing wildly. By the fourteenth calculation, they are completely different. This is "chaos."

Why is chaos important? The problem is significant because of the ability of a computer to use ultra precise numbers. Every computer (even the Simplex 2000) has a characteristic number of digits that it carries in dealing with the numbers it computes. When a computer executes a chaotic formula, the precision of its values becomes crucial. Even a difference in the twentieth decimal place between two starting values can make a world of difference in the output after only a few calculations have been computed.

Consider what happens when, in the course of calculating a chaotic formula, a computer runs into its own lack of precision. Its inability to carry numbers to 21 places, for example, would mean that when 21 or more are required for full precision, the values that it produces for *Xvar* will be slightly off. The slight difference between the true and computed values soon balloons into a huge difference, and we can no longer say that the computer is accurately representing what would really be going on in the real system under study.

When we try to track the behavior of a chaotic system, even by computer, we ultimately fail because eventually the demands for precision outstrip the computer we happen to be using.

By now, you understand that the assignment operator (:=) doesn't mean the same thing as an ordinary equality symbol. The assignment operator does not mean that two quantities are equal to begin with, only that they will be when the assignment is complete. An assignment statement makes the variable on the left side of the := symbol equal to the value of the formula by simply assigning that value to the variable.

As the computer executes the loop body over and over again, it keeps adding 1 to the variable called Count. In the first iteration of the loop, Count equals 1. In the next iteration, Count equals 2, then 3, and so on. Shortly after Count reaches the value of 10, the loop body has been executed ten times. That's when the computer stops. The FOR statement specified that the loop ends when the value of Count equals 10. The computer does not always stop when it comes to an END word. The END in the FOR-loop simply tells the computer that the FOR-loop has no other statements in it.

The last line of the Turbo Pascal program called *Chaos* consists of the Turbo Pascal word END, followed by a period. This not only marks the END of the program's statements, the computer stops here, as well.

You have taken a brief tour of the computer hardware, followed the path of display information back into the box, and arrived finally at one of the memory chips where a program was stored. Here was software in its ultimate home, stored as a stable pattern of 0's and 1's. But only you "saw" the program in its human-readable form called source code. Going over the meaning of the statements has enabled you to begin learning not only a little about programs in general but about Turbo Pascal in particular.

Awakening from the dream, you realize you know the difference between hardware and software. As you progress through this book, however, your grasp of this knowledge will improve. In the meantime, you can review some of the crucial preliminaries of Turbo Pascal programming to which the tour introduced you.

Statements and Syntax

The *Chaos* program contains examples of no less than seven different statement kinds.

```
PROGRAM Chaos;
VAR Xvar: REAL;
VAR Count: INTEGER;
```

```
BEGIN
WRITELN ('Enter a number between 0 and 1.');
READLN (Xvar);
FOR Count := 1 TO 10 DO
   BEGIN
   Xvar := 3.9*Xvar*(1-Xvar);
   WRITELN(Xvar:6:4);
   END;
END.
```

These statements are organized into three distinct sections that all Turbo Pascal programs share.

- Program header. This statement declares the name of a program to the computer. The computer will always refer to the program by this name. The header always consists of the Turbo Pascal word PROGRAM followed by the name of the program, in this case, *Chaos*. A program header is one kind of Turbo Pascal statement.
- Variable declarations. Any program that uses variables must declare them right after the program header. Turbo Pascal programs declare simple variables by using the Pascal keyword VAR followed by the name of the variable (given by the programmer), followed by the *variable type*. You will learn about the types REAL and INTEGER in Chapter 3. The variable declaration is another kind of Turbo Pascal statement.
- Main body. The main body of a Turbo Pascal program is sandwiched between Turbo Pascal words BEGIN and END. These words are called *statement delimiters*. The main body of a program itself happens to be a statement. Within this compound statement, you will find the WRITELN and READLN statements, two more kinds of Turbo Pascal statements. You will also find the FOR-loop, itself a statement with BEGIN and END delimiters. And inside the BEGIN and END of the FOR-loop, you will find an assignment statement, as well as another WRITELN statement.

All Turbo Pascal statements follow rules of *syntax*. Such rules control the form that a statement may take. In general, different kinds of statements follow different forms. Among other things, this generalization means that not all versions of a statement that are meaningful to you will be accepted by the computer. For example, suppose a programmer tried to use a loop control like this:

```
FOR Count := 1 TO 10 DO THE FOLLOWING
```

The computer would not accept this as a valid part of a FOR-loop. The loop control must end with the word DO (and that word alone) right after the limit value 10. The DO, in turn, must be followed by the body of the FOR-loop.

A more general rule states that all Turbo Pascal statements must end with a semicolon (;). You are permitted to omit semicolons only for statements that immediately precede the word END. In this book, I leave such semicolons in. Failure to add the semicolon elsewhere, even once, may prevent a program from running. The very next chapter will begin a process that will continue throughout this book. Each time I introduce a new kind of Turbo Pascal statement, I will also add a precise description of its syntax.

The Invisible Machine

Although hardware has its fascinations, the student of computer science will find that the biggest adventures await in the realm of software. Computers are structured, after all, to make the hardware invisible (and irrelevant). In fact, someone who believed that all programs are executed by genies could still be a perfectly good programmer! The principle is worth stating:

> Computers are designed to execute programs line by line, in sequential order, except as directed by loops and other controlling statements. They are further designed to make software transparent and completely independent of the hardware.

You have already seen this principle in action. The *Chaos* program was executed in sequential, line-by-line fashion. But this sequential scheme was interrupted by the loop in which the two statements of the loop body were executed over and over again, a total of ten times. A program departs from the sequential execution scheme only under the direction of certain Turbo Pascal statements, such as a FOR-loop. You will learn about other statements that affect the order of execution in due course.

Finally, by transparent software, I mean software written in a language that is easy for humans to read and understand (source code as opposed to executable code). A program is independent of hardware when it runs on any computer that supports the programming system on which the program is based, Turbo Pascal in this case.

Bits into Numbers

A simple example of the execution principle in action involves the way a computer stores the numbers with which you are familiar. All information processed within your computer takes the form, ultimately, of bits—short for binary digits. Luckily, it is easy to understand (a) why computers use bits and (b) how bits can be used to represent numbers and all the other kinds of information that a computer might process.

Computers use bits because, as you saw during your tour of the Simplex 2000, they store and transmit information by using electronic elements that are always either in a state of high voltage or low voltage. We call these states 1 and 0. Just as a decimal digit may be 0, 1, 2, and so forth, up to 9 (ten possible values), so a binary digit (or bit) may be 0 or 1 (two possible values). This greatly reduced range of values is not as great a disadvantage as it may seem at first. It all depends on how you put these bits together.

In the computer's memory and in many other places in the computer hardware, the basic binary elements are organized into *registers*, each consisting of a fixed number of such elements. The accompanying figure shows a register that consists of eight binary elements. Each element stores either a 0 or a 1.

11001001

How do these rafts of bits turn into the numbers that we are used to? The answer lies in the *binary number system*. To understand this system, you only need to reflect for a moment on the decimal number system. A decimal number like 209, for example, actually represents the result of adding together the following powers of ten, each multiplied by one of the decimal digits in this number:

$$(2 \times 10^2) + (0 \times 10^1) + (9 \times 10^0)$$

Of course, 10^1 is just 10 and 10^0 is just 1, so the result of adding these numbers together is 209—not a surprise. The point is that all decimal numbers can be thought of as sums of powers of 10, each power multiplied by the appropriate decimal digit from the number.

The same thing is true of binary numbers, except that now you must use powers of 2 instead of powers of 10. Take, for example the binary number 11010001. If you write this number out as powers of 2, you get an expression that is somewhat longer than the previous one involving powers of 10.

$$(1 \times 2^7) + (1 \times 2^6) + (0 \times 2^5) + (1 \times 2^4) + (0 \times 2^3) + (0 \times 2^2) + (0 \times 2^1) + (1 \times 2^0)$$

If you multiply seven 2's together, you get 128. Similarly, 2^6 is 64. The remaining powers of 2 are 32, 16, 8, 4, 2, and 1. If you add together only those powers of 2 that are multiplied by 1 and express the result in the standard decimal notation, you get 209. (I admit that I arranged the bits to come out with this result. But it's a quick way of demonstrating the equivalence of the two number systems.)

Computer registers are often called *words*. Every computer has a typical size of register called its *word size*. The size of a word is just the number of bits in it. In the simplest kind of computer memory, each word would hold one item of information. For example, the eight-bit word shown above is capable of storing 2^8 or 256 different binary numbers, from 0 to 255. If it were to need larger numbers, the computer's words would be linked together systematically to make even larger words.

Besides numbers, a computer must store letters and other keyboard characters. With 256 different binary patterns available, an eight-bit word, for example, has more than enough capacity to represent all the characters of the keyboard (considerably fewer than 256). By international convention, all computers use the same numerical codes to represent keyboard characters and other information. Recall your tour of the computer hardware in which you finally found the E stored in memory as a sequence of bits. The actual sequence, according to this convention, would be 01000101. In decimal notation, this is the number 69.

But who wants to work in binary when it's possible to work in decimal numbers? Your keyboard has decimal digits on it; and these digits also have code numbers so that the computer can translate quickly and efficiently between its own internal binary system and the decimal system that the user is more familiar with. Don't worry exactly how the computer does this. However, I will note in passing that this is just one small example of how computers are structured to make the hardware invisible. You don't see bits, you see ordinary numbers instead.

What Is Computer Science?

I have spoken about hardware and software, but what of the "computer science" in the book's title? Within the discipline of computer science are many divisions, or subdisciplines. Some of these lean toward technology, because they are concerned more or less exclusively with the development of new techniques for handling information. Other subdisciplines lean toward science, because they involve the discovery of new general theories that govern the process of computation. I will discuss the main technological disciplines first.

Many computer scientists take a keen interest in *computer architecture.* Typically, these individuals work with large units within the computer, designing and arranging them to maximize the speed or usefulness of the machine or to minimize the manufacturing cost. For example, a computer architect may look for the best way of organizing memory or the central processing unit (CPU), a chip where programs are interpreted. He or she may also be involved at a higher level of organization, attempting to organize the entire machine for optimum performance. In this book I have very little to say about computer architecture.

Computer scientists involved in *software engineering* seek to develop new techniques for organizing really large programming projects, both in the way that such programs are structured and how human beings can divide up the programming work. In the final chapter of this book you can read about a large programming project suitable for nonmajors and, through it, appreciate what it takes to coordinate a team of programmers.

Compiler design concerns the way that programs in specific languages are translated into executable code for specific types of computers. *Language design* addresses the issue of what instruction types are most appropriate in various programming settings. The compiler that comes with your Turbo Pascal programming system translates Turbo Pascal programs into an executable form.

A few computer scientists may seek to develop new *applications* programs, but this task tends to be the province of programmers working for large and small software firms. Most applications, after all, have commercial potential. It was applications programmers who brought out the first popular spreadsheets like Lotus 1-2-3 and the first widely used word processors like WordPerfect and Microsoft Word. In a wider sense, and with somewhat less commercial emphasis, there is a whole world of applications programs that find more restricted use, such as airline scheduling programs or weather forecasting software. In this book, you will see a number of simple applications programs developed before your very eyes.

Computer scientists who design new *operating systems* find themselves fascinated by the collection of special programs that make it possible for computers to run in the first place. A major program called the *operating system* (disk operating system, or DOS, in IBM-compatible computers) orchestrates all the other programs that read input from the keyboard, compile programs, organize data on the disk, and so on. As you use your computer to explore the projects in this book, you will come to appreciate the myriad functions that operating systems make available.

Database design concerns the organization of data and ways of probing that data. This discipline emphasizes very large collections of data and the investigation of general techniques for recalling database items with various qualities of interest to potential users. Although you will not be designing any databases in the near future, you will learn some techniques for storing and retrieving large amounts of information.

There are also scientific disciplines within computer science. While the foregoing fields use some mathematics, they rarely develop it. The following subdisciplines could well be regarded as branches of mathematics.

Computer scientists working in the field of *data structures* survey the possibilities for storing data in various structures such as tables, trees, networks, and other configurations. Accompanying methods for storing data in the structure, changing it, and retrieving it must be proved fast and effective.

Many who work in the field of *logic design* develop circuits that carry out specific goals such as multiplying or sorting and have an optimum simplicity that can be proved mathematically. In Chapter 4, you will discover the basic elements with which these theorists work, the "gates" of logic.

There are abstract concepts that embrace everything that computers are or ever could be! The discipline of *automata theory* (which you will encounter in the very next chapter) analyzes abstract machines that resemble board games with moving counters.

Another important area, called *complexity theory*, addresses how quickly programs can complete their tasks. In a surprising number of cases, it is the theorists who have the final say, even in areas such as hardware design and software applications. In Chapter 9, you will witness a race between two programs as an illustration of this theory.

The Road Ahead

In the coming chapters, you will not only learn some valuable computer science, you will also learn more about Turbo Pascal. Each chapter will introduce new statement types or deepen your knowledge about statements with which you are already familiar. The vehicle for these lessons will be projects, starting in the very next chapter. There, you will follow the steps of development for a simple program that tutors grade school children in basic arithmetic. In the chapter after that, you will participate in the design of an investment tracking program. Whatever else you study, there is a good chance you will find an area of interest all your own in the pages ahead.

Through it all, expect your knowledge of both computer science and programming to broaden. In the end, not only will you be computer literate in the best and fullest sense, you will even muse, as you type a report on your favorite word processing software, on how the various parts of it might be programmed. In any event, those who know nothing of programming will spend their lives as software slaves, destined always to buy programs written by others. You, on the other hand, will have the option of developing your skills (if you wish) to the point of writing your own special purpose programs.

SUMMARY

In this chapter, you took a brief tour of computer hardware, in search of a program called *Chaos*, locating it at last in the memory chip. This program became a springboard for an advance peek at some typical Turbo Pascal statements and how they function. Along the way, you encountered a plethora of new terminology that you will meet again in later chapters. You also learned enough about the binary number system to

Running Turbo Pascal Programs

If you have Turbo Pascal running under DOS, simply enter and run the program as listed. If you have Turbo Pascal for Windows, on the other hand, merely add the line "USES WinCrt" right after the program header. If your programs are downloaded through a computer network or made available on a diskette, this detail has already been taken care of.

appreciate how computers can use simple binary elements to store and transmit more complex information such as letters and numbers.

This chapter also introduced several fundamental themes, such as the principles that programs execute sequentially, that hardware is designed to be as unobtrusive as possible in the programming process, and that a program as a whole amounts to a large task that is greater than the sum of its parts.

As a humble illustration of how computers are designed to make life as easy as possible for the programmer, you discovered that binary numbers are the basis of all computing. Yet these numbers have been used to represent the more familiar decimal numbers and characters.

Every chapter of this book is richly supplied with explorations, opportunities for students to test their understanding of the material covered in a variety of ways. Some of the explorations are quite simple, being little more than exercises in the testing of programs or concepts. Other explorations take you a little further afield by asking you to modify these programs. Further on, you will encounter explorations that ask you to write completely new programs that, nevertheless, follow closely the structure of programs you have analyzed.

EXPLORATIONS

The following explorations have been graded in difficulty and in the amount of independent work they require, from practically nothing to fairly extensive projects (correlated to the stage of your learning experience). Although most exercises deal with programming in Turbo Pascal, a few require only written answers and address the computer science component of this chapter. This organization will be followed in all subsequent explorations.

1 Here is a list of the italicized technical terms that appeared in this chapter. The list does not include the names of programs, of variables, or of the disciplines within computer science: hardware, software, bits, source code, executable code, statements, header, declaration section, main body, prompt, loop, FOR-loop, assignment statement, assignment operator, expression, formatted output, iteration, variable type, statement delimiters, syntax, registers, binary number system, words, word size, and disk operating system.

Twenty-four terms appear. Select the ten you feel best able to define or describe, then do so. Your description should be (a) different from that in the text, (b) brief, and (c) easily understood by someone who is not taking the course.

2 What decimal number does the following binary number represent?

10101101

3 If you have the *Chaos* program available on your computer, use the appropriate DOS or Windows commands to load the program into your Turbo Pascal system. Run the program. As you know, it will ask you for a number between 0 and 1. Try entering 0.5. Do you get the same numbers that you saw earlier in this chapter? Next, try entering 0.2. Do you get the same numbers or different ones?

4 Using your Pascal editing system, under either DOS or Windows, type in the *Chaos* program and run it. If it does not run, you may have made a syntax error in entering the program. Check the program carefully against the original, as listed in this chapter. When you get the program running, you will be ready to perform some interesting experiments:

- **a** Change the FOR-loop index limit from 10 to 100 by inserting an extra 0. The program will produce 100 numbers. They will look, well, chaotic.
- **b** Next, take out just one semicolon (;) from the end of any line. What happens when you try to run the program?
- **c** Some users might regard the message "Enter a number between 0 and 1." just a trifle abrupt. Change the WRITELN statement in the user interface to read, "Please enter a number between 0 and 1."; then run the program to check that it reflects this change.

d You can even experiment with chaos. Use your Turbo Pascal editing system to change the number 3.9 in the assignment statement to 2.1. Leave the FOR-loop iteration limit at 100. Now, run the program. How do the numbers behave now?

5 The following program is almost identical to the *Chaos* program. Can you spot the slight difference between the two? Run the program, using a variety of different values for *Xvar* when prompted. How does the output behave? When you think you know, try changing the loop index limit from 10 to 20, just to be sure.

```
PROGRAM Chaos;
VAR Xvar: REAL;
VAR Count: INTEGER;
BEGIN
WRITELN('Enter a number between 0 and 1.');
READLN(Xvar);
FOR Count := 1 TO 10 DO
   BEGIN
   Xvar := 2.1*Xvar*(1-Xvar);
   WRITELN(Xvar:6:4);
   END;
END.
```

6 The following program is quite different from the *Chaos* program, yet it follows the same general form. This format should make it easy to analyze. Enter the program by using your Turbo Pascal editing system and then run it. Write a brief report of what it does and how it does it.

```
PROGRAM AgeExpert;
VAR Count, Age: INTEGER;
BEGIN
WRITELN('Enter your present age in years.');
READLN(Age);
FOR Count := 1 TO 10 DO
   BEGIN
   Age := Age + 1;
   WRITELN('In', Count, 'years, your age will be', Age);
   END;
   END.
```

This program uses a slightly more sophisticated form of WRITELN statement than *Chaos* used. From the program's output, can you figure out how the four parts (separated by commas) inside the WRITELN parentheses work?

7 Here is a story that illustrates loops. You may already have heard a variation of it: "It was a dark and stormy night. A Sioux hunting party sat around the camp fire. One of the hunters, bolder than the rest, stood up. 'Tell us a story, oh chief!' he cried. The old chief began. 'It was a dark and stormy night. A Sioux hunting party sat around the campfire . . .'" It should be clear by now how this story ends—or doesn't.

Write a Pascal program called *StoryTime* that goes through ten rounds of this story. Your program will have no variables to declare, so right after the header there will be a BEGIN statement. It will contain a FOR-loop, the body of which will consist only of WRITELN statements, enclosed in a BEGIN–END pair. The first part of the loop body might look like this:

```
BEGIN
WRITELN('It was a dark and stormy night. A hunting party');
WRITELN('of Sioux sat around the camp fire. One of the');
WRITELN('hunters, bolder than the rest, stood up. Tell us');
```

The program will not be able to manage quotes properly, in fact it omits them altogether, for who wants to see a story in which the last part begins with nine quote-marks in a row?

8 What is this INTEGER that the *Chaos* program uses? You know that the word *integer* is just a fancy name for a whole number and you know that there's an infinity of whole numbers. No matter how large an integer you write, you can always think of a larger one. Is the computer infinite, too? To find out, try running the following program:

```
PROGRAM Infinite;
VAR Number: INTEGER;
BEGIN
FOR Number := 1 TO 40000
   WRITELN(Number);
END.
```

As the program runs, the computer will automatically print each new number at the end of the list on the screen. When it reaches the bottom, it will roll all the previous numbers up one line on the screen to make room for the new number. The computer runs so fast that you have no chance to read individual numbers as they roll up the screen. But you may be quick enough to catch what happens after it reaches 32,000. What happens? Discuss.

9 In the DOS-based Turbo Pascal programming system, as soon as your program has run, the system immediately returns you to the edit screen without giving you a chance to see the program's output. This can be annoying and there are two ways to deal with the problem: (a) To see the output again, select the USER SCREEN option from the WINDOW portion of the upper menu bar. (b) To prevent returning to the edit screen at the end of a run, simply add the following statement to your program just before the final END statement:

```
READLN;
```

When it reaches what would otherwise be the end of its run, the program will wait for input from the user, giving you time to inspect the output. When you want to return to the edit window, simply press any key. An alteration that produces a standard effect by nonstandard means is called a "kludge" by programmers.

Add the kludge to your *Chaos* program and check that it works as advertised here.

2 The Automated Teacher

Programs from Algorithms

computer program can give explicit expression to human ideas. A programmer begins with a rough idea for a process, perhaps to compute chaos or to convert temperatures from one scale to another, or even to teach children arithmetic. The programmer then describes the process in terms of an algorithm, a rough outline of the program. Like a sculptor chipping away at a block of stone, the programmer refines the algorithm until a simple translation into Turbo Pascal reveals the program's final shape.

As the program takes shape, however, the informality of the algorithmic description gives way to the formality of rules for shaping actual Turbo Pascal statements. Syntax rules the day. When all the errors, or "bugs," have been eliminated and the program runs exactly as envisioned, the programmer is done. I illustrate the entire process with a program that tutors children in basic arithmetic, a sort of "automated teacher."

The rules of syntax furnish one example of an automaton. This abstraction of automatic behavior is one of the most useful ideas in computer science. You will consider some automata that you already know about (like soft drink machines) and some you don't know about (like language recognizers).

The Programming Process

The programming process consists of three phases: developing an idea by writing a succession of algorithms, turning the final algorithm into a program, then debugging (i.e., to detect, locate, and correct errors) the program. One factor shapes the goal at all stages:

> Programming languages force you to be explicit and precise in formulating computational ideas. A programmer must therefore learn to think formally.

When you first learned English, you had to learn a few rules of grammar to make yourself understood in the first place. Later, you discovered additional rules that, far from restricting your speech, made it more accurate and expressive. Like the rules of English grammar, the rules of programming syntax may seem irritating at first, but they not only become second nature to the programmer, they vastly extend his or her powers to translate human ideas into programs.

The Problem

The idea for a program usually has its roots in a problem of one kind or another. As soon as the programmer has an idea for how a computer might solve the problem, the programming process has begun. To make the process explicit, let's begin with a problem faced by modern schools with high enrollments and a shortage of teachers. In arithmetic class, it would help if the students could work independently, at times, with a tutoring program. It would take some of the burden off the teacher if part of the teaching job, even a small part, could be automated.

As a novice programmer, your ideas should not outstrip your abilities, but you might well decide that it would be possible to write a program that tutored children in addition (for example). You can imagine a program that asks the child for two numbers, along with the answer, then checks whether the child did the addition correctly.

As soon as you have such an idea, you should specify it. There's nothing like writing things down to clarify your ideas! You decide on the following specification.

> Write a program that will accept two numbers from a student, calculate their sum, then ask the student to enter the sum. If the student

is correct, the program will reward the student with a congratulatory message. If the student's answer is incorrect, the program must so inform the student and provide a message of encouragement.

The Algorithm

Before the programmer begins to write a program, he or she usually makes a design in the form of an *algorithm*, a step-by-step outline, mostly in English, of what the program is supposed to do. With a carefully thought-out algorithm in hand, the programmer has less work to do than if he or she simply tried to write the program from scratch. Unplanned programs tend to have a great many mistakes in them, not only in syntax, but in *logic*, that is, how the statements within the program are structured to achieve the computational goal. It can take far longer to find and correct mistakes in logic or syntax than it takes to write a good algorithm that leads quickly to a good program.

Although the word *algorithm* may sound a little formidable, you are probably already familiar with the principles involved. For example, cooking recipes could be described as algorithms, as could directions you might get while driving. My favorite example of a real-life algorithm consists of the assembly directions for the brand-new widget glommer you saved up to buy. You won't understand the directions of course. No one does. But the idea is that by following these directions and by looking carefully at various helpful assembly diagrams, you can eventually figure out how to assemble the widget glommer. Most algorithms are actually much easier to follow than this.

1. Remove widgets, wing-bar, glommer-rolls, bat shield, back plate, pull-cord, struts, and screw package from shipping crate.
2. Fit plastic cap of wing-bar into slot A (Figure 1) of back plate using the screw provided.
3. Slide bat shield half way along wing-bar and clamp in vertical position.
4. Attach first widget to the large glommer-roll with three screws (Figure 2).

The instructions continue, but these four make my point. Someone who has some experience with tools and putting things together should have no trouble assembling the object, given the right algorithm.

The list of assembly instructions is an algorithm because it spells out the assembly informally, relying on the experience of the person

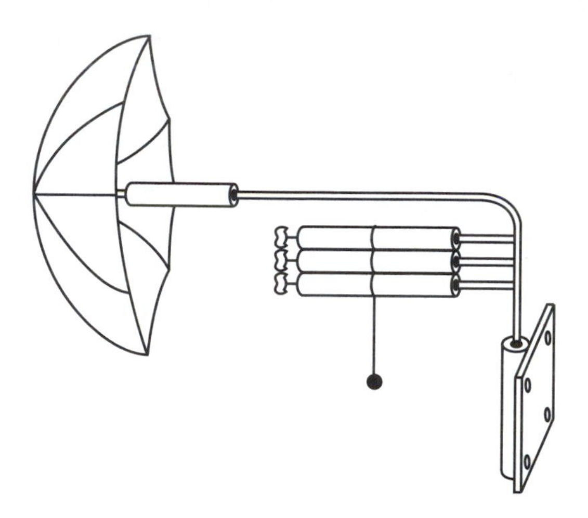

The widget glommer, fully assembled

assembling the object to get it right. You could say much the same thing about a computer algorithm. It spells out the steps that a given program must have, steps that make sense only to a programmer. Unlike the assembly of a new gadget, however, a computer algorithm will result not in hardware but in software. The steps in a computer algorithm are destined to become statements in a program. When the steps have been put in this form, even a machine (the computer) can follow them.

To begin the programming process, let's list the steps the program must follow in order to interact successfully with young students. The actions are considered from the computer's point of view, so to speak. I have numbered the steps to remind you that they must be carried out in this order.

1. Get two numbers from the student.
2. Add the numbers together and save the result.
3. Get the student's answer.
4. If the answer is correct, congratulate the student.
5. If the answer is not correct, advise the student.

The algorithm is written in English, but it already shows some aspects of good algorithmic design. The steps of the algorithm are all in the correct order and what each step really means is fairly clear and unambiguous.

What would it be like to use the program?

The steps of the algorithm, numbered from 1 to 5, follow each other in logical sequence. What is the first thing that must happen? The student obviously has to give the computer something to work with, namely, the two numbers to be added. So, the computer gets two numbers from the student. Next, in step 2 the computer adds the two numbers together and stores the sum away so that it can retrieve it later to compare with the student's answer. In step 3 the computer must get the student's answer, presumably by asking the student to type in the result of his or her own addition effort. In steps 4 and 5 the computer checks the student's answer against its own. If the answer is correct, the computer will congratulate the student (step 4). If the answer is not correct, however, the computer informs the student, but in an encouraging way. Have I left anything out?

The order of steps in an algorithm is usually important, but sometimes the order of two or more steps can be reversed without changing anything essential in the way the resulting program will operate. For example, steps 2 and 3 in the algorithm above can be interchanged: The program could ask the student for the answer *before* finding an answer of its own, instead of *after*; it makes no difference. For one thing, the computer is so blazingly fast that, even with these steps in reverse order, it will have computed its own answer before the student's finger has even left the return key after entering his or her own answer.

Refining the Algorithm

This algorithm lacks some detail. An experienced programmer might be able to turn it into a working program almost immediately, but, as an amateur, you will have to refine the algorithm by expanding some of the steps or even by dividing them into two or more new steps. Because you are using Turbo Pascal, moreover, you must keep Turbo Pascal statement types in mind, at least the ones you already know about (or will shortly).

The only Turbo Pascal statements you have encountered so far are in the *Chaos* program, so I have listed it here as a reminder. A representative statement of each type has been highlighted in boldface.

```
PROGRAM Chaos;
VAR Xvar: REAL;
VAR Count: INTEGER;
BEGIN
WRITELN ('Enter a number between 0 and 1.');
READLN (Xvar);
FOR Count := 1 TO 10 DO
   BEGIN
   Xvar := 3.9*Xvar*(1-Xvar);
   WRITELN(Xvar:6:4);
   END;
END.
```

Obviously, the tutorial program will use a header, and this very thought forces you to think of a name for the program. How about *AddTutor*? Because I am not asking you to write the actual program at this stage, you can abstain from writing the header and declarations. But, in place of the declarations, you should make a list of the variables used by *AddTutor*—as soon as you have finished analyzing the steps of the first algorithm.

To produce a second algorithm, which will be a refinement of the first one, let's go through the first one step by step and look for a Turbo Pascal statement in the program *Chaos* that you might be able to adapt to the tutorial program. What about step 1 of the algorithm? What statement types in the *Chaos* program might be useful here?

1. Get two numbers from the student.

Logically, the program must ask the student for the numbers by sending a message to the computer screen. In other words, the program must employ a WRITELN statement. Recall from Chapter 1 that such a statement is called a prompt. Next, still on the same algorithmic step, the program must read in the numbers that the student types in. The program, in consequence, must use a READLN statement. Armed with these ideas, you can now refine step 1 into two steps:

Write a message to the student, asking for two numbers.
Read the numbers the student enters.

The program will need two variables to hold the two numbers. Let's call them *FirstNum* and *SecondNum*. Now that you know what they will be called, you might as well include them in the second algorithm:

Write a message to the student, asking for two numbers.
Read the numbers the student enters as FirstNum and SecondNum.

What Turbo Pascal statement types might come in handy when you translate step 2 into a program?

2. Add the numbers together and save the result.

This looks very much like an assignment statement. The program will cause the two numbers to be added together by explicitly stating the formula (number + number) and assigning the resulting sum (via the := operator) to a new variable that you might as well name now. How about *Sum*?

You can refine this step by bringing it a little closer to an actual Turbo Pascal statement:

Assign the sum of *FirstNum* and *SecondNum* to *Sum*.

You can almost refine step 3 of the first algorithm by yourself:

3. Get the student's answer.

Because it involves "getting" something from the student, this step also requires a prompt (using a WRITELN statement) followed by a statement that reads in the student's answer (a READLN statement). Let's call the student's answer, well, *Answer*.

Names Programmers Give

As you know, Turbo Pascal generally uses two kinds of words. There are Pascal words like BEGIN and VAR. These cannot be changed nor can a programmer use them for any purpose other than the proper one. But when it comes to naming programs or variables, the programmer has a much freer hand.

A good practice to follow in Turbo Pascal programming is to choose names for programs and variables that are as meaningful as possible. At the same time, very long names make programs less, rather than more readable, so you don't want names that are too long. Who could not guess that the variable name *FirstNum* in the tutorial program is a contraction of "First Number"? The name is short and meaningful.

Write a message to the student, asking for his/her answer.
Read in the number the student enters as *Answer*.

The last two steps of the algorithm ultimately involve a kind of statement that you have not seen before.

4. If the answer is correct, congratulate the student.
5. If the answer is not correct, advise the student.

To turn these steps into Turbo Pascal, you need to know about a new statement type called a *conditional statement*, or IF–THEN *statement*, both terms meaning the same thing at the moment. I will discuss conditional statements further when the time comes to write the program. For the time being, let us refine the steps only slightly by using the word "message" as a reminder that a WRITELN will be needed:

If the answer is correct,
  then send a message of congratulations to the student.
If the answer is incorrect,
  then send a message of advice to the student.

Now you have produced a second algorithm, a stepwise refinement of the first one. Here it is, with all the new steps included. I have added a reminder at the top that a header and declarations will be needed. Because the names of the variables to be used by the program have been chosen, I have listed them under "declarations" without saying anything more about them:

header for **program** *AddTutor*

declarations for **var**iables
FirstNum, SecondNum, Sum, Answer

Write a message to the student, asking for two numbers.
Read the numbers the student types as *FirstNum* and *SecondNum*.

Assign the sum of *FirstNum* and *SecondNum* to *Sum*.

Write a message to the student, asking for his/her answer.
Read in the number the student types as *Answer*.

If the answer is correct,
then send a message of congratulations to the student.
If the answer is incorrect,
then send a message of advice to the student.

In anticipation of translating this algorithm into a Turbo Pascal program, I have placed some of the words or parts of words in boldface. These words are already close to the corresponding Turbo Pascal words that the program will use in the statements that correspond to these steps.

As I mentioned earlier, there is one Turbo Pascal statement that you know nothing about yet, and that statement type will be the subject of a brief excursion into the land of logic.

If . . . then . . .

The title of this section says it all. The simplest form of the Turbo Pascal conditional statement uses two key words, **if** and **then**. You have already used this kind of statement in your own life. Consider a sheet from the daily memo of Morton J. Frogwhistle, attorney at law. The third item on

Morton J. Frogwhistle
Attorney
37 Pond Road
Springfield, DH 37575

1. Breakfast with Mrs. Winslow.
2. Meet Mole & Vole 10:00.
3. If the client of Mole & Vole will settle out of court,
   then advise Winslow to settle out of court.

A day in the life of a busy lawyer

the memo happens to be a simple conditional statement of sorts. **If** the client of Mole and Vole will settle out of court, **then** he, Frogwhistle, will advise his client to drop the lawsuit. Like any conditional statement, there is an expression, "the client of Mole and Vole will settle out of court," which will turn out to be either true or false. If the expression is true, then something will happen: He will advise his client to settle out of court. If the expression is not true, then no such action will be taken and the suit, presumably, will go ahead as planned.

In Turbo Pascal, the IF–THEN statement has a definite form:

```
IF expression
   THEN statement
```

The action part of the IF–THEN statement is normally indented in order to make it easier to read. When such a statement happens to be part of a Turbo Pascal program, the computer first tests the truth of the expression. If the expression is true, the computer will execute the statement following the Turbo Pascal word THEN. If the statement is not true, the computer will skip this statement entirely and go on to the next statement following the IF–THEN statement. The accompanying diagram makes this clear. The arrow shows what happens to the execution of the program in either case.

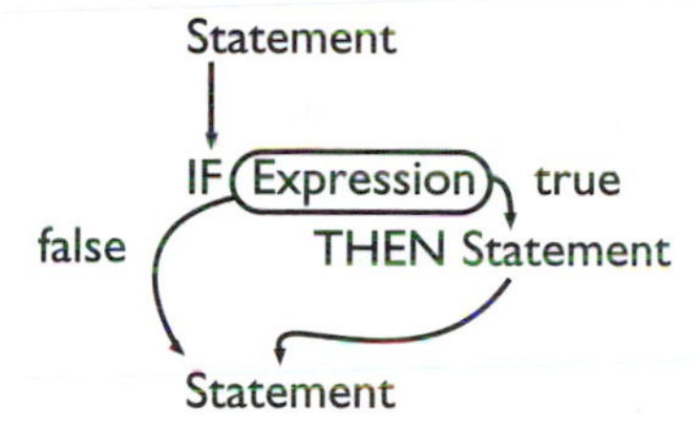

Execution of an IF–THEN statement

What better example of how to use an IF–THEN statement could you find than the *AddTutor* program that you happen to be writing? Now take the second, last step in the second (refined) algorithm.

> **If** the answer is correct,
> **then** send a message of congratulations to the student.

What expression should you use for "the answer is correct"? The student's answer is correct only if it matches the value of the variable *Sum* worked out by the computer. To form such an expression in Turbo Pascal, you have to express that idea in mathematical notation:

$$Answer = Sum$$

As you already know, the message following the THEN will involve a WRITELN statement, so you may as well finish off the example:

```
IF Answer = Sum
   THEN WRITELN('Congratulations! You got that one right.');
```

Besides the equals sign, several other signs can be used to express the relative size of variables or numbers. These signs include > (greater than), < (less than), <> (not equal to), <= (less than or equal to), and >= (greater than or equal to).

The statement above, like all Turbo Pascal statements, ends with a semicolon. (There are exceptions to this rule, but they are not important at the moment.) This is the simplest form of IF–THEN statement. Later, you will encounter a form that is even more useful. Both forms are conditional statements.

To review, an IF–THEN statement has two main parts. Following the Turbo Pascal word IF, there is a logical expression, one that is either true or false. Following the Turbo Pascal word THEN, there is a statement that may be executed. The computer will execute this statement only if the expression is true. If the expression is not true, then the computer will skip the statement.

Writing the Program

You are now ready to write the program. To make it especially easy for you to see what's going on, I will translate the refined algorithm into the program step by step: First write the header and declarations.

```
PROGRAM AddTutor;
VAR FirstNum, SecondNum, Answer, Sum: INTEGER;
```

As you can see, the header for *AddTutor* has the same general form as the header for the *Chaos* program. Because the student will be dealing only with whole numbers, or integers, the program declares all variables to be INTEGER. Note how Turbo Pascal allows you to declare all the variables at once, so to speak. When they are all the same type (such as INTEGER), you can list them on the same line, with a comma and a space after each one.

Now you can translate the rest of the algorithm:

Algorithm

Write a message to the student, asking for two numbers.

Program

```
WRITELN('Please enter two numbers to be added.');
```

On the basis of what you know about Turbo Pascal so far, the only way to send a message to the student is to use the WRITELN statement. Is this the best message to send to the student? One of the explorations at the end of this chapter challenges you to write a better one.

The next step reads in the numbers. Again, on the basis of your previous experience, the READLN statement is the natural one to use here:

Algorithm

Read the numbers the student types as *FirstNum* and *SecondNum*.

Program

```
READLN(FirstNum, SecondNum);
```

Notice how you can read in more than one variable with the same READLN statement. The student must type the two numbers, separated by a space, then press the ENTER key.

The next step of the algorithm is destined to be an assignment statement.

Algorithm

Assign the sum of *FirstNum* and *SecondNum* to *Sum*.

Program

```
Sum := FirstNum + SecondNum;
```

Following this, the program prompts the student for his or her answer:

Algorithm

Write a message to the student, asking for his/her answer.

Program

```
WRITELN('Please add these two numbers and enter your answer.');
```

Again, is this the best way to prompt the student? When you have finished examining this translation into Turbo Pascal, you might wish to read the box on page 44, entitled "The User Interface."

As with the previous prompt, the program must have a READLN statement telling the computer to read in the student's answer:

Algorithm

Read in the number the student types as *Answer*.

Program

```
READLN(Answer);
```

Now come the conditional statements that I explained in the foregoing section. As you can see, the translation has exactly the form I described:

Algorithm

If the answer is correct,

then send a message of congratulations to the student.

The User Interface

The *user interface* of a program consists of all the interactive elements that it offers. The user interface of the *AddTutor* program, for example, consists of two prompts with their associated input (READLN) statements, as well as the informative messages at the end of the program.

Prior to taking this course, you may have already used a program that confused you with its messages and its options. Your confusion was not necessarily your fault! The programmers who created these programs may not have spent enough time anticipating all the problems that ordinary people might encounter with their creation. Designing a good user interface involves one part programming and two parts psychology.

It never hurts to imagine a first-time user of your program, staring at the screen. Imagine, for example, a grade school child who is about to use *AddTutor* for the first time. The teacher has started the program for the child. What does the message on the screen say? What should it say?

Will the child know how to enter numbers from the computer keyboard? It seems safe to assume that such a basic keyboard skill has already been covered by the teacher. Beyond this, further questions remain. What is the best way to word the prompt to minimize confusion? Take the first prompt of the program, the one that will ask the student for two numbers:

```
WRITELN('Please . . . ');
```

Program

```
IF Answer = Sum
   THEN WRITELN('Congratulations! You got the right answer.');
```

The second conditional statement has the same form, but the expression it tests is the opposite of the first expression. This one uses the not-equals symbol (<>), formed by typing first <, then >.

Algorithm

If the answer is incorrect,
   then send a message of encouragement to the student.

You want the child to enter two integers, and you want the child to understand that the two numbers will be added together. To avoid confusion, you particularly want to ensure that the child doesn't try to type two numbers, then press the ENTER key just once. The READLN statement allows a user to do this, but the child may not put a space between the numbers. One prompt that may work fairly well uses two WRITELN statements instead of just one. The first WRITELN states the main idea, that two numbers are needed and that the computer will add them together. At this point, you might indulge in a bit of fantasy by pretending that the computer is a person of sorts. It could refer to itself as "me." The second line of text is all about getting the data entry right, asking the child to enter the two numbers separately.

```
WRITELN('Please give me two numbers to add together.');
WRITELN('Enter the first number, then enter the second one.');
```

At the end of the program, another crucial interaction with the user seeks to reinforce good performance in children who get right answers and, at the same time, encourage children who get wrong answers. Here is one possible solution to the second problem:

```
WRITELN('Oops! You made a mistake. Can you find it?');
```

Program

```
If Answer <> Sum
   THEN WRITELN('Oops! You made a mistake. Can you find it?');
```

Now you can put all these statements together to complete the program. In doing so, you must always remember to include the header and declarations and to sandwich the main body between the words BEGIN and END.

You are now ready to write and test the program called *AddTutor*. Before you do this, however, read the program carefully and ensure that every statement makes sense to you in light of the foregoing discussion. I have altered the prompts slightly in order to take my own advice in the box entitled "The User Interface."

```
PROGRAM AddTutor;

VAR FirstNum, SecondNum, Sum, Answer: INTEGER;

BEGIN
WRITELN('Please give me two numbers to be added.');
WRITELN('Enter the first number, then enter the second.');
READLN(FirstNum, SecondNum)
Sum = FirstNum + SecondNum;
WRITELN('Now, please add these two numbers and enter your answer.');
READLN(Answer);
IF (Answer <> Sum)
   THEN WRITELN('Congratulations! You got the right answer!');
IF (Answer = Sum)
   THEN WRITELN('Oops! You made a mistake. Can you find it?');
END.
```

I have separated the program header, the declarations, and the main body to make the structure of the program a little more transparent. Turbo Pascal makes no objection to blank lines in the middle of a program.

Now it's time to test the program. I certainly hope I haven't made any mistakes . . .

Debugging the Program

To run the program called *AddTutor*, you must first have the Turbo Pascal system running on your computer. If you run Turbo Pascal under DOS or OS/2, you can enter the program as shown. If you run under Windows, however, please be sure to insert the following statement right below the program header:

```
USES WinCrt;
```

Next, using the editing facility of the system, type in the program exactly as you see it printed on this page. Before trying to run your program, you should compile it, however, to check for *syntax errors*, that is, mistakes in the grammar that Turbo Pascal expects you to use. When you compile the *AddTutor* program, you will discover to your horror that the program contains a mistake. The compiler informs you that a semicolon is missing from the end of the third statement in the main body of the program. Using the editing facility, you fix the error by adding a semicolon to the statement.

When you compile the program again, just to be sure that no further errors remain, up pops another. This time, you discover that the fourth statement in the main body also contains a syntax error. The assignment statement, it appears, does not have the right assignment operator. You fix it by inserting a colon (:) just before the equals sign. Once again you compile the program. This time it compiles correctly and you are ready to run it.

The compilation was successful. The program seems to run. The right message appears on your screen:

```
Please give me two numbers to be added.
Enter the first number, then enter the second.
```

You think of two numbers, 35 and 82, say. You enter them separately, as the message advises. As soon as you press the ENTER key the second time, the next message appears:

```
Now, please add these two numbers and enter your answer.
```

Debugging a program can be frustrating

You enter the correct sum, 117. The computer's response shocks you:

```
Oops! You made a mistake. Can you find it?
```

Something's very wrong. It seems there's another error, but this kind of error will never be found by the Turbo Pascal compiler. Instead, you have just discovered a *logical error*, a flaw in the way the program's logic is organized. It turns out that I accidently got the two IF conditions mixed up, placing the = where I meant to put the <> and vice versa.

Use the editing system to exchange the symbols, then run the program again in the same way. Now the computer's response is better:

```
Congratulations! You got the right answer!
```

Also check the behavior of the program on wrong answers. After you have done this step, you will have debugged the program. A program this size usually doesn't need much more checking. It is perfectly normal, however, for students of Turbo Pascal who write such programs to discover some syntax errors and even a logical error or two.

Once a program has been written and debugged for both syntax errors and logical errors, you might be tempted to improve it. For example, when you think about *AddTutor* from the user's point of view, you might suddenly realize that it has one feature that makes it rather hard to use. Immediately after helping a child with a single addition problem, the program quits! To try another addition example or to attempt the same one again, the child will have to restart the program by selecting the RUN option again. Should it be necessary to restart the program every time you want help with an addition problem? You will learn how to overcome this difficulty in Chapter 4 when you learn how to make programs restartable. Such programs give a user the option of running them again, in effect, without exiting.

It's now time for you to become a little more systematic about learning the programming language Turbo Pascal. In particular, it's time to delve into two very important issues, syntax and semantics. *Syntax* means the form that a statement takes—the rules of its grammar, so to speak. *Semantics* means how a statement operates within the context of a program—its meaning, in short. When you understand both the syntax and the semantics of each Turbo Pascal statement in its most general form, you will then be equipped to use it in any setting. You will become, as far as these statements are concerned, a Turbo-charged Pascal Programmer.

Form and Meaning

All Turbo Pascal statements have a special form that is governed by the rules of syntax. They also have a special meaning that is referred to as semantics. You will now pay an extended visit to form, and then drop in briefly on meaning.

Syntax

Algorithms, as you may recall, have almost no rules at all. Sentences written in English, with occasional formulas interspersed, are, however, arranged in a sequence. But programs are completely rule driven. In other words, programs obey a strict syntax. Most of the Turbo Pascal statements that you have already used appear in the following table, each type accompanied by an example from one of the two programs you have already seen. (Can you remember which of the statements belong to which program?)

Type	*Example*
Program header	`PROGRAM AddTutor;` `PROGRAM Chaos;`
Variable declaration	`VAR Xvar: REAL;` `VAR FirstNum, SecondNum, Sum, Answer: INTEGER;`

READLN and WRITELN	`READLN(FirstNum, SecondNum);`
	`READLN(XVar);`
	`WRITELN('Enter a number between 0 and 1.');`
	`WRITELN('Please give me two numbers to be added.');`

Assignment statement	`Sum := FirstNum + SecondNum;` `Xvar := 3.9*Xvar*(1-Xvar);`
IF–THEN statement	`IF (Answer = Sum)` `THEN WRITELN('Congratulations! You got the right answer.');`

Compare the examples from each of the two programs. The paired examples always have something in common, because they reflect the same rules of syntax. Even where they differ, they do so according to these rules.

The program header has the simplest syntax. You can pretty well figure out the rules by merely inspecting the two examples in the table above. A program header appears to consist of the Turbo Pascal word PROGRAM, followed by a name, followed by a semicolon. Stated this way, the rule sounds simple, but other statements in Turbo Pascal are complicated enough to make such descriptions hard to understand. For this reason, the rules of syntax often are summarized in the form of *syntax diagrams*, little follow-the-arrows maps that describe precisely just what forms of each statement are allowed in Turbo Pascal. Here, for example, is the syntax diagram for program headers.

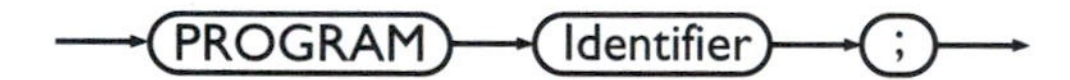

You interpret this diagram by following the arrows, entering the diagram on the left and leaving it on the right. First comes the Turbo Pascal word PROGRAM, then an identifier, then the semicolon. The word PROGRAM and the semicolon never vary, but the *identifier* (a technical word for names) has a syntax diagram all its own.

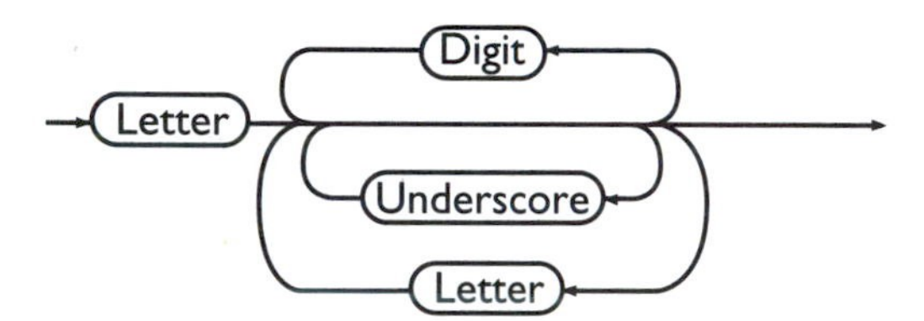

In this syntax diagram the arrows branch out and loop back as well. To discover the power of this syntax diagram, let's check the syntax of a Turbo Pascal identifier by running it, one symbol at a time, through the diagram.

You know that Xvar is a valid identifier because you have already used it successfully to represent the variable *Xvar* in the *Chaos* program, a program that was checked by a compiler before it ran. The letters X - v - a - r may be run through the diagram one at a time. The X takes you from the entrance of the diagram past the "letter" label (X, after all, is a letter) to the point where the arrow divides into branches near its end. To process the v, you must take the back-arrow branch labeled "letter" because v is also a letter. The back-arrow takes you back to the main arrow, and you must travel this arrow forward again to the branch point. The next two letters, a and r, also take you through the same back-loop two more times. After the final letter (r), you take the exit-arrow instead of a back-arrow. The fact that you can trace the syntax diagram successfully, finally exiting after the last symbol of the word *Xvar*, means that *Xvar* is a valid identifier.

If the variable name had started with a digit instead of a letter (say, 3Xvar), you would have been unable to trace the syntax diagram successfully because the very first symbol, a digit, is not allowed. Turbo Pascal identifiers cannot start with a digit. However, after the first, required letter, an identifier can consist of any sequence you like of digits, letters, and even the underscore character (_). In particular, this syntax diagram tells you that if you ever tried to name a program with two separate words, the name would not be accepted. The title Add Tutor, for example, would not work, although the title Add_Tutor would.

The two syntax diagrams, one for program headers, the other for identifiers, together identify which combinations of keyboard characters may be used to form valid program headers and which may not. With this brief introduction to syntax diagrams, you can read the syntax diagrams for all the Turbo Pascal statement types covered so far. These diagrams appear in Appendix A.

Semantics

What do Turbo Pascal statements "mean"? This is a question of semantics, namely, how Turbo Pascal statements work in the context of a program. The question is easy to answer for the program header statement.

```
PROGRAM AddTutor;
```

The key word PROGRAM alerts the computer to the fact that what follows will be the text of a program. The computer responds by storing away the name of the program, *AddTutor*. You may also save the program under this name in order to run it later. The program will appear in the computer directory under the name *Add Tutor*.

Other Turbo Pascal statement types have more complicated semantics. For example, assignment statements mean that the variable on the left of the assignment operator will receive a new value. This value will be the result of a calculation involving the expression on the right of the assignment operator.

The assignment statement below comes from the *AddTutor* program.

```
Sum := FirstNum + SecondNum;
```

In the context of the program *AddTutor*, this statement means that the variable *Sum* will receive a new value after this statement is executed. The value will be the result of adding together the values of the two variables *FirstNum* and *SecondNum*.

On the basis of this even briefer introduction to semantics, you should be able to understand the semantics of all the Turbo Pascal statement types covered so far. This information appears in Appendix A. In subsequent chapters, syntax and semantics will be explained in the manner of the foregoing examples each time you encounter a new statement type or the elaboration of an old one.

Compilers and Syntax

Now you are ready to understand one of the functions of the Turbo Pascal compiler. A Turbo Pascal program does not "run" directly on a computer. It must first be compiled. The *compiler* translates a Turbo Pascal program into *machine language*, that is, a set of commands that control the computer at the most basic functional level. The compiled program, called an *executable program*, is the one that actually runs on the computer.

A compiler is not hardware; it is software. A compiler is a program—a very large program, in fact. To translate your program successfully, the compiler must encounter only statements that rigorously follow the syntax rules. Beyond this, syntax provides a framework for the translation process. For example, the difference between the equals sign (=) and the assignment operator (:=) may seem slight, but the compiler treats these

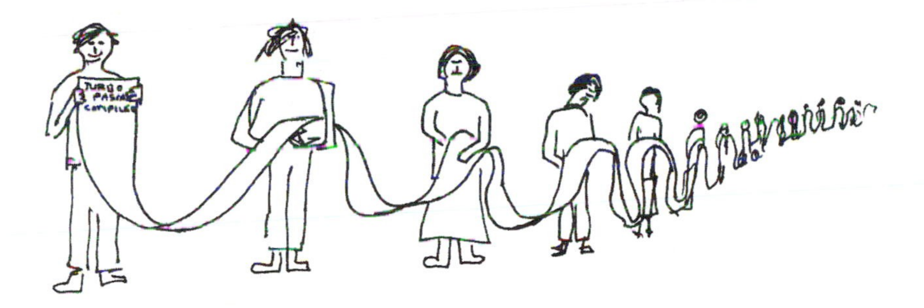

A compiler is a very large program

two symbols very differently. It tries to interpret the equals sign as a test of equality between two expressions that occur on either side of it. It interprets the colon–equals sign as a command to replace the current value of the variable to the left of the sign by the current value of the expression to the right of the sign. If the compiler happens to be processing what it thinks is an assignment statement, only to encounter the equals sign with no colon, it throws up its hands and refuses to go on. It is simply not constructed to guess what you meant.

To see how a compiler works, look once again at the assignment statement from the *AddTutor* program and compare it with the corresponding syntax diagram:

```
Sum := FirstNum + SecondNum;
```

When the compiler processes a line of program like the assignment statement above, it has no idea what it is reading at first. When it reads in the symbols that make up the identifier, it simultaneously traces an internal or built-in syntax diagram. By the time the compiler encounters the blank space between the variable called *Sum* and the next symbol, it "knows" that an identifier is involved. In fact, it has already processed the declaration statement and entered the identifiers in a table. As soon as it sees an identifier in the main body, for example, *Sum*, the compiler checks the table to see if that identifier matches any identifiers in the table. If not, it creates a message such as "Unknown identifier" to send to the programmer.

If the identifier is already in the table, however, the compiler continues its scan. Next, the compiler encounters the two characters that make up the assignment symbol (:=). This new syntactic element matches what it finds in the corresponding part of its own internal version of the syntax diagram for assignment statements. The compiler "expects" a colon–equals at that point. Continuing, it then processes the arithmetic expression to the right of the assignment operator. It scans the remaining symbols, checking to be sure that the identifiers are valid and that the arithmetic operators like plus (+) are in the right place (between the identifiers, for example, and not in front of them). At the end, it checks for a semicolon.

Automata Theory

The idea of a compiler tracing its way automatically through a syntax diagram has been a major motivation for the development of a major discipline within computer science. The area of computer science called *automata theory* studies the behavior of abstract machines that consist of nothing more than *states* (static configurations of a machine) and *transitions* between states (abrupt changes from one static configuration to another). Perhaps you can think of a number of machines (besides computers) that have this property.

The Pop Automaton

How about the soft drink machine into which you must pump three quarters to receive a can of pop? The accompanying diagram shows an automaton (pronounced aw taw' muh tuhn) that summarizes the operation of the soft drink machine in abstract form. The automaton consists of just three states, which I have labeled 0, 1, and 2. Each of these states represents a configuration of the soft drink machine. State 0, for example, means that no money has been put into the machine. State 1 means that someone has put in a quarter. State 2 means that someone has put in 2 quarters. (By the way, this kind of diagram is called a *state diagram*.)

If you drop by the machine in a thirsty frame of mind, you will normally find it in state 0, the so-called *initial state* of the machine. If you put a quarter into the machine, the quarter causes a transition from state 0 to state 1. You can trace this effect by following the arrow from state 0 to state 1 in the accompanying figure. Another quarter moves the automaton into state 2 and a third quarter causes a third and final transition from state

Warning: This machine only takes quarters.

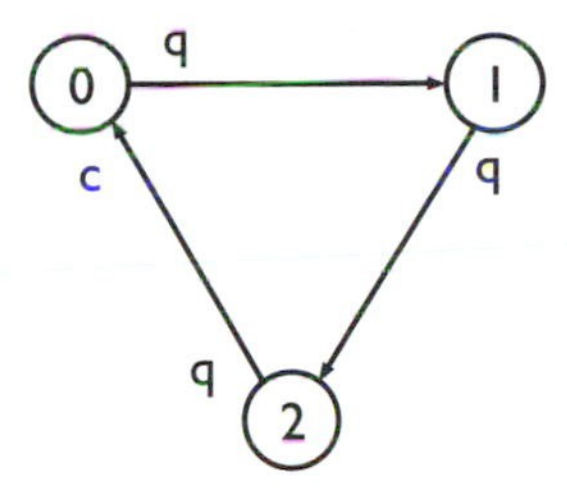

The soft drink automaton

2 back to state 0, in the process triggering a mechanism that drops a can of your favorite drink into the receptacle at the bottom of the machine.

Besides states and transitions, an automaton also has inputs and outputs. I have labeled the transition arrows in the diagram with a q, which stands for "quarter." I have labeled the third transition arrow not only with the input q but also with the output c, which stands for "can."

I could complicate the state diagram for the soft drink automaton by dragging in other functions, such as making change, being out of cans, or even being unplugged, but not many more states would have to be added. When you view a soft drink machine as an automaton, you know immediately that from a computational point of view, it is a very simple machine.

Modern computers, on the other hand, are very complex machines, as the number of possible states attests. Modern computers have so many states that I must resort to a special symbolism just to write the number down. If you look at the memory of a computer, without even considering the central processing units or other parts, you may be looking at over 50,000 separate memory elements. Each element is capable of containing either a 0 or a 1, independently of what all the other elements may contain. To find out how many states this leads to, you multiply the number of possible configurations for each memory element, namely, 2, as many times as there are elements. This means $2 \times 2 \times 2 \times \ldots \times 2$ fifty thousand times. In mathematical shorthand, this turns out to be

$$2^{50,000}$$

Do you have any idea how big this number is? It boggles the mind. The only other big number I know of is minuscule by comparison, that is, the number that roughly estimates the total number of fundamental particles (electrons and basic constituents of atoms) in the known universe:

$$2^{64}$$

Automata, besides illustrating the complexity of machines, are also useful because they describe some of the basic functions of software, like the compiler. The syntax diagrams that you have seen so far resemble the state diagrams of automata but are slightly different. Nevertheless, each syntax diagram may be recast as an automaton.

The accompanying figure, for example, shows the automaton that corresponds to the syntax diagram for program headers. Note that I have built in the automaton that checks for identifiers, as well as the letters of the word PROGRAM and the final semicolon. This automaton is somewhat more complicated than the soft drink automaton. The beginning of each transition is labeled with the symbol that triggers it. None of the arrows are labeled with an output because only the states are important in a compiler's syntax automata.

Every automaton has two special states with self-explanatory names, the *initial* state and one or more *final states*. At the beginning of its operation, an automaton must be in its initial state. As it happens, state 0 is also the final state of the pop machine automaton, because it enters this state when the third and final quarter is inserted.

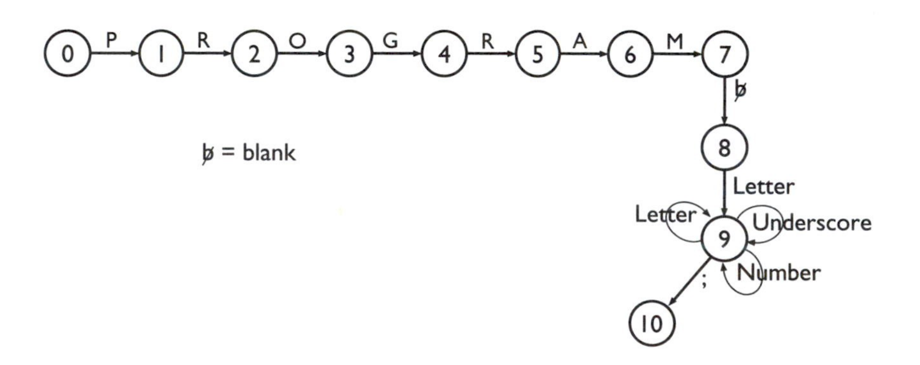

Automaton for header syntax

The transition arrows in the state diagram on page 56 have been labeled "letter," "digit," and "underscore." These are the inputs to the automaton. You won't be surprised, after reading these names, to realize that this automaton corresponds to the syntax diagram for identifiers, that I presented in the section on syntax.

To see the header-checking automaton in action, you can try it on the program header for *AddTutor*. The letters of the word PROGRAM take the automaton from its initial state to state 7, where only a blank will trigger a transition to state 8. At this point, the automaton begins to process the name of the program. Here is where the identifier syntax automaton lives. When the automaton reaches state 9, it has only to process the semicolon before exiting to the final state.

A Taste of Theory

Automata theory also yields insights into the relative powers of different sorts of machines. But first you need to know a little more terminology. Any string of symbols that you submit to an automaton is called a *word*. Some words take an automaton from its initial state to its final state. Such words are said to be *recognized* by the automaton and make up its *language*. Suppose that, in recognizing a word, an automaton is allowed to enter its final state more than once. Under these conditions, the language of the soft drink machine, for example, consists of the following words:

qqq, qqqqqq, qqqqqqqqq, qqqqqqqqqqqq, . . .

Then the number of such words—those having three q's, six q's, nine q's, and so on, is infinite.

By the same token, the language of the program header syntax-checking automaton consists of all valid combinations of keyboard symbols that spell out Turbo Pascal program headers. Thus the combination

```
PROGRAM Chaos;
```

is just *one* word in the language recognized by the header-checking automaton. This language is also infinite, as far as the checking automaton is concerned.

On the face of things, it sounds quite impressive to say that some automata have infinite languages, even though they have a finite number of states. Just how powerful are automata? Some people might think that no automaton could recognize the English language, but this would not be true. If you had about three decades and half a ton of paper to spare, you could design a syntax-checking automaton that recognized all (and only) English words. I can get you started with a hint. Below is the state diagram for an automaton that recognizes the language consisting of the four words, "dog," "cat," "parrot," and "penguin."

Alas, there are some things that automata can't do. For example, no automaton can recognize all palindromes, words or phrases that look the same when you reverse them. The following examples are well known: mom; wow; dad; able was I ere I saw elba. The last palindrome, which includes blanks, as well as regular alphabetic characters, is attributed to Napoleon, but I doubt that Napoleon actually said it.

The most important thing to know about the word *science* in computer science is that it proceeds along largely mathematical lines. Automata theory, in particular, is a mathematical subject. To understand how scientists know what they know lies at the foundation of any scientific subject. Whereas the physical sciences establish their truths by induction (observation and experiment), the mathematical sciences establish their truths by deduction. In other words, if I claim that no automaton can recognize all palindromes, I will have to prove my claim deductively. I will put my proof not in formal terms, but in informal ones. No automaton can recognize palindromes.

Suppose that an automaton that can recognize all palindromes does exist. Let's give it a name, say, PR. If the automaton PR can recognize

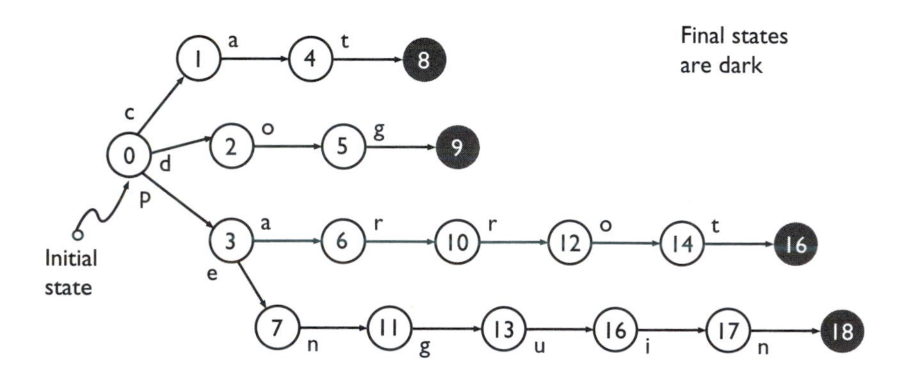

Animal automaton

palindromes (and nothing but palindromes), then it will certainly recognize these: b, aba, aabaa, aaabaaa, aaaabaaaa, and so on. Like all automata, PR has only a finite number of states, say, n of them. I select one of the palindromes from the list above, the one with n a's, followed by a b, followed by another n a's. When I give this palindrome to PR, it starts to process the word. But after PR processes the first n a's, it is forced to repeat one of its states, that is, to reenter it after passing through it earlier. (If it did not repeat one of its states, it would have to have more than n of them, right?) Let's suppose that it makes k further transitions before returning to the repeated state. The figure below illustrates the situation.

Now, form a new word from this palindrome, a word from which k a's have been removed from the first string of n a's. If you compare how PR processes the new word with how it processed the original one, you will find that it does exactly the same thing with both words up to where it enters the repeated state for the first time. Now, let PR process the original string until it returns to the repeated state. From this point on, PR behaves exactly the same on both words because, from this point on, they are identical. The automaton PR ends up in the same (final) state with both words. The blow comes when you realize that in this final state, PR has recognized a nonpalindrome. This contradiction can only mean that the automaton PR could not have existed in the first place. No automaton can recognize *all* palindromes.

In case the failure to recognize palindromes does not strike you as a very severe limitation, let me point out that automata cannot even add! Indeed, there are many things that no automaton can do. Automata are certainly not as powerful as computers, even though both have states.

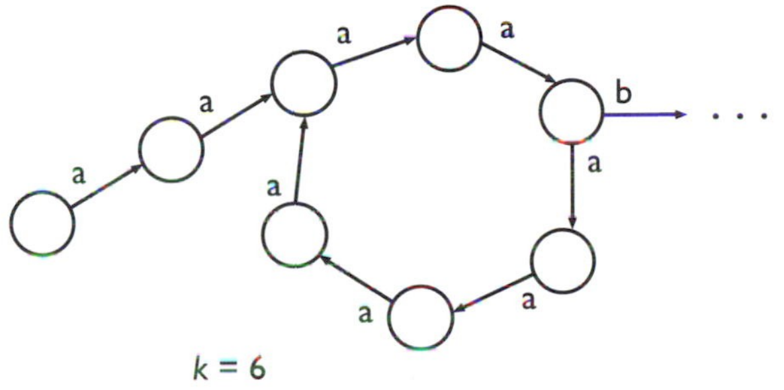

The palindrome checker is forced to repeat a state

Yet, as the discipline called complexity theory (see the summary of computer science disciplines in Chapter 1, page 23) has discovered, there are limits on the powers of computers as well. For example, there are problems that simply cannot be solved by any computer. There are other problems that, although they *can* be solved by computers, would require the lifetime of the universe (or longer) to be solved. Knowledge of the limits of machines is just as valuable, in the long run, as knowledge of their powers.

SUMMARY

You have learned about the programming process and the key role played by algorithms in that process. Algorithms form a critical bridge between the conception and the execution of a program design. The *AddTutor* project provided you with an opportunity to take part in the programming process.

The syntax of Turbo Pascal programs must be adhered to very carefully in writing a program. Syntax diagrams make it easy to see what forms of statements are permitted by Turbo Pascal and which are not. And syntax itself makes an interesting subject, not only because it leads directly to the function of compilers, but because it leads also to automata theory, an important discipline within computer science.

In automata theory, you learned that, in spite of their obvious powers, automata have limitations as well. Computers also have their limitations.

EXPLORATIONS

1 With the aid of your Turbo Pascal editor, type the incorrect version of the *AddTutor* program into the Turbo Pascal system and try to compile it. What happens? Now correct the syntax errors but leave the logical error in place. This program will compile, but it will not run correctly. Demonstrate this with an example. Finally, correct the program and run it with two examples, one with the correct answer and one with an incorrect answer. Does it appear to work correctly now?

2 On the basis of the *AddTutor* program, write a new program called *TimesTutor*. Instead of drilling a student in addition, *TimesTutor* helps the student practice multiplication. Consequently, you will need to replace the addition operation by a multiplication, as well as carry out other modifications. After writing your program, debug it and test it in the manner of exploration 1.

3 Here is a program that resembles the *AddTutor* program very closely. Analyze the program and then write a description of it that follows the form below:

a Write a one-paragraph description of what the program does.
b Write out each statement of the program separately and, below each statement, name the Turbo Pascal statement type involved and describe how it works in the context of the program.

```
PROGRAM SquareTutor;
VAR Number, Square, Answer: INTEGER;

BEGIN
WRITELN('Please give me a number to square.');
READLN(Number);
Square := Number*Number;
WRITELN('Now, please square the number and enter your answer.');
READLN(Answer);
IF (Answer = Square)
   THEN WRITELN('Congratulations! You got the right answer!');
IF (Answer <> Square)
   THEN WRITELN('Oops! You made a mistake. Can you find it?');
END.
```

4 Here is another program that resembles the *AddTutor* program. First analyze the program and then write a description of it that follows the form given below:

a Write a one-paragraph description of what the program does.
b Write out each statement of the program separately and, below each statement, name the Turbo Pascal statement type involved and describe how it works in the context of the program.

```
PROGRAM LottoWizard;

VAR Age: INTEGER;
BEGIN
```

```
WRITELN('Hello. I am the lottery wizard.');
WRITELN('Please enter your age. I will tell');
WRITELN('you what lottery number to play.');
READLN(Age);
WRITELN('Your lucky number is:');
IF Age < 20
   THEN WRITELN('2 12 25 28 36 41');
IF Age >= 20
   THEN WRITELN('1 22 32 39 40 45');
END.
```

5 Suppose you wish to write a version of the *AddTutor* program for a child who can read but has never used a computer before. Rewrite the WRITELN statements of *AddTutor* to make it possible for even this child to use the program. Try to give complete instructions but, at the same time, try to be as economical as possible in your use of additional WRITELN statements. Test your program, if possible, on someone who has never used a computer.

6 Modify the *AddTutor* program so that when the student gets the answer wrong, the program gives the student the correct answer along with the message of encouragement.

7 Here is an algorithm for a program that helps carpenters with their measurements (not that they need any help). The program takes two measurements as input, each given in feet and inches. It computes the sum of the two measurements, reduces it to standard feet-and-inches units (the latter less than 12 inches), then reports the results to the user.

1. Ask the user for the first measurement.
2. Input the measurement as two variables, *Feet1* and *Inches1*.
3. Ask the user for the second measurement.
4. Input the second measurement as two variables, *Feet2* and *Inches2*.
5. *Feet* := *Feet1* + *Feet2*
6. *Inches* := *Inches1* + *Inches2*
7. If *Inches* > 11, then *Inches* := *Inches* – 12 and *Feet* := *Feet* + 1.
8. Report the new measurement to the user.

Step 1 will be a prompt, naturally. In step 2, two variables, *Feet1* and *Inches1*, will hold the values entered by the user. Steps 3 and 4 are essentially a repeat of the first two steps, except that two new variables are involved. Steps 5 and 6 are straightforward assignment statements of a type that you are already familiar with. Step 7 is critical. It adjusts the answer in the case where the two inches measurements add up to 12 or more. Note that if "*Inches* > 11" is true, there are two things the program must do. In a case like this, you must follow the THEN portion of the conditional statement with not one but two statements. Turbo Pascal syntax demands that in such a case, you must place a BEGIN–END pair around the two statements. Indent all four lines to the same extent. Debug the program and test it on as many different distinct *kinds* of input as you can think of.

8 In this exploration, you will write your own algorithm and then write a program based on that algorithm. You are probably familiar with the 24-hour clock. Times range from 00:00 to 23:59, 24:00 being considered identical to 00:00. Your program must accept two such times as input from a user, the greater time first, the lesser time second. It must then compute the difference or elapsed time, in hours and minutes, and report that time difference to the user. You will need two variables for each time.

a Write an algorithm for this program, naming all variables to be used and being as explicit as possible about how to handle the case where the second minute figure is larger than the first.

b Write a program based on the algorithm. Then debug it and test it on as many distinct cases as you can think of.

9 Listed below are several examples of Turbo Pascal statements. Some of them will be accepted by the Turbo Pascal compiler as valid; some will not be accepted. Can you determine which? If you are uncertain about the exact syntax of any particular statement type, you can compare the statement with examples in this chapter or look it up in Appendix A.

a `PROGRAM Addition Tutor;`

b `PROGRAM WrongSyntax;`

```
c  WRITELN('#!*@;&%?');
d  WRITELN('Please enter a number.');
e  READLN(FirstNum);
f  READLN(SecondNum);
g  58 := Num1*Num2;
h  Average := First*Second*Third/3;
i  IF XPert <> Task;
      THEN XPert := Task;
j  FOR Index := 1 TO 15 DO
      WRITELN('Now I'm at iteration number', Index);
k  FOR Count := 1 TO
      READLN(NumBirds);
```

10 If you examine the syntax diagram for variable declarations in Chapter 3 (see page 90), you will discover that it allows any number of identifiers of the same type. Alter the diagram by adding a single back-arrow. The altered diagram should permit different types within the same VAR statement.

```
VAR Temp, Humidex: INTEGER; Pressure: REAL;
```

11 Redesign the soft drink automaton to allow the user to select a drink. Signal the selection with the letter s. By adding a new state, a new transition, and a new input, you can complete the design in the form of a new state diagram.

12 Design an automaton that recognizes all two-letter English words. You can find these words in a regular dictionary, but a Scrabble dictionary will enable you to find them more quickly.

13 This may sound strange, but there's something to be learned from a program you don't understand. Turn to Chapter 3 and examine the program on page 75. Try to understand it by reading the various Turbo Pascal statements that make up the program and attempting to figure out how they work together. How long do you think it would take to understand the program fully? I will explain why I asked you to do this near the end of the next chapter.

3 A Variable Named *Money*

Input, Output, and In Between

This chapter provides a lively metaphor to explain how computers store variables. The metaphor, a cubbyhole in a storage cabinet, helps you to understand how variables vary. To drive the ideas home, you follow the life of a particular variable, one called *Money*, after developing a program that tracks the real value of investments. Along the way, two boxes explain the input and output devices by which computers communicate with the outside world. Variables often get their first values through input devices and also provide values for output devices. Thus input and output form part of the life of a variable. (In this course, your main input device will be the keyboard, your main output device the screen.)

After developing a program called *RealInvest*, a sample run reveals some details of the life of a variable called *Money*. Besides providing an understanding of how variables work, the programming project suggests a new topic, the life of a program. Although the program called *RealInvest* has met all of its objectives, a number of improvements suggest themselves. In the course of watching the program grow and improve like a living organism, your programming skills develop to a new level when you learn about formatting output, the CONST statement, the WRITE statement, CHAR variables, and how to add comments to a program to make it more readable.

This chapter bears an intimate relationship to the next chapter, which is devoted to computer graphics. There, you will see *RealInvest* reincarnated as a graphics program in which the value of an investment becomes a colorful display of vertical green bars and the variable called *Money* takes on a new life.

The Life of a Variable

The life of a variable begins when it is declared in a program. It is not truly born, however, until the program begins to run. At first the variable has no value, but, sooner or later, through either an assignment statement or a READLN statement, it gets its first value. Thereafter, its value may change. For example, the *Xvar* variable in the *Chaos* program (Chapter 1) changed its value with every iteration of the program's FOR-loop. Some variables may never change their values. For example, the variable *FirstNum* in the *AddTutor* program (Chapter 2) never changed after the user entered a value for it.

Sometimes in the course of its existence, a variable's value is output to the user. The variable *Xvar*, again, had its value output frequently to users of the *Chaos* program. As you can already see, the life of a variable is closely linked to input and output statements.

Before following the life of a particular variable called *Money*, it is important to understand how the values of variables are actually stored in a computer. Then you will grasp the meaning of the word *vary*.

A Metaphor for Memory

The memory of a computer can be pictured as a very tall tier of cubby-holes, some of which contain a piece of paper. Each piece of paper has a number or some other datum, like a word, written on it. From time to time something removes the paper from one of the cubbyholes and replaces it by another. Such cubbyholes are the homes of particular variables. As you can see in the accompanying illustration, one of the cubbyholes is labeled *Money*. If the variable called *Money* lives anywhere, it is here. The paper currently in the cubbyhole holds the current value of the variable *Money*.

When a program is first compiled, the computer sets up a cubbyhole for each variable declared in the program. The computer knows where every variable lives because it keeps an address book, of sorts. A variable gets its first value in a number of ways. As I have already mentioned, the value may be input by the user. The initial value of *Money*, for example, might come when a READLN statement is executed.

```
READLN(Money);
```

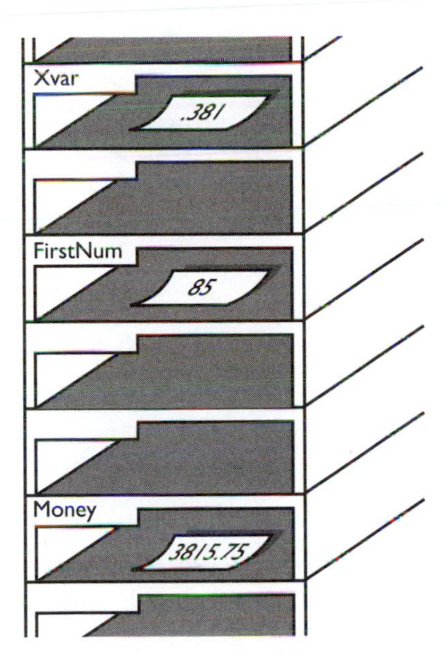

The cubbyholes of memory

As soon as the computer executes this statement, it looks up the address of *Money* and puts whatever value the user entered directly into the cubbyhole for this variable. The initial value of another variable, however, might well come from an assignment statement. The variable *Xvar*, you may recall, had its value continually changed by an assignment statement in the *Chaos* program:

```
Xvar := 3.9*Xvar*(1-Xvar);
```

Every time the computer executed this statement, it looked up the address of *Xvar*, took out the slip of paper stored in that cubbyhole (so to speak) and replaced it by another. In the forthcoming program, called *RealInvest*, you will see that the variable called *Money* also changes its value when an assignment statement is executed. The accompanying illustration shows how a variable varies. When a program is being executed, the value stored in the cubbyhole may change just once or many, many times. It all depends on the program.

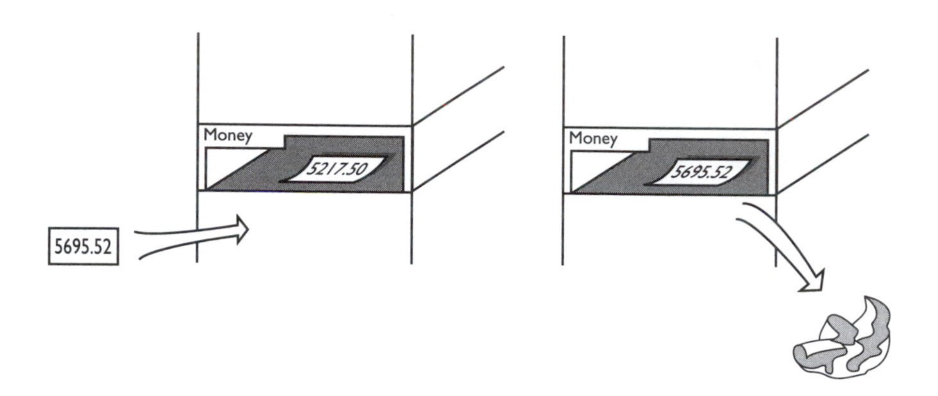

How a variable changes its value

An Investment Program

The project for this chapter centers on a program that tracks the value of an investment. As you know, a term deposit in a bank grows over the years because the bank pays a certain annual rate of interest, say, 5%. At the same time, however, money inflation decreases the value of the investment. It is rather hard for the average person to do these important calculations even with the aid of a hand calculator. The program I have already named *RealInvest* should solve this problem.

> Write a program that determines how the real value of an investment changes with time. The program must take, as input from the user, four pieces of information:
>
> 1. the initial amount of the investment
> 2. the number of years the money is to remain in the bank
> 3. the annual rate of return, or interest rate
> 4. the expected inflation rate
>
> The program must calculate and display both the nominal value of the investment, year by year, and its "real" value (when inflation is taken into account). Finally, the program must warn the user if the value of the investment is actually declining, owing to inflation.

Let's begin the design process by listing all the variables we anticipate will be used by relying solely on the project specification.

Name	*Description*
Money	"Real" value of the investment (example: 10,000)
Term	Number of years of investment (example: 5)
Return	Annual rate of return (example: 8.25%)
Inflat	Predicted annual rate of inflation (example: 3.1%)

The specifications for *RealInvest* state that certain information will be provided by the user. In other words, the program will require prompts, all of which can be at the beginning. Here is one way that the prompts might be organized:

1. Prompt the user for *Money* and *Term*.
2. Input *Money* and *Term*.
3. Prompt the user for *Return* and *Inflat*.
4. Input *Return* and *Inflat*.

You might ask why I broke up the user interface into two separate prompts. Well, nobody wants to be prompted for four separate items in one go: "Hmm, okay. Next I have to input the third item. Now what item was that again?"

After the program has received the four items of information from the user, it will proceed to the main calculation. How does the amount of the investment (stored in the variable *Money*) change, year after year after year? If the phrase, "year after year" reminds you of a loop, you'd be right. The number of times the calculation must be done will be found in the value of *Term*, the number of years that the money is to be invested.

5. For every year in the *Term*,
   calculate the effect of *Return* on *Money*,
   calculate the effect of *Inflat* on *Money*,
   display the value of *Money* on the screen.

At your stage of development as a programmer, a loop means using a FOR statement. This, in turn, means that a loop index variable must be added to the list of variables. Let's call it *Year*.

Name	*Description*
Year	An index to the current year being calculated

Input: The Devices

A program variable may receive its initial value through a number of different input devices. Although this course focuses mainly on input from the keyboard, you ought to be familiar with the other possibilities. Our hypothetical but typical computer, the Simplex 2000, has four input devices, as shown in the accompanying illustration.

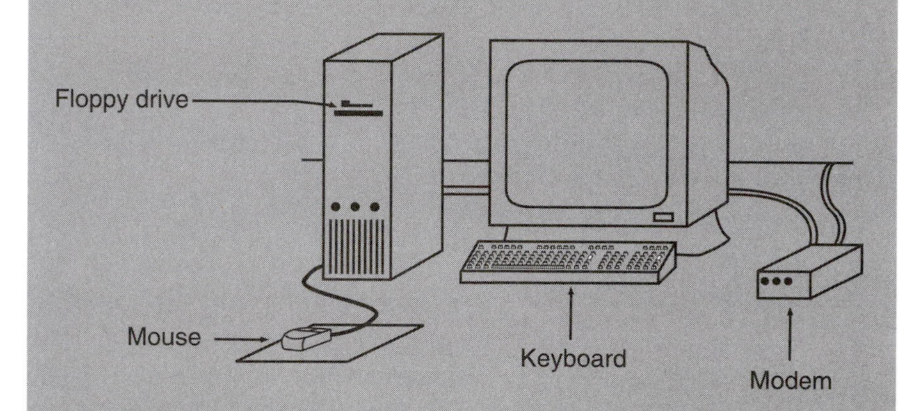

Four input devices for the Simplex 2000

Keyboard. When the user presses a key on the keyboard, an electronic signal encoding the key that was pressed is sent to the hardware inside the box. Suppose a program happens to be running on the Simplex 2000 and is in the middle of executing a READLN statement. The character or number that was sent to the hardware will become the value of a particular variable in the program.

The final mission of *RealInvest*, to warn the user of a declining investment value, can be accomplished by comparing the final value of the investment with the initial value.

6. If final amount < initial amount,
 then warn the user.

Floppy drive. The Simplex 2000 comes equipped with a drive into which the user can insert a disk, often called a floppy disk. (This piece of hardware should not be confused with the hard disk, a permanent part of the machine's memory system.) Floppy disks are very useful for holding large amounts of data; when a program reads such a disk, the characters or numbers contained in the disk are transferred to the computer's central processing hardware, where they become the values for one or more variables in a program that is running. Floppy disks are also popular input vehicles for the entry of whole programs into a computer.

Mouse. This device consists of a housing that contains a ball, which rotates like a wheel under a mechanical car and rolls one way or another across a pad. The rolling motion of the ball is translated into two signals that control the horizontal and vertical positions of a cursor on the screen. Many commercial programs use the position coordinates of the cursor, as well as "mouse clicks" (button presses), as input values for their variables. Equivalent devices include the trackball, where the user rolls the ball by hand, and the joystick, where the spherical motion of a vertical lever replaces the ball altogether.

Modem. With the advent of the "information highway," this device has come into its own. Indeed some computers (but not the Simplex 2000) have a built-in modem. A modem connects the computer to a telephone line. Within the hardware, special connections give a program access to the telephone signals, and many programs have been written to supervise this connection to the outside world, automatically handling the dialing of numbers and transfer of data. Other programs take the data that arrives by modem and use it directly for values of its variables.

This task calls for one more variable. If you use *Money* to store away the value of the investment at every yearly cycle, then at the end of the investment term, *Money* will contain the final value of the investment. Let's use a variable called *MoneyIn* to hold the initial value until the program reaches the stage represented by step 6. The test in the IF–THEN statement will simply compare *Money* with *MoneyIn*.

Name	*Description*
MoneyIn	Holds the initial value of the investment

Small changes, made during the algorithmic design process, often reverberate throughout the program, causing little changes elsewhere. Because you now have a new variable that will hold the initial value of *Money*, the program will obviously have to include an assignment statement right after step 4:

Set *MoneyIn* to the value of *Money*

By "setting" one variable to a specific value, I mean assigning that value to the variable.

Stepwise Refinement

You are now ready to refine the steps of this algorithm. Anticipating the translation of the algorithm into the program *RealInvest*, first write the name of the program and list the variables:

Program name: *RealInvest*
Variables: *Money*, *Term*, *Return*, *Inflat*, *Year*, *MoneyIn*

To speed things up, I write two pairs of prompt/input steps, all in one fell swoop:

output: "Please enter the amount of the investment and the term."
input: *Money*, *Term*
output: "Next, enter the rate of interest and the rate of inflation."
input: *Return*, *Inflat*

Note that I used a simplified way of indicating the prompts and the accompanying input steps in the algorithm by using the words *output* and *input*.

Here is a good place to insert the step in which *MoneyIn* gets assigned the initial value of *Money*.

Set *MoneyIn* to *Money*

In case you forgot what it looked like, I have reproduced below the next step of the original algorithm. It was an algorithmic version of a loop:

For every year in the *Term*,
  calculate the effect of *Return* on *Money*,
  calculate the effect of *Inflat* on *Money*,
  display the value of *Money* on the screen.

Let's refine this loop only partially, for the moment, then go on to refine the remaining steps of the initial algorithm.

For Year running from 1 to *Term*,
  calculate the effect of *Return* on *Money*,
  calculate the effect of *Inflat* on *Money*,
  display the value of *Money* on the screen.

The final step of the first algorithm called for a warning to the user in case the final value of the investment was less than the initial value. Having named the two relevant variables makes it easier to write this step.

If *Money* < *MoneyIn*,
  then output: "WARNING! The value of your investment will fall."

A Little Knowledge . . .

Very often, writing a program involves the use of special knowledge that has nothing to do with programming or computer science. After all, to the extent that a program must solve a real-world problem, it may well draw upon specialized knowledge to solve it. You will not be expected to draw upon such knowledge for this course; it will be supplied, as now. But it is important to realize that the creative process of programming continually calls on all kinds of specialized knowledge. The refinement of the three steps in the loop of the first algorithm illustrates this crucial point.

For example, what calculation should you use to "calculate the effect of *Return* on *Money*"? Suppose the rate of return is 8%. Then an amount worth $1 at the beginning of a given year will be worth $1.08 at the end of the year, inflation aside. In this particular case, the annual calculation would look something like this:

```
Money := Money*1.08;
```

Because the program *RealInvest* must be able to handle *any* rate of interest, and not just 8%, note that 1.08, which is actually 1 + 0.08, can be generalized to

```
Money := Money*(1 + Return);
```

The variable *Return* must be specified as a decimal number and not as a percentage. This refinement causes another reverberation. You must make sure that the user understands that a decimal fraction is required as input. Note that when you later come to translate the refined algorithm into a program, the second prompt will require an extra WRITELN statement or two to explain the requirement to the user.

The second step within the annual calculation loop is more troublesome. Even though almost everybody has done simple interest calculations in high school, how many have calculated inflation? When prices inflate (the normal meaning of "inflation"), the value of money deflates. In spite of what an amazing number of financial reporters seem to think, the two percentages are not the same. The box on page 76 explains the difference and ends by giving you a formula to apply. The formula turns out to be exactly as simple as the interest calculation. As explained in the box, the following formula expresses the change in the value of money over a year: 1/(1 + Inflat). This expression means that the annual calculation of the ravages of inflation will look like this in the program:

```
Money := Money/(1 + Inflat);
```

This step introduces a new arithmetic operator. Just as the symbol * means "multiply" in Turbo Pascal, the symbol / means "divide." Because Turbo Pascal classifies the result of division as a real number, you should only employ division in an assignment statement when the assigned-to variable (the one on the left-hand side) is real.

Before continuing to the final, translation stage, it wouldn't hurt to run a little bench test of these formulas. Suppose, then, that someone invests $10,000 at 7.7% for one year and that over that year the rate of inflation is expected to be 4%. First, apply the rate of return formula:

$$10{,}000*(1.077) = 10{,}770$$

At the end of the year, the investor should receive $10,770, but there is inflation to consider. To calculate the effect that an inflation rate of 4% would have on the purchasing power of this money, apply the following inflation formula:

$$10{,}770/1.04 = 10{,}356$$

In other words, some $414 of purchasing power was lost to this investment because of inflation. Enough!

Translating into Turbo Pascal

If you read the following program over carefully, you will see that every statement accurately reflects a step in the refined algorithm. The most radical difference will be found in the user interface. In the program, the prompts give more detail to the user about what is expected of the input. The first prompt ensures that the user will employ units of dollars and years. The second prompt explains by way of an example (which is often the quickest way) what the decimal fraction versions of percentage numbers are.

```
PROGRAM RealInvest;

VAR Term, Year: INTEGER;
VAR Money, MoneyIn, Return, Inflat: REAL;

BEGIN
WRITELN('Please enter the amount of the investment, in dollars,');
WRITELN('and the term of the investment, in years.');
READLN(Money, Term);
WRITELN('Now enter the rate of interest and the rate of inflation,');
WRITELN('both as decimal fractions, e.g., 0.08 instead of 8%.');
READLN(Return, Inflat);
```

A Bit of Economics

When the government announces an inflation rate of, say, 5% in a given year, it means that the average price of goods and services rose by 5% over the year. To be specific, let's suppose that a pair of socks that cost $1.00 at the beginning of the year cost $1.05 at the end of the year. Just as the price of the socks went up as a result of price inflation, the purchasing power of the dollar went down. This is money deflation. The same dollar doesn't buy as much as it used to.

To make a precise statement of just how inflation of prices affects the purchasing power of a dollar, let's suppose that you ask how many pairs of socks a dollar will buy at the end of the year as opposed to how many it would have bought at the beginning. In other words, you are working in socks, instead of dollars. At the beginning of the year, $1000 would have bought 1000 pairs of socks, but at the end, $1000 will buy

$$1000/1.05$$

```
MoneyIn := Money;

FOR Year := 1 to Term DO
   BEGIN
   Money := Money*(1 + Return);
   Money := Money/(1 + Inflat);
   WRITELN('After ' , Year, ' years, the value is ', Money);
   END;

IF Money < MoneyIn
   THEN WRITELN('WARNING: The value of the investment will decline!');

END.
```

You may have noticed that I have broken up the program into pieces. There is no harm in inserting blank lines into a program. This practice can make a program easier to read.

pairs of socks, namely, 952 pairs of socks, to the nearest pair. You can already see that the value of the $1000, as far as socks is concerned, has slipped from 1000 pairs to 952 pairs. Scaling this down to a single dollar, you could say that at the end of the year the dollar has slipped in purchasing power from $1.00 to $0.952, a drop of about 4.8%. In other words, there is a difference between the rate of inflation and the corresponding rate of deflation. At the level of 5%, it isn't much, but (a) when compounded, as in a term deposit, the difference can get quite large, and (b) higher rates of inflation lead to even larger differences between inflation and the corresponding money deflation.

If you look closely at the purchasing power of $1000, you will see the formula you want, in embryo form. To calculate the new value of an amount of money after inflation, simply divide it by the following little formula:

$$1 + \text{Inflat}$$

The WRITELN statement within the FOR-loop demonstrates the great flexibility of this statement. Within the parentheses of such a statement, the programmer can insert either a variable name or a string of text enclosed by single quotes. The two kinds of components can be inserted in any order, as long as they are separated by commas. This facility enables the programmer to have a message in which some parts change as the loop churns on. You will notice that the strings of text that are adjacent to variables have one or two extra spaces inserted into them. Without these spaces, the output of the program would look like this:

```
After5years, the value is2500.00
```

Because you already know how the rest of the program works, let's return to the variable *Money* and revisit its life via a particular example. I have reproduced a skeletal version of the *RealInvest* program below. The only statements left are those that have a direct bearing on the value of this variable.

```
–
–
–
READLN(Money, Term);                          Money gets its
                                               first value.
–
–
–
FOR Year := 1 TO Term DO
   –
   –
   Money := Money*(1 + Return);               Money increases.
   Money := Money/(1 + Inflat);               Money decreases.
   –
   –
```

Suppose the user enters an investment of $1200 over a three-year term at an interest rate of 4% and an inflation rate of 6%. In other words, at the beginning of the program, four of the variables have been initialized.

Term = 3
Return = 0.04
Inflat = 0.06

The variable *Money* is born when the user inputs the value of $1200.

Money = 1200

The program then enters the FOR-loop, where *Money* takes on successive values, increased by the rate of return, then sacked by inflation:

Money = 1248.00	First assignment statement
Money = 1177.36	Second assignment statement
Money = 1224.45	First assignment statement
Money = 1155.14	Second assignment statement
Money = 1201.35	First assignment statement
Money = 1133.35	Second assignment statement

If you could chart the changes in this variable as the program runs, you would see it jump upward every time the computer executes the first assignment statement in the loop, only to drop further than it climbed when the computer executes the second assignment statement. You don't need a chart, however, to appreciate that at the end of the program's run, the value of *Money* is lower than the value the investor began with. This triggers the alarm.

```
WARNING: The value of the investment will decline!
```

The foregoing technique of following the fortunes of a particular variable is called a *program trace*. You will find this technique very useful in debugging your own programs. It constitutes one of the programmer's arts.

Speaking of debugging, you haven't tested *RealInvest* yet, so let's run it under precisely the conditions mentioned. The output that appears on the screen is shown in the accompanying figure. What went wrong? The answer is "Nothing." If the programmer does not specify the format to be followed when the value of a REAL variable is output, the computer automatically assumes that the user wants *floating point notation*, such as 1.1773584906E+03, for example. In spite of its formidable appearance, the number is easy to decipher. It simply means

$$1.1773584906 \times 10^{+3}$$

```
Please enter the amount of the investment, in dollars,
and the term of the investment, in years.
1200 3
Now enter the rate of interest and the rate of inflation,
both as decimal fractions, e.g., 0.08 instead of 8%.
0.04 0.06
After 1 year the value is 1.1773584906E+03
After 2 years the value is 1.1551441794E+03
After 3 years the value is 1.1333490062E+03
```

Output of the *RealInvest* program

or

1177.3584906

That's better; but who wants to see the value of their investment to the ten-millionth of a penny?

Formatting Real Output

To put the values of the variable *Money* into meaningful form, it is necessary to use the *colon notation*, a system of colons and numbers that determines the format of a real number when the program outputs it. It consists of two colons that are appended to the name of a variable in a WRITELN statement. The number following the first colon is the total number of spaces that will be allocated to the displayed version of the value (including the decimal point). The number following the second colon determines how many decimal digits will be allowed in the answer. You may recall the WRITELN statement from the middle of the FOR-loop in the *Chaos* program:

```
WRITELN(Xvar:6:4);
```

This format specifies a total of six spaces, one for the whole number digit, one for the decimal point, and four for the decimal digits. Flip back to page 3 for a moment and confirm that this format is actually followed by all the values of *Xvar* output by *Chaos*.

With this brief description of formatting real output under your belt, you can make a definite improvement to *RealInvest* by altering the WRITELN statement inside the FOR-loop to

```
WRITELN('After ', Year, ' years, the value is ', Money:7:2);
```

This format leaves room for seven spaces: 4 for dollars, one for the decimal point, and two for the cents. This leaves up to four digits for the dollar part of the answer. If *Money* has a three-figure dollar value, the program will simply print one leading blank to bring the total number of characters to seven. If *Money* has a five-figure dollar value, on the other hand, this format will still print all the digits, but it will leave no blanks.

If the program is expected to deal with larger investments in six figures, say, the first format number should be increased to nine.

This refinement puts the program *RealInvest* into final form. Or does it?

The Life of a Program

Once a program has been written, it is not unusual for the programmer to make changes that improve the performance of the program in some way. Your experience with *RealInvest* will be typical in this regard.

CONSTant Inflation

If you think about how *RealInvest* will be used, you will quickly realize that interest rates will vary continually, even within the same day. Different financial institutions may offer different rates. At the same time, the predicted rate of inflation may not change for months. For this reason, it makes sense not to prompt the user for the expected rate of inflation every time the program is used, but to keep this value in the form of a constant. Superficially, a constant looks like a variable because it carries a value in a name, but constants never change their value unless the programmer changes their declaration.

For example, let's add the following statement to the declaration block of *RealInvest*. This statement declares a constant called *Inflat*.

```
CONST Inflat = 0.04;
```

At the same time, because *Inflat* is no longer a variable, you must remove this name from the VAR declarations. Finally, you must also change the prompts, removing all references to inflation and the variable *Inflat* from them and from the accompanying input statement. I have reproduced the first half of the program below, highlighting those statements that have changed.

```
PROGRAM RealInvest;

VAR Term, Year: INTEGER;
VAR Money, MoneyIn, Return: REAL;
CONST Inflat = 0.04;
```

```
BEGIN
WRITELN('Please enter the amount of the investment, in dollars,');
WRITELN('and the term of the investment, in years.');
READLN(Money, Term);
WRITELN('Now enter the rate of interest as a decimal fraction,');
WRITELN('e.g., 0.08 instead of 8%.');
READLN(Return);
```

The rest of the program remains the same, even the statement in which the constant *Inflat* appears.

```
Money := Money/(1 + Inflat);
```

When the computer executes this statement in the new version of *RealInvest*, it looks up the value of the constant *Inflat* instead of that of the variable *Inflat*. These values are stored in separate areas of memory.

The Turbo Pascal CONSTant statement forms part of a program's declaration block and has the following syntax:

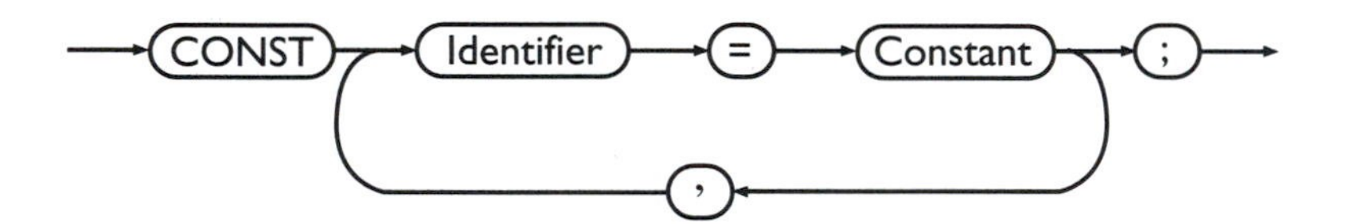

The statement tells the computer to reserve space in memory for a constant named "identifier," just as it would reserve space for a variable. Because constants cannot change, it is illegal to make an assignment to a constant. The compiler will tell you about such a syntax error if you should forget this rule.

Here is another example of the use of a constant. You may recall from Chapter 1 that the program *Chaos* uses a specific number, 3.9, in the calculation of its assignment statement:

```
Xvar := 3.9*Xvar*(1 - Xvar);
```

If you change this value, the program will generate various different kinds of output. Some values will produce "chaotic" output and some will not. In order to change this number, it makes sense to introduce a new constant:

```
CONST Drive = 3.9;
```

The name *Drive* is meant to suggest that high values of this constant will drive the chaotic process harder than low values. Naturally, the assignment statement must be modified to accommodate the constant:

```
Xvar := Drive*Xvar*(1 - Xvar);
```

Now you can change the constant to any other value you like. If you change it to 2.5, for example, you will drive the process more slowly and the program will produce very different, well-behaved, output.

A CHARacter for Currency

The life of the program involves a little growth sometimes, especially when you add features. For example, it would seem desirable for the program *RealInvest* to work not only in dollars but in any currency, as symbolized by a single keyboard symbol.

You are already familiar with two data types in Turbo Pascal, namely, INTEGER and REAL. The discussion on page 90 explains in detail how these types differ. There is a third data type in Turbo Pascal called CHAR, short for "character." My vehicle for the introduction of this new data type will be another improvement to the *RealInvest* program, namely, to allow currency symbols.

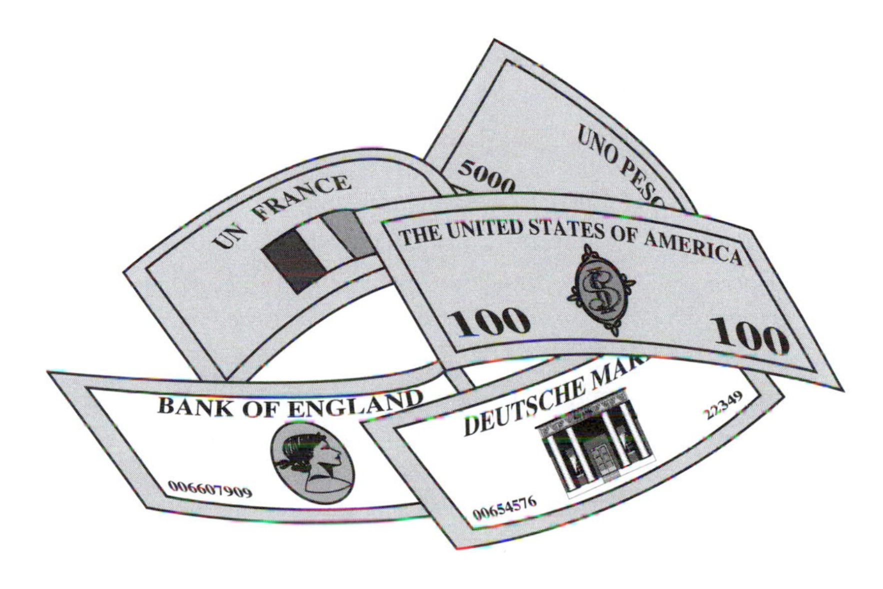

An assortment of currencies

The syntax of a CHAR declaration statement is exactly the same as that of an INTEGER or REAL declaration statement:

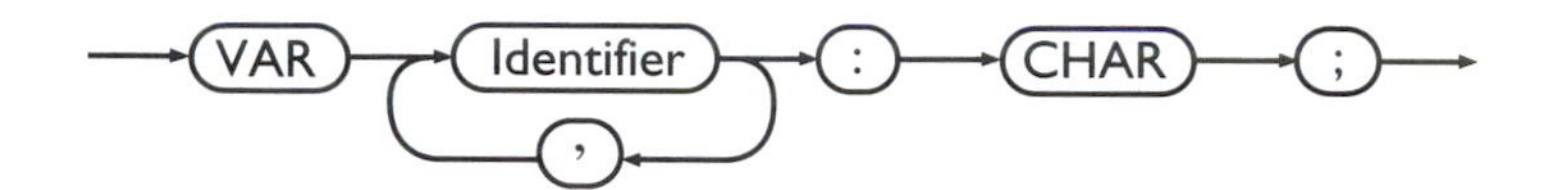

Semantically speaking, this statement tells the computer that the program will use a variable that will take on character values. To some people, this may sound strange, but why not? Let's take an example of a character variable called *Crncy*. The *RealInvest* program could use this variable to place the symbol of any type of currency next to a money amount. The declaration for this variable must be added to the program in the declaration section:

```
VAR Crncy: CHAR;
```

In the user interface section of the program, you must also add a new prompt to ask the user to input a character that represents the units of currency in which the program must work.

```
WRITELN('Please enter a single symbol that represents the currency');
WRITELN('of the investment, e.g., $ for dollars, p for pesos.');
READLN(Crncy);
```

Finally, the variable *Crncy* makes an appearance in the WRITELN statement in the middle of the annual calculation loop.

```
WRITELN('After ', Year, ' years, the value is ', Crncy, Money:7:2);
```

When the computer executes this statement, it will print the character currently in *Crncy*, then, without any intervening space, the value of the variable *Money*. Thus if *Crncy* = '$' and *Money* = 2303.21, the final part of this WRITELN statement would produce

```
the value is $2303.21
```

These changes illustrate the actual use of a CHAR variable in a program. The fact that I decided not to use it after all should not detract from the value of this illustration. As it turns out, the ability to work in different currencies at the drop of a hat adds value to the program *RealInvest*, but it also makes it slightly harder to use. For this reason, I would prefer to keep the currency symbol as a constant. A typical user of the program, after all, is not likely to change currencies more frequently than he or she changes inflation.

The following CONST declaration takes care of the matter, assuming that the user will work in dollars:

```
CONST Crncy = '$';
```

Notice that a specific value for a character constant or variable always involves a single character surrounded by single quotes.

WRITEing a New Prompt

The program *RealInvest* will mature further once you understand how to make the prompts operate a little more effectively from the user's point of view. The WRITELN statement has a close cousin called WRITE. You can replace some of the WRITELN statements in the *RealInvest* program by WRITE statements in order to enhance the user interface slightly. You will see exactly how in a moment.

The Turbo Pascal WRITE statement has exactly the same syntax as the WRITELN statement but a slightly different effect in a running program. To understand this difference, you need to know about the *screen cursor*. This display element is the little flashing underscore that you see racing ahead of the text or numbers when a program outputs a message or data to the screen. The cursor simply gives the position where the next character, be it number or letter, will be placed on the screen.

Let me illustrate the difference between WRITELN and WRITE statements by using the *AddTutor* program from Chapter 2. In that program, a WRITELN statement asks the user to input two numbers:

```
WRITELN('Enter the first number, then enter the second.');
READLN(FirstNum, SecondNum);
```

When the computer executes this statement, it prints the following message on the screen:

```
Enter the first number, then enter the second._
```

For a split second, the cursor appears at the end of the line of text; then it skips down to the beginning of the next line. The numbers input by the user therefore appear at the beginning of the next line. Consider what happens when we use a WRITE statement instead:

```
WRITE('Enter the first number, then enter the second.');
READLN(FirstNum, SecondNum);
```

In this case, the cursor remains next to the last character of the output message. When the user enters the two numbers, they appear right beside the message.

So let's use the WRITE statement to effect a mild improvement in the appearance of the user interface in the *RealInvest* program. As it currently stands, one of the prompts has the following appearance:

```
WRITELN('Please enter the amount of the investment, in dollars,');
WRITELN('and the term of the investment, in years.');
READLN(Money, Term);
```

I want to preserve the first WRITELN statement, because it sends the cursor to the beginning of the next line in order to complete the message to the user. However, I want to change the second WRITELN statement to a WRITE statement so that the cursor will sit expectantly at the very end of the prompt. The final version of this prompt will therefore have the following form:

```
WRITELN('Please enter the amount of the investment, in dollars,');
WRITE('and the term of the investment, in years: ');
READLN(Money, Term);
```

You will see one subtle change in addition to the obvious one. I changed the period at the end of the message to a colon, indicating an expectant condition, and I added a space before closing the message with the single quote. This space will prevent the user's input from colliding visually with the message.

Comments on Comments

The final event in the life of *RealInvest* involves the addition of a feature that all good programs must have, namely, documentation. So far, the programs presented in this book have been "naked," fit only for the eyes of someone who understands Turbo Pascal fairly well. The rest of the world needs comments in programs. In the larger programs that you will see in later chapters, even an expert would appreciate comments.

Any bunch of keyboard symbols that is enclosed in curly brackets is, technically speaking, a comment. Here are two examples of comments:

```
{jh4q3iufo%Dk-iac z c[c opK c [0 ;mr29!$#*(CV}

{Calculate growth of investment due to return.}
```

The first comment is hardly a "comment" in the ordinary sense of the word. I included it to illustrate that the computer couldn't care less what symbols appear between the curly brackets (except for more curly brackets, of course). The symbols are for humans only. They have no effect on a program's operation. In fact, I will include as comments only English sentences or phrases between the curly brackets. You can insert a comment anywhere you like in a Turbo Pascal program. During compilation and later, during execution, the computer will completely ignore whatever appears between the curly brackets.

There are two reasons for putting comments into a program. First, comments help other people to understand your program. To see the trouble an undocumented program makes, imagine trying to understand the *RealInvest* program as it appeared earlier, without the accompanying explanation. In fact, I asked you to do this in Exploration 13 of Chapter 2.

The first reason becomes apparent when several people get together to write a large program in a software engineering project. Documented code makes it possible for team members to understand one another's programs. It also makes it much easier to change the code a few years later when, perhaps, there is a whole new gang of programmers who would be quite literally lost without the comments. It might cost a software company only a few thousand dollars to upgrade a software package that is well documented. But it could easily cost the same company hundreds of thousands of dollars to upgrade the same program if it had never been documented. It might even have to be rewritten from scratch.

Undocumented programs are hard to understand

The same upgrade scenario leads to the second reason for documenting your programs. You yourself may want to read and modify them later, only to realize that you no longer understand your own program! This happens all the time, and it only takes a few weeks for much of your memory of the process (including your reasons for doing things the way you did) to disappear.

In this textbook, I will adopt the convention of beginning each major section of a program with a comment that explains what that section does. At the same time, any individual statements that might otherwise be difficult to understand should also receive comments.

Finally, the Improved Program

I'm now ready to incorporate all the improvements described above and to add comments. Read the following program over carefully and see if you can spot all the changes due to the addition of the following new features of Turbo Pascal: formatted real output, the CONST and WRITE statements, and comments.

```
PROGRAM RealInvest;
{This program tracks the real value of an investment, taking}
{both the rates of return and inflation into account.}

{declaration section}
VAR Term, Year: INTEGER;
```

```
VAR Money, MoneyIn, Return: REAL;
CONST Inflat = 0.041;
CONST Crncy = '$';

BEGIN {program}

{user interface}
WRITELN('Please enter the amount of the investment');
WRITE('and the term of the investment, in years: ');
READLN(Money, Term);
WRITELN('Now enter the rate of return as a decimal.');
WRITE('fraction e.g., enter 0.08 instead of 8%. ');
READLN(Return);

{initialization section}
MoneyIn := Money;

{main loop: Calculates yearly increase on}
{return and yearly decrease on inflation.}
FOR Year := 1 to Term DO
   BEGIN
   Money := Money*(1 + Return);
   Money := Money/(1 + Inflat);
   WRITELN('After ', Year, ' years, the value is ', Crncy, Money);
   END;

{warning section}
IF Money < MoneyIn
   THEN WRITELN('WARNING: The value of the investment will decline!');

END. {of program}
```

This program will run as is under a DOS-based system. To run it under Windows, you must add the USES statement

```
USES WinCrt;
```

right after the program header. You should feel free to run *RealInvest*, trying it with different inputs that bring out different features of the program. For example, try it with such a low value of *Return* that the warning statement is triggered. Next, edit the program by changing the constant *Crncy* from '$' to 'Y', the closest thing your keyboard will give you to the actual symbol for the Japanese yen. Then run the program and notice how the symbol Y appears in front of all money amounts.

RealInvest has now "matured" as a program. You might even say that it will continue to live as long as someone runs it.

Variable Reprise

The development of the *RealInvest* program enabled me to introduce a new type of variable, the character variable. This addition brings to three the total number of variable types that you now understand. I have incorporated their declarations into the following combined syntax diagram.

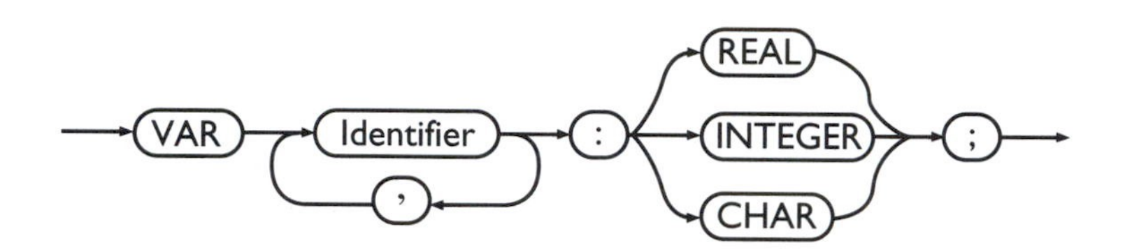

Because you already understand the semantics or meaning of these three kinds of declarations, you are ready to probe a little further beneath the surface to explore how these three kinds of variables are stored within the computer. Among other things, this exploration will help you appreciate how variables of type CHAR are variables in exactly the way that those of type REAL and INTEGER are.

Integer variables These variables take on only whole number values. In other words, you could write out a list of all possible values, as follows:

. . . –9, –8, –7, –6, –5, –4, –3, –2, –1, 0, +1, +2, +3, +4, +5, +6, +7, +8, +9, . . .

The list is open at both ends, meaning that it is potentially infinite. Computers, on the other hand, have only a finite amount of memory. Not surprisingly, then, a computer is only able to deal with so many integers, and no more. It all depends on the size of words or registers that contain the integers.

The Simplex 2000 is a fairly typical computer, so it has a 16-bit word. Here, for example, is a 16-bit integer:

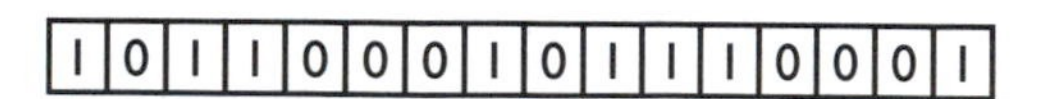

Because integers can be either positive or negative, one of these bits, the first, is reserved for storing the sign, encoding it as either a 1 or a 0. The remaining bits, 15 of them, are devoted to the numerical part of the integer. The largest binary number with 15 bits is obviously

111111111111111

This binary number represents the decimal number 32,767. The way most 16-bit computers get around this apparent limitation is to string words together into 32-bit combinations. Thus, even though the largest value that a Turbo Pascal INTEGER variable can take on is 32,767, you can get around this limitation by being able to declare a *double-precision integer* of 32 bits (one of which must be a sign bit).

Real variables A real variable takes on real values, that is, those with a fractional part, in addition to a whole number part. Examples of real numbers include 362.916, 23.00, and −7.631. The whole number part of 362.916, for example, is 362 and the fractional part is .916. It may happen that the whole number part of a real number is 0, of course; and the same conclusion holds for the fractional part. Obviously, the total number of real numbers is infinite, yet the computer is finite. This simple fact means that a limited number of real numbers can be stored; although by stringing words together, you can again obtain much larger numbers or ones with very large numbers of decimal digits in them.

In a computer the value of a real variable is stored in two components called, respectively, the *mantissa* and the *exponent*. The mantissa represents the number with a decimal point that appears right after the leading digit. The exponent carries the information of how far to the right or left the decimal point appears in the actual number. For example, the real number 1,259.712 will be represented with the following mantissa and exponent:

Mantissa	*Exponent*
1.2597120000	+03

In other words, if you shift the decimal point +3 units (to the right), you will get the number as I wrote it earlier. If the exponent had been −03, then you would have had to shift the decimal point three places to the left, obtaining the number 0.001259712.

Output: the devices

Output from a program is no less important than input to it. The computations of a program can be made available to a user in several ways. The Simplex 2000 has four output devices. Two of them have already appeared at the beginning of this chapter because they also happen to function as input devices.

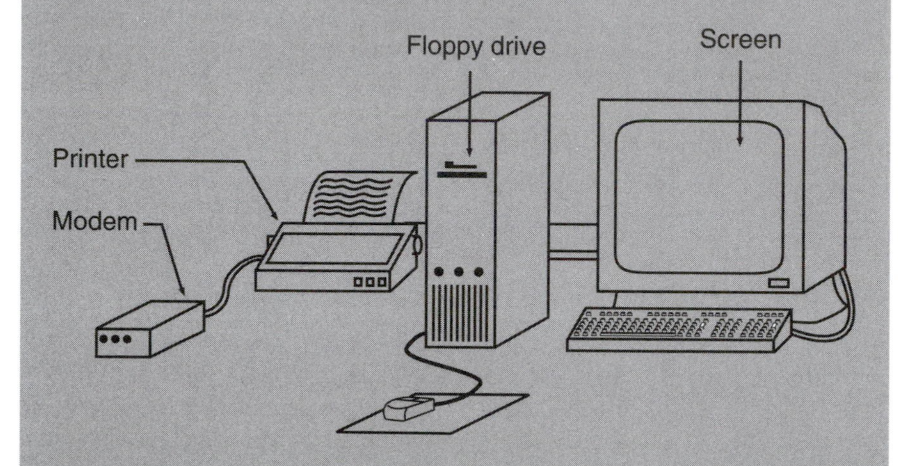

Four output devices of the Simplex 2000

Screen. As you learned in Chapter 1, signals to the screen arise in the computer's memory, where it stores either the text of a message (such as a prompt) or the value of a variable. The basic element in screen output is the pixel, a point on the screen that can be given any one of a wide range of colors. A typical screen, composed of hundreds of thousands of pixels, therefore becomes a powerful tool for the production of graphic images. A program can access any or all

Character variables If you thought that the storage of the values of character variables would present a special obstacle to the computer, you may not have thought of the encoding power of numbers. Unlike the number of integers or the number of real numbers, the number of characters is not infinite. Here is a sampling of them:

'a' 'A' '$' ':' '@' '5' '+' 'B' 'Z' 'z' '7' '='

of these pixels, changing their colors as the result of special commands to the screen. Variables that hold the coordinates of pixels, or their colors, are essential to this vital output device.

Printer. The Simplex 2000 is connected to its printer (a standard affair) by a cable that transmits one character at a time from the computer to the printer. At some point in the process, many characters transmitted to the printer might be values of variables in some program. A program can send either text information, such as a message to the user, or numbers, such as the values of output variables. The Simplex 2000's printer does nothing more than this, but some printers, such as laser printers, can also reproduce screen graphics.

Floppy drive. You have already read a description of the floppy disk and its drive on the Simplex 2000, but the description was confined to the use of disks as input devices. A program can also send output to a disk. It does so, typically, when a program produces a lot of data that someone else may wish to use, transporting the data to his or her computer, if necessary. You can also store whole programs on a disk, and this transfer represents another form of output that a computer has.

Modem. Modem communication software, mentioned at the beginning of this chapter, can send information as well as receive it. Perhaps the biggest single use of modems these days is to facilitate communications on the Internet. After reading your e-mail, you may want to reply to some of it. When the communications software is running, you merely type the message, specify the receiver, and the software (including the modem) does the rest. Some communications programs also permit you to transmit the output of a program directly via a modem. The Simplex 2000 can be connected with another computer that will analyze the data.

In fact, all characters can be stored as special combinations of 0s and 1s in eight-bit words called *bytes*. The following figure shows just two samples of the scheme.

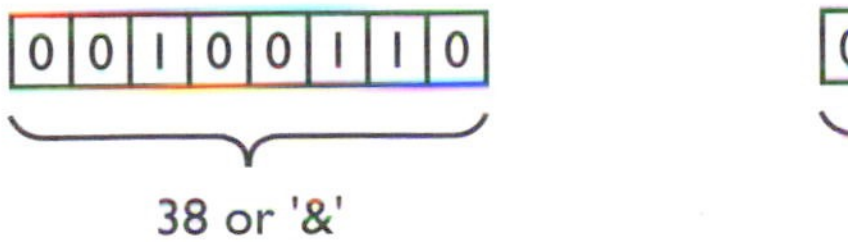

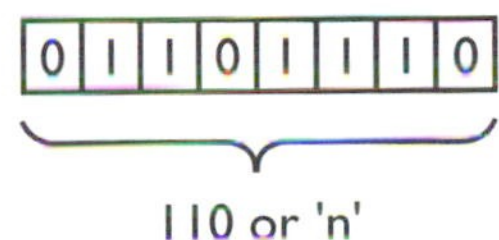

The character & is represented by the binary number for 38, and the character n is represented by the binary number for 110. This encoding scheme is universal to all computers and represents one of the few aspects of computer design that is not likely to change in the years to come. The scheme is called the ASCII code, where ASCII means the American Standard Code for Information Interchange.

SUMMARY

You have followed the life of a variable called *Money* by building a program that used it. When you ran the program, you found that *Money* fluctuated a good deal. The fluctuation was visualized as a series of changes in the computer's memory, where the cubbyhole labeled *Money* received a succession of slips of paper with different values written on them. Each slip replaced the one that was there before. By the time *RealInvest* was completed, you learned that variables are not the only things with "lives" in the world of computing. Programs have lives, too.

The subsequent improvements to *RealInvest* allowed you to learn about some important and useful Turbo Pascal statements, including the CONST statement, the CHAR declaration, and the WRITE statement. These Turbo Pascal lessons revolved, in one way or another, around input or output devices. The two boxes on input and output devices provided a wider context in which you could visualize the physical means by which input to and output from a computer connected to the outside world.

Finally, you learned something about the importance of documenting your programs in order to make them readable later by others and by yourself. This chapter contained no computer science to speak of, but the stage is now set for future chapters to do so.

EXPLORATIONS

1 Neglecting the sign bit, what integer is stored in the 16-bit word shown in the figure on page 91? Don't forget that, counting from the right, a one in the *n*th position represents a contribution of 2^{n-1} to the (decimal) sum.

2 Rewrite the numbers represented in floating point form below in standard real number notation:

1.83527390E+05
5.66828177E–03

3 For each of the following formatted output statements of the real variable *Luminance*, write out the form the output would take if *Luminance* equals 35.9116.

```
WRITELN(Luminance:2:1);

WRITELN(Luminance:6:3);
```

4 Add some flexibility to the sample program below by introducing a constant called *Scale* that takes the value 0.425. Be sure to use the new constant in the appropriate statement of the program.

```
PROGRAM ScaleChange;

VAR MeasureIn, MeasureOut: REAL;

BEGIN

WRITE('Enter the measurement: ');
READLN(MeasureIn);

MeasureOut := 0.425*MeasureIn;

WRITELN('The scaled measurement is ', MeasureOut);

END.
```

5 Reproduce the effect on the screen of the following sequence of WRITE and WRITELN statements when executed by a computer. Use an underscore to show the position of the screen cursor when all the statements have been executed.

```
WRITE('Peter');
WRITELN('Piper');
WRITE('picked a');
WRITELN('peck');
WRITE('of pickled');
WRITE('peppers');
```

6 Test the *RealInvest* program by running it with the following inputs: *Money* = 5000, *Term* = 5, *Return* = 3.9. Set the constant *Crncy* to 'D' for deutsche marks and leave the constant *Inflat* as it is. Do all aspects of the program seem to function correctly? Because the rate of inflation is higher than the rate of return, should you not expect to receive a warning that the value of the investment is decreasing?

7 Rewrite the RealInvest program so that it does not print the intermediate values of an investment, rather only the last value. This revision will mean removing the WRITELN statement from the loop, among other things.

8 What does the following program do? Analyze it and then run it. When you are quite sure of its purpose and understand the role played by each section of the program, add comments that would have made the program much easier to understand had they been part of the program to begin with. As part of this process, you should also separate the program into sections by adding blank lines, in the manner of the final version of *RealInvest*.

```
PROGRAM Population;

VAR Birth, Death, Pop: REAL;
VAR Year, Period: INTEGER;

BEGIN
WRITELN('Please enter the initial population and the period, in years.');
READLN(Pop, Period);
WRITELN('Now, enter the rates of birth and death per thousand.');
READLN(Birth, Death);
FirstPop := Pop;
FOR Year := 1 to Period DO
   BEGIN
   Pop := Pop*(1 + Birth/1000);
   Pop := Pop*(1 - Death/1000);
   WRITELN('After ', Year, ' years the population is ', Pop);
   END;
IF FirstPop > Pop
   THEN BEGIN
      WRITELN('Warning: At the current birth rates and');
      WRITELN('death rates, the population will decline!');
   END;
END.
```

9 Rewrite the *RealInvest* program so that the user can input percentages for *Return* instead of decimal fractions. This revision will mean making two kinds of changes, one in the user interface, the other in the loop body of the program, where *Money* is calculated.

10 Write a program called *RadioActive* that takes as input the amount of radioactive waste at a nuclear dump site and the number of years of storage. The half-life of this material happens to be one year, meaning that after every year half of the radioactive material present at the beginning of the year continues to be radioactive at the end of the year. *RadioActive* must use the half-life figure to calculate the degree of natural decay of the material in question and to report to the user how much radioactive waste remains *after* the period in question. Use units of tons for the amount of radioactive waste and units of years for the half-life.

Write an algorithm for the program, refine it if necessary, then translate the refined algorithm into Turbo Pascal. Consult the *RealInvest* program for some programming details but be aware that the structure of *RadioActive* will not be identical to that of *RealInvest*.

11 Using the experience gained with FOR-loops in this chapter, modify the *AddTutor* program so that it becomes restartable. This revision means that after attempting an addition question, the student-user will automatically be prompted to try a new problem without having to restart the program.

Refine the following crude algorithm to design the program, then write it, giving it a name that reflects its restartable nature.

1. Prompt the student for the number of questions.
2. Input as *Tries*.
3. For *Index* := 1 to *Tries*,
   Prompt and test the student.
   Report the results, including the correct answer.
4. Inform the student that the session has ended.

Note that the body of the loop consists essentially of the program that was formerly called *AddTutor*. (This is not an ideal kind of loop to use for a restartable program, but it will do for now.)

12 With either the *AddTutor* program of the previous question in hand, or the original one, improve the program further by allowing the program to select the numbers to be added. For this you can employ the statement

```
FirstNum := RANDOM(100);
```

It will have the effect of assigning a random integer between 0 and 99 to the variable *FirstNum*. Use the same kind of statement to allow the program to select a value for *SecondNum*.

13 Write a program that accepts a temperature in either Celsius or Fahrenheit from a user, then converts it to the other temperature and reports it. As in the program of Exploration 11, the user will first specify how many temperature conversions he or she wishes to perform. You should use the formulas $F = 1.8*C + 32$ and $C = (F - 32)/1.8$, where F and C represent the value of a temperature in Fahrenheit and Celsius degrees, respectively.

Begin by making a complete algorithmic design, ensuring that the computer will have the information that it needs from the user at each stage of the computation. Then translate the algorithm into Turbo Pascal and debug the resulting program.

4 Electronic Visions

The Color of *Money*

The most dramatic output of computers, what makes them spectacularly easy and informative to use, is their ability to draw pictures on the screen. Rare is the program that would not benefit from the addition of graphics output.

In this section, I will develop a computer graphics version of *RealInvest* called *RealInvest_Graph*. To set the stage, I outline the essentials of Turbo Pascal graphics, showing how to set up the computer in graphics mode. Then I introduce a few of the most basic and useful Turbo Pascal graphics statements, especially the ones that will permit the variable *Money* to march across the screen as a succession of vertical bars, charting an investment.

When it comes to storing computer graphics images, some systems are better than others. Computer scientists have developed many techniques, including the use of trees. Every leaf in the structure called a quad-tree contains a piece of the image.

Getting into Graphics

So crucial are computer graphics today that a commercial, scientific, or industrial program that doesn't use them is scarcely thinkable. Even word processing programs have interfaces that fill the screen with lively icons and images. More typically, computer graphics range from charting variables (as illustrated in the *RealInvest_Graph* program to come) to portraying weather systems, human faces, golf courses, game scenarios, virtual reality, star maps, and encyclopedia images. As the old saying goes, a picture is worth a thousand words.

Speaking of words, Turbo Pascal makes available two kinds of screen systems. In the one you have been using so far, called *text mode*, the screen is set up to display only keyboard characters, typically in the form of words and numbers. In this chapter, you will explore the capabilities of *graphics mode*, in which the individual points of a screen, called pixels, become the basic elements.

You may recall the brief tour of hardware that you took in Chapter 1. It began at the screen of the Simplex 2000 computer. Like the screen of the computer you use, this screen is composed of pixels, thousands of them, each with its own position numbers, or coordinates. Even characters are composed of pixels. In the new milieu called graphics mode, the pixels can be illuminated individually or in preformed arrangements such as lines, circles, and bars.

Portrait of a Variable

There are many ways to display the progress of a variable as the computer calculates new values for it. Suppose, for example, that a run of the *RealInvest* program produces the following values for the variable called *Money*.

Year	*Money*
1	5,250.00
2	5,512.50
3	5,788.13
4	6,077.53
5	6,381.41

These values can be represented on the screen in a variety of ways. Three possibilities are: (a) as a succession of points, or pixels; (b) as a succession of points joined by lines; or (c) as a succession of vertical bars. The accompanying figure illustrates the three possibilities.

The height of each point, line, or bar in relation to a baseline called a *horizontal axis* represents the actual value of the variable at a specific stage in the computation. The vertical axis on the left of each graphics display includes values that make it possible to read off the values of the variable. Because relatively few values are involved, the point display is hard to see. Even the line display looks a little thin. You will probably agree that the bar display on the right is the easiest to read. Although I will ultimately use the bar display in the *RealInvest_Graph* program, all three forms are used as examples in the graphics excursion to come.

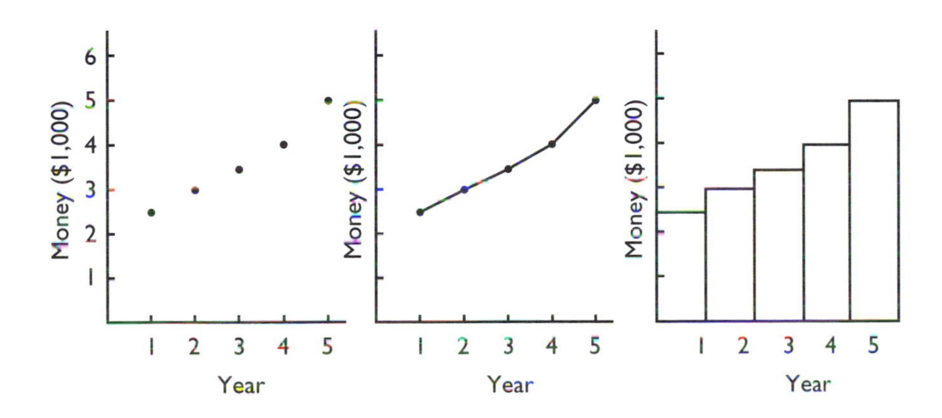

Points, lines, and bars represent the growth of *Money*

The Screen

There are four possible types of computer screens. The type of screen you are using depends on which graphics card (one of those circuit boards you flashed by in the introductory tour of Chapter 1) your computer uses. Here are the standard options:

Graphics type	*Size of pixel grid*	*Number of colors*
CGA	320×200	4
EGA	640×(200 or 350)	16
VGA	640×480	16 or 256
SVGA	800×600 or 1024×768	16 or 256

The size of the pixel grid consists of two numbers, which represent the width and the height of the screen, as measured in pixels. As you go from CGA to SVGA, the number of pixels in the screen grid increases. For this to happen, the hardware must pack more and more pixels into the same screen area. This packing squeezes the pixels together, thereby resulting in images that have greater sharpness, or *resolution*.

Every pixel on the screen has its own special pair of numbers that are called coordinates, which locate the point precisely. You are already familiar with the basic idea of coordinates. Who, after all, hasn't tried to find a feature on a map? After looking up the place name in the index, you find either a pair of map coordinates, such as grid numbers (like E-7) or latitude and longitude (like 81 W, 43 N). The first coordinate tells you how far across the map you must go horizontally (east or west). The second coordinate tells you how far you must go vertically (north or south). Screen coordinates work exactly like this; and they typically are specified as a pair of numbers enclosed by parentheses. The point that is 155 pixels to the right of the left edge of the screen and 240 pixels down from the top will have coordinates (155, 240), for example.

The next illustration shows the layout of a VGA screen. If you have a VGA computer, you should make a copy of this page. Otherwise, you should prepare a similar map of your own particular screen. Either way, you will want to refer to your layout when writing a graphics program

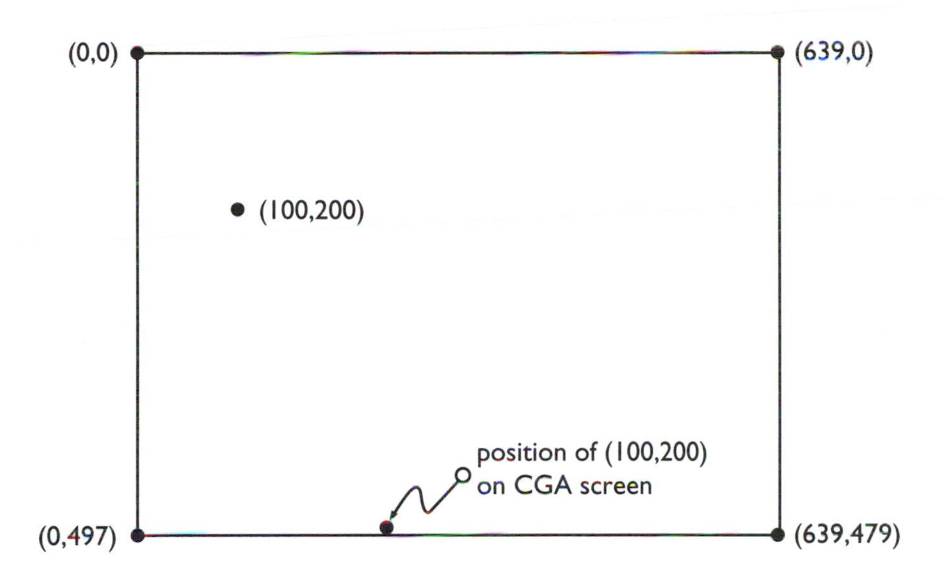

VGA screen layout

in Turbo Pascal. On any screen, the pixel (0, 0)—called the *origin*—is located in the upper left-hand corner of the screen. The coordinates of the lower right-hand corner is different for different screens, however. The CGA screen's lower right-hand corner has coordinates (319, 199), for example, whereas the VGA screen's lower right-hand corner has coordinates (639, 479). In both cases these ultimate coordinates are one less than the given screen dimensions, because the numbering for both coordinates starts at 0 instead of 1.

Which system you work in will make a big difference when it comes to making objects appear on the screen. For example, if your program draws a point at (100, 200), the point will appear near the bottom of the CGA screen but much closer to the upper left-hand corner in the VGA screen. In addition, high-resolution screens have more available colors than low-resolution ones.

At the same time, the numbers that you want to represent on the screen may be too large or too small to work with directly. How, for example, would you plot the values for the variable *Money* given on page 101? The answer lies in a scaling process that converts the raw data to screen data. Let's take another look at the table.

Year	*Money*
1	5,250.00
2	5,512.50
3	5,788.13
4	6,077.53
5	6,381.41

Let's suppose that your screen is a VGA screen; in other words, it is divided into 640 × 480 pixels. Therefore, all horizontal coordinates must lie between 0 and 639, and all vertical coordinates must lie between 0 and 479. I will tackle the problem of scaling the two coordinates by considering them one at a time.

First, the horizontal coordinates 1 through 5 (representing *Year*) are much too small to display effectively. A display of five pixels, lines, or bars that were separated by a single pixel would clearly be unreadable. To spread them out horizontally, let's multiply them all by 40, say. The horizontal coordinates then become 40, 80, 120, 160, and 200. To place the first coordinate further away from the left edge of the screen, let's also add 60 to all of the numbers. You end up with 100, 140, 180, 220, and 260 as the positions for your five *Year* numbers.

Next, a height of 5,250 is impossible to portray directly on the screen as a vertical coordinate. However, if you divide each of the *Money* numbers by 25 and truncate them to integers, you get the following values.

Year	*Money*
100	210
140	220
180	231
220	243
260	255

You are still not quite done. You have yet to establish a horizontal axis, or baseline, which will act as a reference for the points, lines, or bars that will represent the values of *Money*. If you pick this reference line a comfortable distance above the bottom of the screen, say, at vertical coordinate 450, then you only have to recall that vertical coordinates are measured from the top of the screen, not the bottom. To establish the correct height of the individual pixels above the horizontal axis, you must subtract each pixel's vertical coordinate, or each *Money* value, from the vertical coordinate of the horizontal axis (450) to get the right "height."

Year	*Money*
100	240
140	230
180	219
220	207
260	195

I used the scaling factors of 40 in the horizontal direction and 1/25, or 0.04, in the vertical direction. The exact sizes of scaling factors that you use are to some degree a matter of taste. How big, exactly, would you like the display to be? As can be seen by visualizing the numbers in the preceding table as screen coordinates, they use only about half the screen vertically and a third of the screen horizontally. At the same time, it is important to remember that future values of the variable *Money* might well be much larger and that the user may want to see a display that extends beyond five years of investment history. I have therefore cut myself some slack by choosing scaling factors no larger than these.

Graphic Elements

Now let's consider just how Turbo Pascal might be used to arrange each of the three kinds of image displays that were illustrated earlier. Elementary graphics statements within Turbo Pascal enable a program to draw points, lines, and bars (among other things). The syntax of all three graphics statements allow for little variation. The programmer only has to fill in the numbers, called *parameters*. Here, for example, is the first kind of statement.

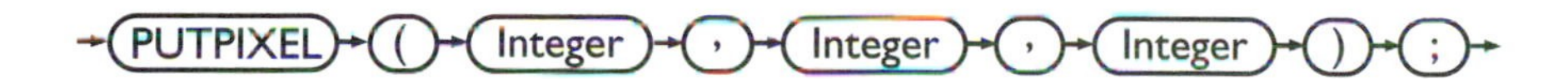

I have used the word "integer" to indicate the parameters that must be filled in. However, Turbo Pascal also permits identifiers such as names of integer variables in these places, an important generality that gives great flexibility to graphics programs.

The PUTPIXEL statement, when executed, paints a pixel on the screen at the coordinates specified by the first two integers. For the third integer, use the integer 2 (the code for green, as I will explain presently). You can use this statement to draw the first pixel for the variable *Money* at the coordinates (100, 240):

```
PUTPIXEL(100, 240, 2);
```

When the computer executes this statement, it will produce a green pixel situated 100 pixels to the right of the left-hand screen boundary and 240 pixels down from the top of the screen. In other words, the point will be 239 pixels up from the bottom of the screen, right in the middle of the screen. As for other options for color, here are just a few of the many colors available in Turbo Pascal. Each color has its own code number.

Color	*Code*
black	0
blue	1
green	2
cyan	3
red	4
magenta	5
brown	6
yellow	14
white	15

The second kind of graphics statements causes a line to appear on the screen. But recall that a line always connects *two* points. As the following syntax diagram shows, this graphics statement has more parameters than the PUTPIXEL statement.

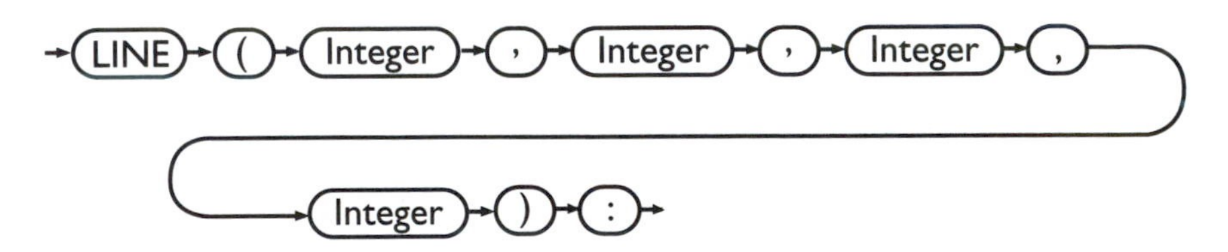

Like the PUTPIXEL statement, this one will take variable parameters in place of integer parameters. Unlike the PUTPIXEL statement, however, it contains no color parameter. Color can be assigned to the line by using a separate statement called SETCOLOR. With the appropriate color number inside parentheses, this statement will cause any line that is subsequently drawn to have the color whose number appears in the SETCOLOR statement. For example, the statement

```
SETCOLOR(2);
```

when placed in the program right after it enters graphics mode (see the next section), will cause all subsequent LINE statements to draw green lines.

Let's suppose, therefore, that the color has already been set to green (2) and that you wish to draw a line from the first point for *Money* at (100, 240) to the second one at (140, 229). The following statement will do precisely this:

```
LINE(100, 240, 140, 229);
```

Note how the two pairs of coordinates are entered. First comes the horizontal coordinate of the first point, then the vertical coordinate. Next comes the horizontal coordinate of the second point, then its vertical coordinate. On a VGA screen, this statement would produce the effect shown in the next figure.

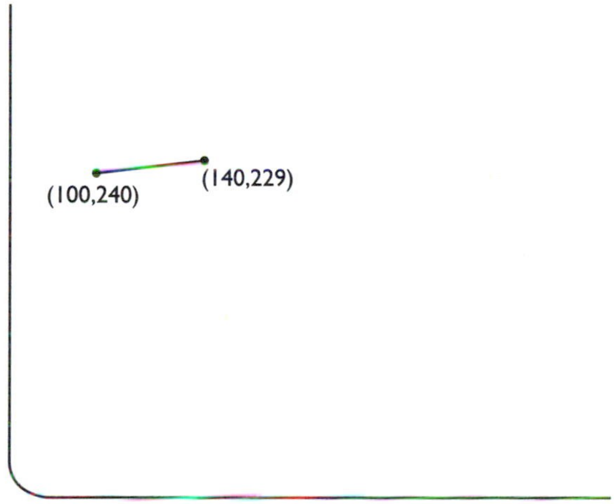

(100,240)
(140,229)

A line joins the first two values of *Money*

The third and final graphics element in this introduction to Turbo Pascal graphics is the BAR statement. The syntax is very similar to that of the LINE statement.

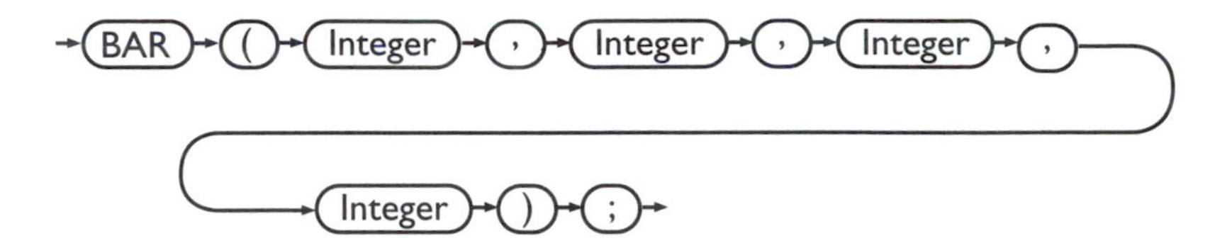

Like the LINE statement, BAR takes no color parameter, the color being determined by a separate statement. Also, the integer coordinates that enter the statement represent two points: one of these lies at the upper left-hand corner of the bar, the other at its lower right-hand corner. Two such points, after all, serve to specify the bar completely, as the examples in the next figure show.

To make a bar that represents the values of the variable *Money*, you must find two points at opposite corners of the bar. The vertical coordinates of these points are easy: one will be at the baseline you established earlier and the other will have the coordinate given in the table on page 105. To

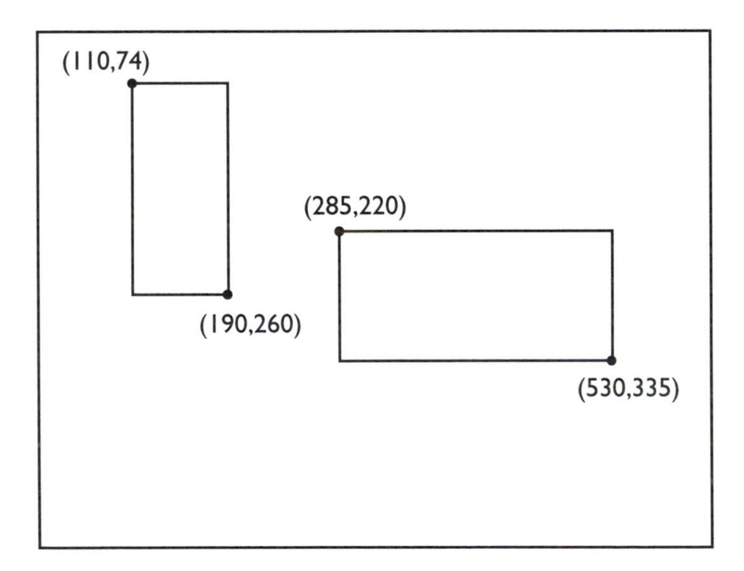

Two points specify a rectangle

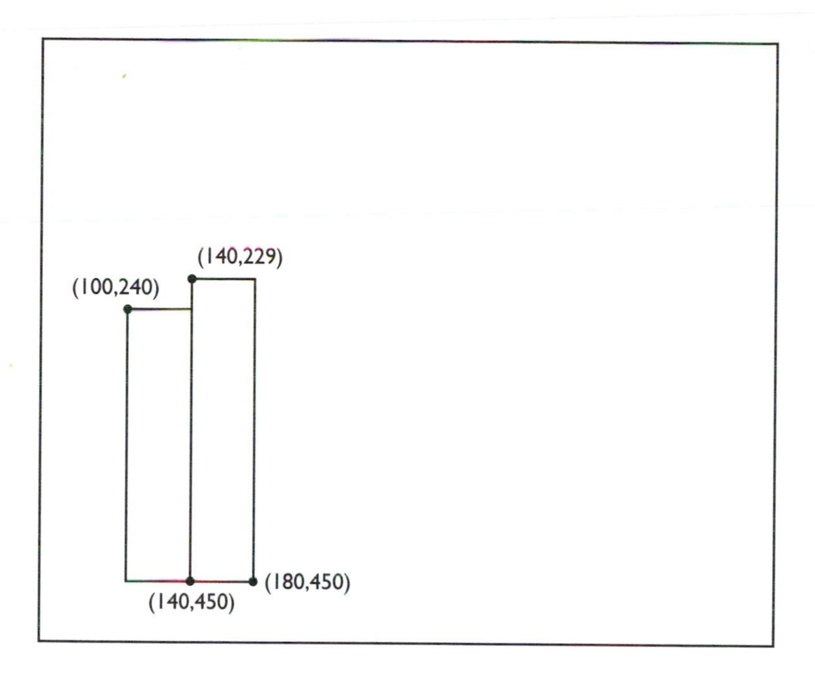

The first two bars for the variable *Money*

make the horizontal coordinates as easy as possible, let the first bar extend from 100 to 140, the next from 140 to 180, and so on, across the screen. Here, then, are the BAR statements for the first two values of the variable *Money*:

```
BAR(100, 240, 140, 450);

BAR(140, 229, 180, 450);
```

Turbo Pascal offers a statement called SETFILLSTYLE that enables you to fill the bars in with a variety of solid colors, hatching, and so on. Let's use the horizontal shading, specified by the statement

```
SETFILLSTYLE(LINEfill, 2);
```

Once again, let's use the color green (2). There is one final requirement: This statement must appear in the program before the BAR statement to which it refers.

RealInvest as a Graphics Program

RealInvest is converted to a graphics program in five stages. First, I explain the new graphics mode in which the converted program operates and how it differs from the text mode in which *RealInvest* operates. Next, I display the initial part of the new program as an illustration of graphics mode. The program is not complete, however, until special graphics initialization statements are included in the fourth stage. In the third stage, I present the main loop and its calculations. Finally, after explaining a Turbo Pascal graphics procedure, I return to the program, displaying the complete product.

Text Output in Graphics Mode

Now that we have developed all the components, it's time to install them in *RealInvest* and get the graphics engine running. It would be convenient if the conversion of *RealInvest* to a computer graphics program simply involved adding a few graphics statements. However, a number of restrictions in Turbo Pascal force you to modify the program in other ways.

For one thing, Turbo Pascal will not allow a program to run in text mode and graphics mode simultaneously. Because you have already written a program with a text-oriented user interface and because that interface does not require graphics images, it seems reasonable to begin the program in text mode, then switch it to graphics mode (see later section on how to do this). However, the WRITELN statement used to output text to the screen in text mode will not work when the computer is in graphics mode. To place text on the screen when the computer is in graphics mode, Turbo Pascal offers the OUTTEXTXY statement. This statement has its own syntax, as illustrated by this syntax diagram:

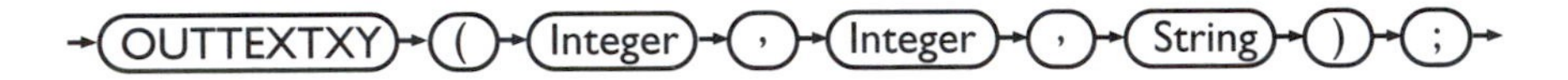

The word OUTTEXTXY is followed by parentheses that enclose three parameters: Two coordinates (the integers) and some text in single quotes (the string), all three items separated by commas. The coordinates locate the point on the screen where the text begins. Whatever text you specify in the third component of the statement will begin at that location on the screen and proceed off to the right.

Stubs

You are now ready to write the first half of the program. Notice that I have inserted two comments labeled STUB in the program below. These represent missing portions of the program that will be filled in after your introduction to the special requirements of Turbo Pascal graphics under DOS or OS/2. If you use Turbo Pascal graphics under Windows, however, you will have to wait until Chapter 7 to do a computer graphics project.

For example, to provide a title for the screen on which the bars will appear, the following text might be appropriate:

```
OUTTEXTXY(10, 10, 'CHART OF INVESTMENT GROWTH');
```

This statement will cause the message CHART OF INVESTMENT GROWTH to appear near the top of the VGA screen. The letter C will appear right beside the point at (10, 10), namely, 10 pixels to the right of the left edge of the screen and 10 pixels down from the top.

You can also use the OUTTEXTXY statement to label the screen so that users can read off the value of *Money* (as represented by the height of vertical bars) by merely glancing at the left edge of the screen. The following block of statements do just this:

```
OUTTEXTXY(10, 46, '10,000');
OUTTEXTXY(10, 146, '7,500');
OUTTEXTXY(10, 246, '5,000');
OUTTEXTXY(10, 346, '2,500');
OUTTEXTXY(10, 446, '0,000');
```

These statements will display reference numbers, from 10,000 down to 0,000, evenly distributed every hundred pixels from a point 46 pixels from the top of the screen all the way down to a point that is 446 pixels from the top of the screen. The 4-pixel difference between the vertical coordinate of the label and the line it refers to enables the OUTTEXT statement to center the label on the (invisible) reference line.

```
PROGRAM RealInvest_Graph;
{This program tracks the real value of an investment, taking}
{both the rates of return and inflation into account, then displays}
{the values as a succession of vertical green bars on the screen.}
{STUB: a section that declares graphics mode}

{declaration section}
VAR Term, Year, Height, ulX, ulY, lrX, lrY: INTEGER;
VAR Money, MoneyIn, Return: REAL;
CONST Inflat = 0.041, Crncy = '$';

BEGIN {program}

{user interface}
WRITELN('Please enter the amount of the investment');
WRITE('and the term of the investment, in years: ');
READLN(Money, Term);
WRITELN('Now enter the rate of return as a decimal fraction,');
WRITE('e.g., enter 0.08 instead of 8%. ');
READLN(Return);

{STUB: a section that initializes the screen for graphics}

{initialization section}
SETFILLSTYLE(LINEfill, 2);

{set up chart labels}
OUTTEXTXY(10, 10, 'CHART OF INVESTMENT GROWTH');
OUTTEXTXY(10, 46, '10,000');
OUTTEXTXY(10, 146, '7,500');
OUTTEXTXY(10, 246, '5,000');
OUTTEXTXY(10, 346, '2,500');
OUTTEXTXY(10, 446, '0,000');
```

It will come as no surprise that, with the addition of new Turbo Pascal statement types, new variables must be added to the program. A glance at the declarations for *RealInvest_Graph* reveals several new variables, namely, ulX, ulY, lrX, and lrY. These variables carry the coordinate information for the corners of the bar that will be drawn once per iteration of the main loop (to come). You will find it easy to remember what these variables do when you realize that the prefixes ul and lr stand for "upper left" and "lower right," respectively. In other words, they refer to the upper left and lower right corners of the bar to be drawn. The X and Y simply refer to the horizontal and vertical coordinates, respectively.

Among the remaining changes to *RealInvest*, you will notice that the initialization statement

```
MoneyIn := Money;
```

has been removed. The warning to the user that the value of his or her investment has declined in value is no longer necessary, because a decline will be perfectly obvious from a glance at the heights of the bars. To the initialization section, I have added a new statement that determines the style and color of the bars. "LINEfill" means horizontal hatching, and the number 2 stands for green. Your bars will be covered with attractive, horizontal green stripes:

```
SETFILLSTYLE(LINEfill, 2);
```

Now let's examine the second half of the program, which begins at the main loop.

```
{main loop: calculates yearly increase on}
{return and yearly decrease on inflation}
FOR Year := 1 to Term DO
   BEGIN

   {calculate values of Money}
   Money := Money*(1 + Return);
   Money := Money/(1 + Inflat);

   {calculate bar variables and draw bars}
   Height := TRUNC(Money*0.04);
   ulX := 40*Year + 60; ulY := 450 - Height;
   lrX := 40*Year + 100; lrY := 450;
   BAR(ulX, ulY, lrX, lrY);
   END; {of main loop}

END. {of program}
```

You are already familiar with the calculations for the variable *Money* in the first section of the loop body. You have also read enough about the VGA screen dimensions to make the second section understandable. The main calculation centers on the variable *Height*, which represents the height of the bar, which in turn represents the current value of *Money*. In the first statement the scaling factor 0.04 is applied to the value of *Money* to convert it to appropriate dimensions for the screen. The TRUNC function simply converts the resulting real number to an integer by TRUNCating the decimal part.

With an appropriate value for *Height* in hand, the program can proceed to draw the bars. First, it must determine the coordinates of the upper left (ul) corner of the bar; then it must determine the coordinates of the lower right (lr) corner. The next figure illustrates the bar and its coordinates as they appear in the program.

Imagine that the computer is executing the loop for the first time and that *Money* happens to equal 5,312.00. In this case, *Year* = 1, and and we can readily calculate *Height* = 212. With these numbers in hand, you can easily predict the values the computer will arrive at:

ulX = 40*Year + 60 = 100

ulY = 450 - Height = 238

lrX = 40*Year + 100 = 140

lrY = 450

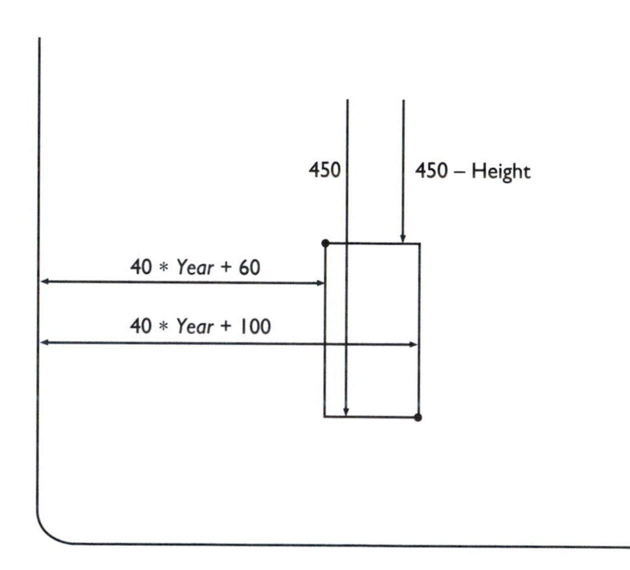

A bar and its coordinates

In other words, the left-hand edge of the bar lies 100 pixels in from the left-hand boundary of the screen and the top of the bar lies 238 pixels below the top of the screen. At the same time, the right-hand edge of the bar lies 40 pixels to the right of the left-hand edge. The bar, in other words, is 40 pixels wide. Finally, the bottom of the bars rests on your (imaginary) horizontal axis at 450 pixels from the top of the screen, 29 pixels from the bottom edge of the screen.

With each iteration of the loop, *Year* increases by 1 and the horizontal coordinates of the two bar corners each increase by 40. In other words, each bar will be plotted 40 pixels to the right of the previous bar.

Finally, the BAR statement uses all four coordinate variables to draw the bar. The computer will automatically fill the bar in with horizontal green hatching, as specified by the SETFILLSTYLE statement in the graphics initialization section of the program.

Now you have completed the graphics version of the investment program. As always, improvements are needed. The program will only handle values of *Money* up to 10,000, and the number of years for which you can view investment results is limited by the screen width in relation to the width of the bars. You can overcome some of these limitations by following Exploration 6 at the end of this chapter.

Setting up Graphics

To run the program *RealInvest_Graph* under DOS or OS/2, you must first fill in the stubs that appeared in the listing above. The Turbo Pascal statements required are the subject of this section.

To run any graphics program under DOS or OS/2, a Turbo Pascal programmer must include two elements in it. Right under the program header, there must appear a USES statement and a procedure called *SetGraph*. As you will learn more fully in Chapter 7, a procedure is like a miniature program that accomplishes a particular computational goal. Turbo Pascal contains many procedures, each organized into a group called a unit. The CRT unit, for example, contains procedures that clear the screen, reposition the cursor, even read keys on the keyboard. The Graph unit, on the other hand, contains procedures that examine your hardware to see which type of screen you have (CGA, VGA, etc.), to procedures that carry out special graphics functions such as drawing points, lines, or bars.

When I add the following USES statement

```
USES CRT, Graph;
```

to *RealInvest_Graph*, it has the effect of making all the procedures in the CRT and the Graph units available to the program.

As a DOS-based Turbo Pascal programmer, however, in addition to a USES statement you must also use the following *SetGraph* procedure in any of the graphics programs that you write whenever you do an exploration. This particular procedure is not part of the Graph unit, so you must define it at the head of the program, right after the USES statement. You can blindly type it in, or you can read the comments that I have added to the procedure.

```
{set up graphics}
PROCEDURE SetGraph;
VAR GraphDriver, GraphMode: INTEGER;
BEGIN
GraphDriver := Detect;
{Detect finds out what kind of graphics card your computer has}
InitGraph(GraphDriver, GraphMode, '\tp\bgi');
{InitGraph sets up graphics for your particular computer}
END;
```

To save yourself the trouble of laboriously typing out this procedure every time you write a new Turbo Pascal graphics program, you can store it as if it were a separate program under a name like *NewGraph*. Every time you want to write a new graphics program, use the Turbo Pascal system to call up *NewGraph*, then add a proper header and the rest of your graphics program. When you have completed your new graphics program, store it under a different name, and *NewGraph* will always be ready for incorporation into a new graphics program. (See Exploration 7 at the end of this chapter.)

The second stub can now be replaced by a graphics initialization section.

```
{graphics initialization section}
SetGraph;
ClrScr;
```

The statement

```
SetGraph;
```

amounts to a *call* to the procedure called *SetGraph*. This causes the computer to execute the procedure by that name and switches the computer to graphics mode. The statement

```
ClrScr;
```

clears the screen of any previous text or graphics, preparing it for new graphics output. When you add these statements to *RealInvest_Graph*, it will operate as advertised.

Here is the finished graphics version of *RealInvest*. I have made a few changes to improve the program. First, I reinstated the section that prints investment values on the screen (from the first version of the program) before the new program enters graphics mode. Second, I decided to narrow the bars by 10 pixels each, making each bar more prominent in the display. The calculation for the horizontal coordinate of the lower right-hand corner of a bar has therefore changed from 40*Year + 100 to 40*Year + 90.

PROGRAM RealInv_Gr;

```
{The graphics version of RealInvest}
USES Crt, Graph;

{Set up graphics.}
PROCEDURE SetGraph;
VAR GraphDriver, GraphMode: INTEGER;
BEGIN
GraphDriver := Detect;
InitGraph(GraphDriver, GraphMode, '\tp\bgi');
END;

{declaration section}
VAR Amount, SaveAmount, Rate: REAL;
VAR Year, Term, Height: INTEGER;
CONST Inflat = 0.041;
CONST Crncy = '$';
```

```
BEGIN{main program}

{user interface - advisory section}
WRITELN('This program calculates the real return on an investment.');
WRITELN('It consists of a text display and a graphic display. To');
WRITELN('continue from one display to the next or to exit from the');
WRITELN('program after the graphics, press the ENTER key.');

{user interface - prompt/input section}
WRITELN;
WRITELN('Please type in the amount to be invested');
WRITE('and the rate of interest (as a ratio): ');
READLN(Amount, Rate);
SaveAmount := Amount; {Save Amount for graphics section.}
WRITE('How many years is the investment to run? ');
READLN(Term);

{Calculate and print amounts.}
For Year := 0 TO Term DO
   BEGIN
   WRITELN('After ', Year, ' years the amount is: ', Crncy, Amount:6:2);
   Amount := Amount*(1+Rate);
   END;

READLN;

{Calculate and display amounts graphically.}

{Initiate graphics mode, clearscreen, and bar style.}
SetGraph;
Clrscr;
SetFillStyle(LINEfill, 2);

{Draw labels.}
OutTextXY(10, 10, 'CHART OF INVESTMENT GROWTH');
OutTextXY(10, 46, '$10,000');
OutTextXY(10, 146, '$7,500');
OutTextXY(10, 246, '$5,000');
OutTextXY(10, 346, '$2,500');
OutTextXY(10, 446, '$000');

{Calculate and display bars.}
Amount := SaveAmount;
FOR Year := 0 TO Term DO
   BEGIN
   Height := TRUNC(Amount*0.04);
```

```
   Bar(40*Year+60, 450-Height, 40*Year+90, 450);
   Amount := Amount*(1+Rate);
   END;

READLN;

END. (of RealInv_Gr program)
```

Storing Images in Trees

Computer science has much to say about the theory and practice of computer graphics, from the creation of graphics images to their manipulation and storage. Despite the great usefulness of graphic images, they have a number of drawbacks. For example, they involve very large amounts of information. A VGA screen image, for example, has 640 × 480 = 307,200 pixels, each with its own color. In other words, over 300,000 memory locations are needed to store such an image. Such a demand would swamp the working memory of most computers, and it would not take many such images to completely fill a floppy diskette.

In this section, you will learn about just one approach to the problem of storing large images. Called the *quad-tree technique*, it substantially reduces the amount of memory space needed to store most images. I will illustrate the technique by using much smaller "screens" that consist of 16 × 16 pixels. In doing so, I will identify two important thought patterns that characterize much of computer science. The *divide-and-conquer* thought pattern has solved many important problems in computer science by dividing them into subproblems and then "conquering" them. The *generalization* thought pattern involves working with small examples (like the 16 × 16 screen) and then drawing conclusions that apply to much larger examples (like the VGA screen).

Simple Screens

The illustration on the next page shows our super-simple screen. Individual pixels have become visible squares. Can you make out the image stored here? Perhaps you are having some trouble making out exactly what this two-color screen is trying to portray. This difficulty merely illustrates the severe restrictions of very low-resolution screens or perhaps you can just make out the silhouette of a cat. On a VGA screen, the image would be unmistakable.

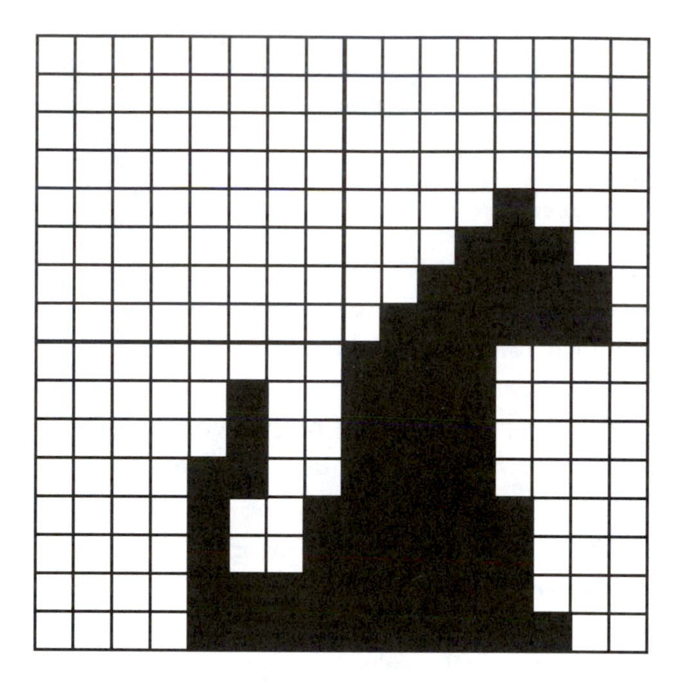

What is it?

If this image were stored away in a computer memory, one pixel per memory location, it would require 256 memory locations. But once you have learned the arcane and seemingly unrelated art of storing a "tree" in a computer's memory, you will understand how to store the cat image there by using far fewer than 256 locations.

Trees in Memory

On the left side of the next figure is an abstract tree consisting of *nodes* (the rectangles) and *pointers* (the arrows). Nodes that have no pointers emanating from them could be called data nodes. The tree looks abstract, but its components are simple enough. It consists of just five nodes. Some of the nodes have pointers to other nodes, and some nodes have no pointers, but contain data, for example, the number 371.

An advanced programmer could install such a tree in memory by taking advantage of the fact that all locations in memory have addresses,

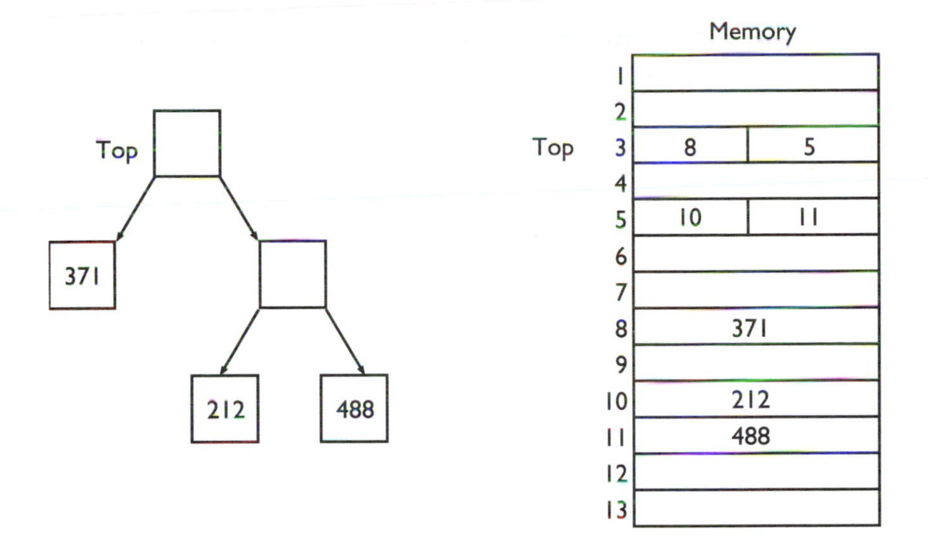

A data tree (left) and the same tree in memory (right)

as indicated on the left-hand side of the memory diagram by the numbers 1 through 13. For example, the programmer could place the top node in location 3. The numbers stored at that location would be the addresses (8 and 5) of the nodes pointed to by the top node. One of these nodes, the one at address 8, is a data node. It contains the number 371. The node at address 5, however, contains two pointers, one to address 10, the other to address 11. If you look down at those addresses, you will see the data from the bottom two nodes of the tree, namely, 212 and 488. Not only are there programs that will create such trees in memory, there are programs that will read out the data they contain.

If you inspect the tree in memory, you will see that as far as the data and pointers it contains are concerned, it is identical to the abstract tree on the left. This simple example should convince you that any tree that consists only of nodes and pointers can be installed in the memory of a computer. This fact is important because now you will understand that any tree I draw from now on can be placed in memory. Thus, any claim I make about the number of nodes in such a tree is automatically a claim about how many memory locations I would need to store such a tree in memory.

The Cat in the Quad-Tree

I will now use the divide-and-conquer thought pattern to reduce the problem of storing the cat image efficiently to a set of new problems, but smaller ones. I will end by converting the entire image to a tree called a *quad-tree* for what will soon be obvious reasons. I begin by dividing the 16 × 16 screen into four quadrants, numbered 1 through 4. The numbering begins in the upper right quadrant and proceeds counterclockwise around the screen.

The adjacent figure shows not only the quadrant scheme but also a small tree with one top node and four pendant nodes. Each of the four pointers to the pendant nodes has been given the number of the quadrant it represents. I have placed the letter W inside the second pendant node because the entire second quadrant consists of nothing but white pixels. All the information about this particular quadrant now resides in that one node: The quadrant consists of nothing but white pixels. The remaining three nodes, however, must be divided anew before they too can be conquered.

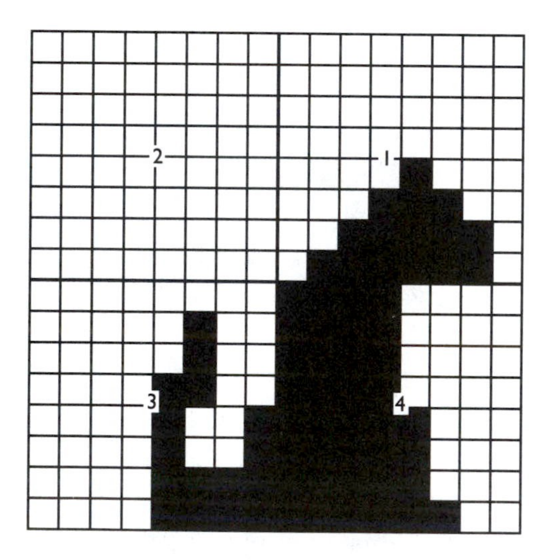

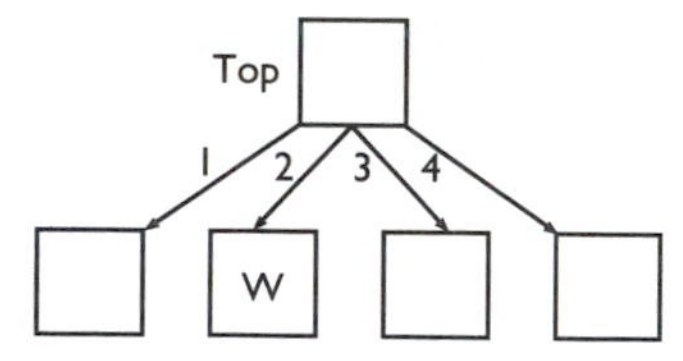

First stage of constructing the quad-tree

I will illustrate the process with the 8 × 8 screen that inhabits the fourth quadrant. This screen can be further subdivided into quadrants of its own, as illustrated in the next figure. When you examine the four smaller quadrants, you will readily see that one is all white, two are all black, and the fourth is mixed. At this stage of tree construction, this portion of the tree appears on the right-hand side of the second stage figure.

The third stage of construction applies to all the nodes at the second level that are not marked B or W. For example, continuing to illustrate the method on the same branch—the 4 × 4 screen in the fourth quadrant of quadrant 4—you see that the corresponding node branches into four new nodes representing the four subquadrants shown in the third stage figure.

Now the nodes represent tiny, 2 × 2 "screens," and each of these can be subdivided one more time to yield the final nodes for this branch. One set of nodes descends from the second node at the third level, the second set of nodes descends from the third node. As far as this branch of the

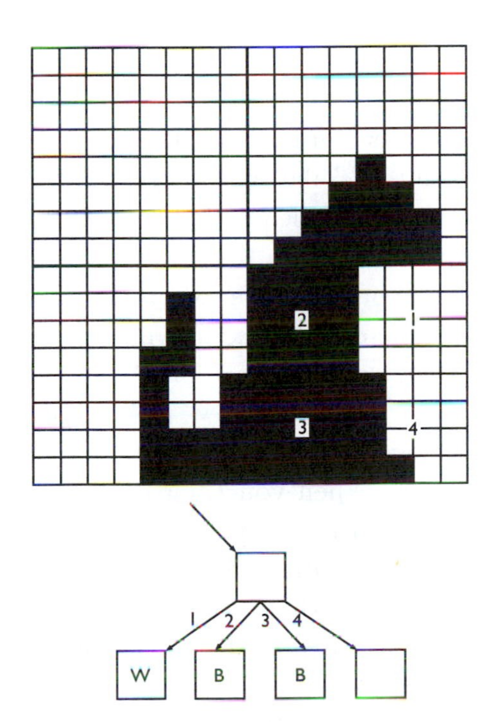

Second stage of constructing the quad-tree

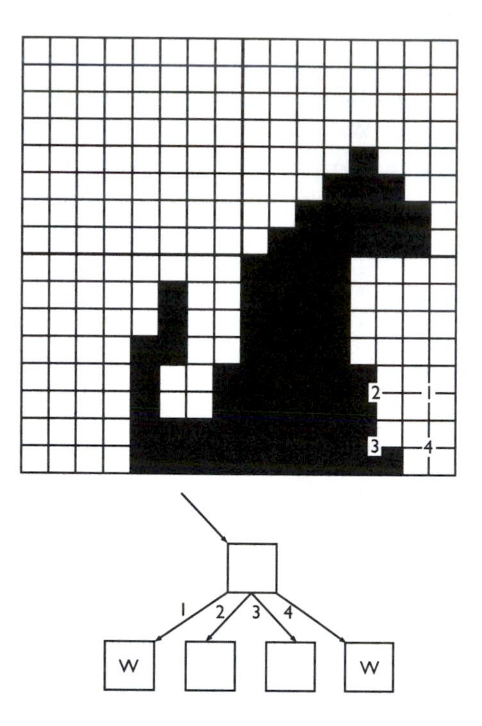

Third stage of constructing the quad-tree

quad-tree is concerned, I will have conquered it completely once I have expanded these two nodes. You can easily check the figure to confirm that one of these third stage nodes will have nodes labeled W, B, B, W hanging from it, and the other will have nodes labeled W, B, B, B.

On the basis of this example, you should be able to complete the conversion of the cat image to a complete quad-tree in which every node that does not have pointers contains either the label W or the label B. You could, of course, use 0 and 1 instead of W and B. Your final quad-tree should contain 77 nodes, 19 of which are pointer nodes and 58 of which are data nodes. When you compare the 77 nodes of the quad-tree with the amount of memory it would take to store all 256 pixels of the original image, you must agree that the quad-tree method has created a substantial savings in memory space. Indeed, the cat in the quad-tree takes only 30% of the space that the cat stored directly in memory would take.

The other landmark in this excursion into computer science country is generalization. How can you know that what has just worked for a mere

16 × 16 screen will work for much larger ones? Well, any screen that has dimensions that are a power of two can be divided into quadrants, and these quadrants can be divided into subquadrants, and so on. The process ends only when you reach subsubsub- . . . -quadrants that are all 1 × 1. A VGA screen with dimensions 640 × 480 does not have dimensions that are powers of two, obviously, but it can certainly be located inside a screen that does. Consider a screen that has dimensions 1024 × 1024. You can comfortably place the VGA screen inside this larger one and proceed to build a quad-tree, automatically making any areas off the VGA screen (but within the larger one) all one color.

How big would such a quad-tree be? The maximum *depth* of the quad-tree for the 16 × 16 screen was 4; that is, it took no more than four pointers, or links, to reach any bottom node from the top one. To calculate the depth of a quad-tree, simply see how many times you can divide the dimension of the original screen by 2 before reaching 1. You can only divide 16 by 2 four times before you reach 1, so, as just noted, the depth of the quad-tree for the 16 × 16 screen is 4. By the same reasoning, it will take no more than ten links to get from the top node of the 1024 × 1024 quad-tree to a bottom node. You can only divide 1024 by 2 ten times before you reach 1.

The conclusion from this process of generalizing is that the quad-tree method will work on *any size* of screen image. The storage efficiency, however, can vary tremendously. In highly detailed images for which the pixels are continually changing color, even within tiny regions, you cannot expect large savings from the quad-tree method. But in images that contain large areas or many areas for which the color does not change, you can expect substantial savings.

SUMMARY

In the course of converting the program *RealInvest* to display its output as vertical green bars, you have made your first foray into Turbo Pascal graphics programming. First, you discovered that all screens are not created equal. Some have more pixels than others, thereby allowing higher resolution graphics.

For the VGA screen, a typical type, you then learned about three basic Turbo Pascal graphics statements—PUTPIXEL, LINE, and BAR—and you saw how the latter graphics element was suited to the display of *Money* in the *RealInvest_Graph* program. You also found that *Money* is not green, but 2, so to speak. Every color used in Turbo Pascal graphics has its own code number. Any graphics statement that does not specify its own color must have either a SETCOLOR or a SETFILLSTYLE statement preceding it.

The final version of *RealInvest_Graph* not only incorporated many of these statements, but required some additional elements drawn from the units that Turbo Pascal makes available. Every DOS-based Turbo Pascal program, it turns out, must carry a special graphics procedure at its head, as well as a USES statement and a call to the procedure inside the program body. The call signals the change to graphics mode. After this, any messages to the user must be carried by the OUTTEXTXY statement and not by WRITE or WRITELN statements.

The computer science portion of this chapter switched the emphasis from generating computer graphics to storing them. A pretty method of storing graphic images efficiently introduced you to several ideas at once. You learned how trees can be stored in memory and how images can be stored in trees. The use of this method illustrated one of the most powerful thought patterns used in computer science, that of the divide-and-conquer strategy. Some problems can only be conquered when they are divided—again and again.

EXPLORATIONS

1 Calculate the number of pixels in the following screens:

CGA: 320×200
EGA: 640×350
VGA: 640×480
SVGA: 1024×768

2 Make a drawing of a VGA screen as a rectangle that is 6.4 inches wide and 4.8 inches high, approximately, and mark the positions of the following pixels on the screen, as closely as you can locate them:

(350, 10) (320, 240) (320, 479) (25, 460) (100, 100)

3 A program must draw points on a screen corresponding to the following values of a variable called *Level*. This variable spells out the level of a lake on the following dates in April:

Date	*Level*
7	53.2
14	58.9
21	75.6
28	79.1

a Find scaling factors that produce appropriate horizontal and vertical coordinates for a VGA screen. The coordinates must fall within a rectangle that is 300 pixels high and 500 pixels wide. The vertical extent of the retangle must correspond to values of *Level* from 50 to 80 and the horizontal extent should embrace the numbers from 7 to 28. Next, determine two numbers that, when added to the scaled coordinates, will center the 500×300 rectangle in the screen.

b Write a fragment of graphics code that will draw all four data points as three line segments in the manner of the illustration on page 101. You do not need to use a loop or include the SETCOLOR statement or any other graphics initialization statements; merely use a series of LINE statements that have the appropriate effect.

c Write OUTTEXTXY statements that display labels such as "April 7" through to "April 28", each directly below the proper data point. Add other OUTTEXTXY statements that display a vertical scale of values, from 50 through to 80, in jumps of 10.

4 Here is a program that draws a figure on the screen. The figure consists of lines. What figure does the program draw and what color will it be? (The special DOS-based graphics statements have been omitted for clarity.)

```
PROGRAM Figure;

BEGIN

SETCOLOR(3);
```

```
LINE(100, 100, 100, 200);
LINE(100, 200, 200, 200);
LINE(200, 200, 200, 100);
LINE(200, 100, 100, 100);

END.
```

5 Analyze the following program. Make a drawing of the VGA screen as described in Exploration 2 and then reproduce as accurately as you can the image that the program produces. I have omitted the appropriate screen initialization statements, including the *InitGraph* procedure.

```
PROGRAM Parabola;

VAR Index, Horiz, Vertical: INTEGER;

BEGIN

FOR Index := 1 TO 15
   BEGIN
   Horiz := 20*Index + 30;
   Vertical := 2*Index*Index + 15;
   PUTPIXEL(Horiz, 479 - Vertical);
   END;

END.
```

6 Given the width of the bars in the *RealInvest_Graph* graphics display, as well as the distance of the first bar from the left boundary of the screen, calculate the maximum number of years that the display can handle before the bars fall off the screen. What happens when you try such a value for *Term*?

7 Type the *SetGraph* procedure into your Turbo Pascal editing system and make a separate "program" out of it by saving it under some meaningful name such as *NewGraph*. The fact that *NewGraph* is not an independent program doesn't matter because Turbo Pascal will save it as if it were one. After this, any time you're ready to start writing a Turbo Pascal program that uses graphics, you can begin by loading *NewGraph* when you run Turbo Pascal from the DOS. That way, you never have to type out this little procedure again. Merely build the new program around it, being sure that when you save the new graphics program, you do not try to call it *NewGraph*.

8 Having saved the *SetGraph* procedure according to the advice in Exploration 7, retrieve it and build the new *RealInvest_Graph* program around it. Debug the program, if necessary, and then run it. What happens when you enter an investment of more than 10,000?

9 Modify the *RealInvest_Graph* program so that it issues a warning to the user about limitations on the term and amount of investments. You already know that the program is not set up to display amounts exceeding 10,000 units of currency, but you must use the results of Exploration 6 to determine how many years the program will handle.

10 Modify the *RealInvest_Graph* program so that it will display the legends Year 1, Year 2, and so on, right across the bottom of the screen, in the appropriate positions under their respective bars. Use the number of years that the last part of Exploration 6 reveals to you. The program will then always display this number of years, regardless of the value of *Term* that the user inputs.

11 Change the *RealInvest_Graph* program by reinstalling the warning to the user if the value of the investment declines. Because the computer will be in graphics mode when the warning is issued, you will have to use the OUTTEXTXY statement instead of a WRITE or WRITELN statement. Bear in mind that there is ample space, about 30 pixels, for the warning message below the bars.

12 Here is an algorithm for a program that imitates a TV raster scan by covering the screen with lines. The program assumes a VGA screen. If you do not have this type of screen, adjust the loop limit accordingly.

```
initialize a variable called Next to 0
within a loop of 96 iterations
   draw a line from (0, Next) to (639, Next)
   add 5 to Next
```

Refine the algorithm and translate it into a Turbo Pascal graphics program that functions according to specifications.

13 Draw a complete quad-tree for the cat image described in the last section of this chapter.

14 The adjacent figure shows an 8×8 screen containing an image of a house and a tree beside it. State how many memory locations would be required to store the image without special treatment.

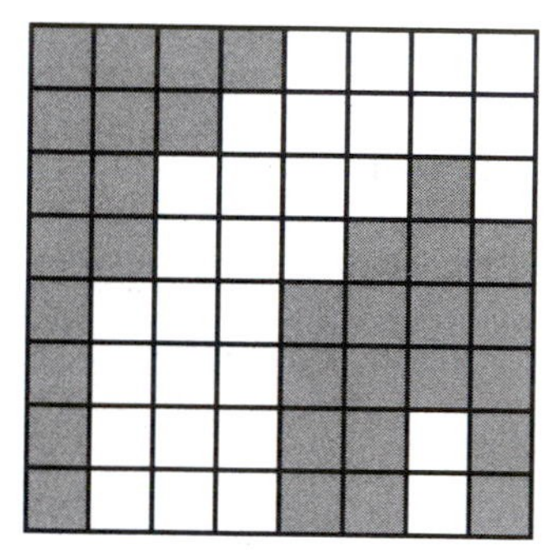

Next, develop the complete quad-tree for this image and state how many memory locations will be required to store the quad-tree. What percentage of image storage space does the quad-tree *save* in this case?

5 The Ground Floor of Computing

Logic in Software and Hardware

Programs make logical decisions when they choose between alternatives, as they do in conditional statements. Computers, on the other hand, do nothing else but make logical decisions. This chapter explores the logic of both software and hardware. Programs contain logical expressions and computers contain logic circuits.

I begin with a project to write a program that controls a simple elevator. To write this program, however, I need a new kind of variable called a *logical*, or *Boolean*, *variable*. I also need a new kind of conditional statement, the IF–THEN–ELSE statement. Conditional statements, as well as assignments to Boolean variables, both require an excursion into Boolean expressions. With this background, I quickly complete the elevator program.

The hardware portion of the chapter explains gates, the basic decision-making elements of computer hardware. I use the gates to design a circuit that controls the elevator. From the exercise, it becomes clear how whole computers can consist of nothing but gates.

Finally, a basic insight of computer science demonstrates the fact that expressions of Boolean variables and circuits of gates are simply two ways of looking at the same thing.

You are now on the ground floor of computing.

An Elevating Project

Programs use logic in a variety of ways. You are already familiar with the IF–THEN statement in which the logical value of the condition (the part following the IF) determines what the computer does next. If the condition is TRUE, the computer executes the statement following the THEN. If the condition is not true, the computer does not execute that statement.

The program I'm about to design and write takes you into the world of logic in software by expanding your ability to use conditional statements in Turbo Pascal. In addition, it expands your knowledge of the "conditions" that conditional statements use. Called *Boolean expressions,* they constitute a world of logic in themselves.

The Elevator Program

Computers live in the strangest places these days. There is one small computer, for example, that you might find near an elevator shaft in the basement of a large, 50-story office tower. Unlike its lucky colleagues that get to run a great variety of programs, this computer has only one purpose in life—to run an elevator control program. Increasingly these days, jobs that used to be done by special purpose hardware are being done by software.

The elevator control computer has both inputs and outputs. The inputs come from two kinds of sources, a control panel on each floor (right by the elevator shaft) and a control panel in the elevator itself. As you know, each floor panel sports two important buttons, labeled UP and DOWN. If a user pushes the UP button, for example, a signal is sent to the control computer that someone pushed the UP button on a certain floor. The panel inside the elevator is more complicated. It contains a button for each floor in the building. If a passenger pushes a floor button inside the elevator, this signal is also sent to the control computer.

The computer's output signals control the elevator. Included among these outputs are signals to stop the hoist, to start it moving in the up direction, to start it in the down direction, and to open and close the elevator doors. In this section I will design and write a control program for the elevator, but to simplify matters, I will not bother to program the doors, the display in the elevator, or a dozen other niceties of elevator control.

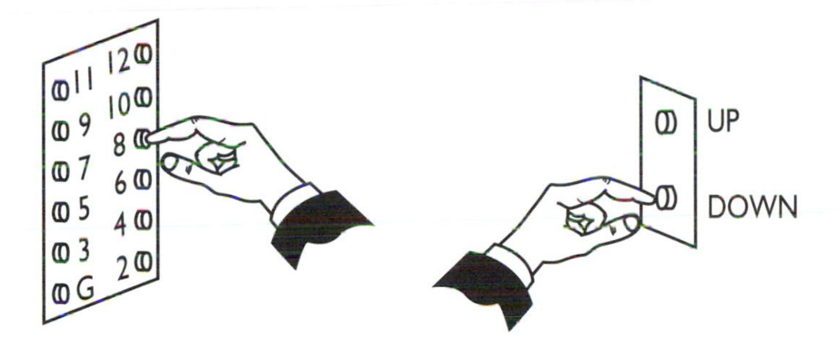

Selecting a floor

> *Design and write a Turbo Pascal program that accepts floor commands from the user, analyzes them, and sends appropriate control signals to an elevator. Because I will not have an actual elevator to control, the program must print or display the values of any key control variables that change values in the course of a run. Such variables would be commands to the elevator to move up, move down, or stop. The program must also display the current floor position of the elevator, including all the floors it passes while moving. I assume that just one passenger will use the elevator at a time.*

This is your first example of a program that is based on a *real time application*. Such application programs must operate with inputs from, and outputs to, external events. If the events happen quickly, the program's response must be equally quick. Examples of real time applications include the process control programs that operate steel mills or chemical factories. The computers that operate various aircraft systems, especially the autopilot, must also run in real time. Such programs must be fast enough to make decisions on the fly, as it were. The elevator control program, were it to operate an actual elevator, would easily be fast enough to operate in real time. In fact, as you will presently discover, I will have to slow the program down, just to follow it!

Beginning the Algorithmic Design

To begin, let's lay out a simple algorithm that captures the main missions of the program to be written. The program makes no distinction between service requests that come from the floor and those that come from the elevator itself. Because the program controls a pretend elevator in any case, all new floor requests will come from the user. Let's call the program *Elevator*.

Algorithm for *Elevator*

get new floor number from user

calculate number of floors to go

if number of floors is positive
  then set hoist variables to up values
    inform user of values
    set increment to +1
  else set hoist variables to down values
    inform user of values
    set increment to −1

in a loop that counts through the floors
  add increment to the current floor number
  report floor number to user

reset hoist variables to stop values

This algorithm describes what the program will do during just one cycle of operation. What if the user wishes to "run" the elevator several times? In this case, you must do what you did to make the *AddTutor* program restartable in Chapter 2. I must add an outer loop around the algorithm above. But we're not ready to do it now, so I will add the outer loop in the next stage of refinement.

In the unrefined algorithm above, the program will do different things, depending on whether the elevator is to go up or down. For example, if the elevator is to go up, the program must set the hoist variables to values that are appropriate for upward motion. It must report these values to the user and it must set an increment to +1. The increment will be a key ingredient of the loop that follows. To go up one floor at a time, the program must add 1 to the current floor number. The opposite things happen if the elevator is to go down. The algorithm assumes that the user will not request service for the floor where the elevator is currently stationed.

Inside the elevator motion loop, the floors must be counted off and reported to the user. When this loop terminates, the elevator will be at the desired floor, and the algorithm provides for resetting the hoist variables to values that reflect the stopped condition.

With this algorithm in hand, I can make a provisional list of variables for the program:

program name: *Elevator*

variables: *FloorNum*, current position of elevator
NewFloor, new floor requested by user
NumFloors, number of floors to go (+ or −)
Increment, +1 for up, −1 for down

In addition to these variables, the algorithm also mentions hoist control variables. I will call them *Up*, *Down*, and *Stop*.

Logic in Turbo Pascal

The three elevator control variables *Up*, *Down*, and *Stop* will each have only two possible values, namely, TRUE or FALSE. These are called *Boolean values*, or *truth values*, and the variables are called *Boolean variables*, or *logical variables*. The program will set these values according to the following table:

Up	*Down*	*Stop*
Up = TRUE	Up = FALSE	Up = FALSE
Down = FALSE	Down = TRUE	Down = FALSE
Stop = FALSE	Stop = FALSE	Stop = TRUE

So far, you have learned about three kinds of variables, namely, real variables, integer variables, and character variables. Boolean variables almost complete the list of variables that you will use in this course. To declare a Boolean variable, you must use essentially the same syntax you would use with any of the other three kinds of variables.

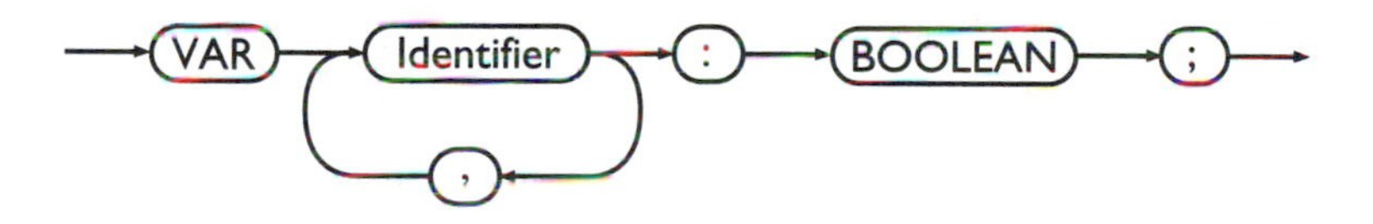

Syntax diagram for declaring a Boolean variable

Just as you can assign values to an integer, a real, or a character variable, so you can assign values to a Boolean variable. But the values must, of course, be Boolean. Consider the statement

```
Up := FALSE;
```

When the computer executes this statement, the variable *Up* will take on the Boolean value FALSE. But, like real or integer variables, Boolean variables can be assigned values other than constant values. You can also assign *Boolean expressions* to Boolean variables. Such expressions consist of Boolean variables joined together by *Boolean operators* such as AND, OR, and NOT. Imagine a more elaborate elevator program, one, for example, that accepts both floor requests (*UpButton*) and elevator panel requests (*NextFloor*):

```
Up := UpButton OR (NextFloor > FloorNum);
```

The expression to the right of the assignment operator will be TRUE if either the UP button on one of the floors has been pushed OR the floor requested inside the elevator is higher than the current floor. To interpret any and all such formulas, you must now follow a byway into the wonderful world of Boolean expressions.

Expressing Logical Ideas

Boolean expressions enable a programmer to express an enormous range of logical ideas. It is worthwhile to explore this world of expressions for two reasons. Boolean expressions are used in Boolean assignment statements. They are also used as the conditions in conditional statements. For example, recall the IF–THEN statement from the *AddTutor* program:

```
IF Answer = Sum
   THEN WRITELN('Congratulations! You got the right answer!');
```

The expression "Answer = Sum" is Boolean because it can be only one of two things—it can be either TRUE or FALSE. Either *Answer* equals *Sum* or it doesn't. There's no in-between.

In case Boolean expressions seem a little esoteric, it might help to realize that people use such expressions implicitly every day. Consider the following somewhat inflated example: "Either you come up with some money or we don't eat tonight, unless you don't mind going to the bank and you fix that car of yours."

Let's make up some logical variables to fit this situation:

Money	TRUE if the accused can find some money
Eat	TRUE if "we" eat tonight
Bank	TRUE if the accused is willing to go to bank
Fix	TRUE if accused can repair automobile

These variables lead to an expression of the speaker's sentiments:

Money OR (*Bank* AND *Fix*) OR NOT *Eat*

For this statement to be true, at least one of the three component expressions must be true. Clearly, the accuser wants "NOT Eat" to be false, so for the whole expression to be true, one of the remaining components had better be true: The accused must find some money or make sure that "(*Bank* and *Fix*)" is true. To ensure the latter, the accused must be willing to go to the bank AND fix the car.

Two kinds of *basic Boolean expressions* can be identified

a Boolean variable
a relational expression

You already know that Boolean variables have names, just as other variables do. A relational expression simply consists of three components: a numerical variable or constant, a relational operator (<, <=, >, >=, =, <>), and another numerical variable or constant. The expression

$$Answer = Sum$$

is a relational expression. So is $A < 7$.

All Boolean expressions are constructed from these two elements. First, you start with any two basic expressions and join them by one of the Boolean operators, AND or OR. There is an additional Boolean operator, NOT, but it applies only to single expressions. You can build up Boolean expressions of arbitrary complexity by following these simple rules. In what follows **X** and **Y** will stand for Boolean expressions.

1. Given a Boolean expression **X**,
NOT **X** is also a Boolean expression
2. Given two Boolean expressions **X** and **Y**,
X AND **Y** and **X** OR **Y** are also Boolean expressions.

It is a good idea to enclose Boolean expressions in parentheses before combining them into new, more complex Boolean expressions. For example, in combining the basic expression "Up Button" with "NextFloor > FloorNum" via the OR operator, you should write

```
Up := UpButton OR (NextFloor > FloorNum);
```

You should also add parentheses whenever there is danger of ambiguity, as I shall presently explain.

To illustrate the rules in action, let's build up a rather abstract expression that consists entirely of two integer variables, *A* and B, as well as two Boolean variables, **X** and **Y**.

```
X OR (A < 7)

(X OR (A < 7)) AND NOT X
```

You do not have to parenthesize single variables or single variables with a NOT in front of them, but if you fail to parenthesize other elements of a Boolean expression, the result can be an incorrect evaluation. For example, without the outside set of parentheses in the second example above, you would have something quite different:

```
X OR (A < 7) AND NOT X
```

Turbo Pascal follows specific rules for evaluating Boolean expressions. For the preceding expression, it will first evaluate the component "($A < 7$) AND NOT **X**". Then it goes on to consider the **X** OR part. (As you will see in the next section, the resulting expression is not the one you want.)

Continuing with the example, let's expand the current expression with yet another OR operator:

```
Y OR ((X OR (A < 7)) AND NOT X)
```

It is one thing to construct a Boolean expression, another to evaluate it. For each possible combination of its component truth values, a Boolean expression will have a truth value of its own.

Truth Tables

Truth tables are simple but effective ways to check the truth or falsity of Boolean expressions, no matter how complicated. Let's begin with truth tables for the three Boolean operators, AND, OR, and NOT. In these tables, **X** and **Y** represent Boolean variables. To streamline the tables, I have replaced the words TRUE and FALSE by the letters T and F. For each combination of truth values for **X** and **Y**, the third column of the first two tables gives the corresponding value of the Boolean expression. In the third table there is only one variable. The application of NOT to a Boolean variable (or expression) simply reverses its truth value.

A glance at the first table reveals that the expression **X** AND **Y** is true only when both of the Boolean variables are true. The expression **X** OR **Y**, in the second table, is false only when **X** and **Y** are both false. In a sense, then, AND and OR are opposites. It is not difficult to remember these tables. For one thing, they are already stored in your head, because the meanings of AND and OR already correspond to how you use these words as logical connectives in ordinary speech. "If I pass this course and I win the lottery, then I'll buy a new Simplex 2000

AND Operator

X	Y	X AND Y
F	F	F
F	T	F
T	F	F
T	T	T

OR Operator

X	Y	X OR Y
F	F	F
F	T	T
T	F	T
T	T	T

NOT Operator

X	NOT X
F	T
T	F

Truth tables for the three Boolean operators

computer." The word "and" in the expression "I pass this course and I win the lottery" has exactly the same meaning as its logical counterpart. The expression will be true only if both the components (concerning passing and winning) are true.

To check the truth value of more complicated expressions, you can build larger tables in which the smaller component expressions are evaluated first, then the whole expression itself. Take, for example, the expression

```
(X OR (A < 7)) AND NOT X
```

This expression can be laid out in a truth table as shown in the next figure. You can plainly see that the final expression is true for just one combination of truth values. Because you have no idea of the truth value of the relational expression "*A* < 7," you treat it like a Boolean variable and examine all possibilities. The pattern of T's and F's below the expression "**X** OR (*A* < 7)" reflects the earlier OR table. To determine the truth value of the final expression, use the truth table for AND. For example, in the first line if **X** is F, then NOT **X** is T. On the other hand, if "**X** OR (*A* < 7)" is F, then one of the components in the final expression is T and the other is F. According to the truth table for AND, the resulting value must be F.

Now let's consider the alternate expression "**X** OR *A* < 7 AND NOT **X**" in which the parentheses that enclose "**X** OR *A* < 7" have been stripped away. If you work out the truth table for this expression, the truth values in the last column will not be F, T, F, and F, but F, T, T, and T. Without parentheses, this is a different expression altogether!

X	A < 7	X or (A < 7)	[X or (A < 7)] and Not X
F	F	F	F
F	T	T	T
T	F	T	F
T	T	T	F

Truth table for evaluating (X OR (A<7)) AND NOT X

A New Conditional Statement

In the crude algorithm for the *Elevator* program, you may have noticed an unusual way of framing conditional statements. It involved the words "if," "then," and "else." The IF–THEN–ELSE statement extends your abilities to control the logic of Turbo Pascal programs. The syntax is only slightly more complicated than that of the IF–THEN statement. If the Boolean expression is true, then the first statement will be executed. If the Boolean expression is false, then the second statement will be executed. In the context of a program, you could summarize the flow of control by a diagram. Note how the IF–THEN–ELSE statement is laid out spatially in the figure on the next page. I will follow this layout whenever I use this form of the conditional. For clarity, I have numbered the statements 1, 2, 3, and 4. The first and last statements represent parts of the program that precede and follow the IF–THEN–ELSE statement. After the computer executes statement 1, it begins to execute the IF–THEN–ELSE statement. First, it tests the value of the Boolean expression. If the expression is true, then the computer executes statement 2 but not statement 3. If the expression is false, it executes statement 3 but not statement 2. In either case, the computer then goes on to execute statement 4.

As usual, the syntax diagram below gives no hint of preferred layout on a program page, but it does make the rules of formation crystal clear. If these statements seemed a bit cumbersome, you were absolutely right.

Let's use the IF–THEN–ELSE statement to enhance an earlier program. Recall that *AddTutor*, the program that helped grade school children with their math, contained two consecutive IF–THEN statements:

```
IF (Answer = Sum)
   THEN WRITELN('Congratulations! You got the right answer!');
IF (Answer <> Sum)
   THEN WRITELN('Oops! You made a mistake. Can you find it?');
```

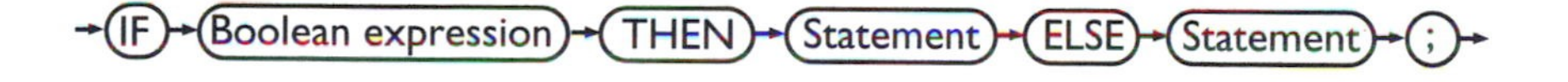

Syntax diagram for IF–THEN–ELSE

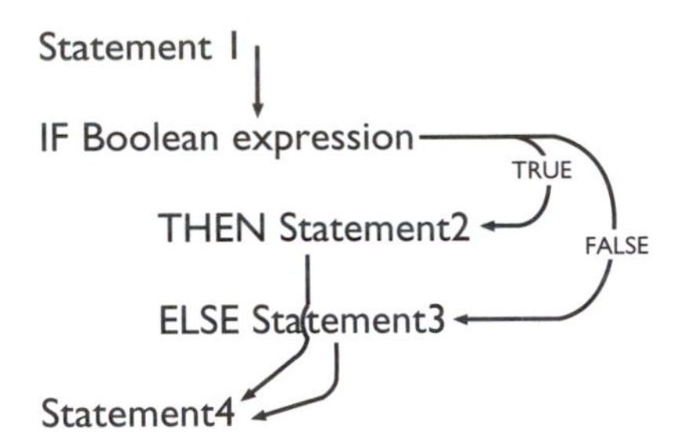

Execution of IF–THEN–ELSE statement

You can simplify this part of the program by combining the two IF–THEN statements into one IF–THEN–ELSE statement:

```
IF (Answer = Sum)
   THEN WRITELN('Congratulations! You got the right answer!')
   ELSE WRITELN('Oops! You made a mistake. Can you find it?');
```

Notice that the statement following the THEN is *not* followed by a semicolon. When the compiler sees the ELSE, it knows very well that a statement has just ended and so doesn't need the semicolon. In addition to simple statements, you can also use compound statements (having a BEGIN and END) inside an IF–THEN–ELSE, just as you can with the IF–THEN statement. You will use compound statements inside the IF–THEN–ELSE statement of the *Elevator* program.

Completing the Algorithmic Design

Now that you understand Boolean variables, Boolean expressions, and the IF–THEN–ELSE statement, I can finish writing the *Elevator* program. The stepwise refinement of the original algorithm had barely begun, when I pulled you aside to explore logic in Turbo Pascal. To complete the refinement, let's add an outer loop that allows ten rides on the elevator. Because I might want to change this number, I will store the number of rides as a constant called *Trips*.

Inside the outer loop, the steps yet to refine look like this:

```
get new floor number from user
calculate number of floors to go

if number of floors is positive
   then set hoist variables to the up combination
      inform user of values
      set increment to +1
   else set hoist variables to the down combination
      inform user of values
      set increment to -1

in a loop that counts through the floors
   add increment to the current floor number
   report floor number to user

reset hoist variables to stop combination
```

The refinement will bring me very close to a Turbo Pascal program.

```
output: "The next request comes from floor:"
input: NewFloor

set NumFloors to NewFloor - FloorNum

if NumFloors > 0
   then set Up, Down, and Stop to TRUE, FALSE, and FALSE
      output: "Sending "Up" signal to hoist."
      set Incr to +1
   else set Up, Down, and Stop to FALSE, TRUE, and FALSE
      output: "Sending "Down" signal to hoist."
      set Incr to -1

for Step (an index) running from 1 to NumFloors
   add Incr to FloorNum
   delay
   output: "At floor: ", FloorNum
```

Set *Up*, *Down*, and *Stop* to FALSE, FALSE, and TRUE.
output: "Sending "Stop" signal to hoist."

The calculation of *NumFloors* uses the fact that if *NewFloor* (the requested floor) is greater than *FloorNum* (the current floor), the difference between them will be positive. Otherwise it will be negative. At the end of the algorithm, a message is sent to the user that the elevator has arrived and the appropriate signals have been sent to the hoist.

Inside the loop, I have also added a mysterious-looking step called "delay." Earlier I remarked that the program will be so fast that the astonished user will witness a blur of reports on where the elevator is. The run will be finished in a millisecond. Turbo Pascal has a DELAY statement that allows a programmer to introduce a delay of any specified length of time into the actual running of the program. For example, every time the computer executes the statement

```
DELAY(5000);
```

all further execution halts until the computer has counted off 5000 milliseconds, or 5 ordinary seconds. Because the DELAY statement is part of the CRT unit (see page 115), you must also add the statement

```
USES Crt;
```

to the program, just below the program header.

The translation of the refined algorithm into a Turbo Pascal program is now more or less imminent. No doubt I will think of some last minute changes that are either necessary or merely desirable.

```
PROGRAM Elevator;
{This program demonstrates the ability of software to}
{make the logical decisions needed to control an elevator.}

USES Crt; {The Crt unit contains the DELAY procedure.}

VAR FloorNum, Cycle, NewFloor: INTEGER;
```

```
VAR NumFloors, Step, Incr: INTEGER;
VAR Up, Down, Stop: BOOLEAN;
CONST Trips = 10;

BEGIN {program}

{Initialize variables.}
FloorNum := 1;

{Inform user of current elevator position.}
WRITELN('The elevator is currently at Floor 1.');

{main loop}
FOR Cycle := 1 TO Trips DO

   BEGIN {main loop}

   {Prompt the user for a floor.}
   WRITE('The next request comes from floor: ');
   READLN(NewFloor);

   {Go to that floor after}
   {deciding which way to go.}
   NumFloors := NewFloor - FloorNum;
   IF NumFloors > 0
      THEN BEGIN
         Up := TRUE; Down := FALSE; Stop := FALSE;
         WRITELN('Sending "up" signal to hoist.');
         Incr := 1;
         END
      ELSE BEGIN
         Down := TRUE; Up := FALSE; Stop := FALSE;
         WRITELN('Sending "down" signal to hoist.');
         Incr := -1;
         END;

   {Make NumFloors positive.}
   NumFloors := ABS(NumFloors);

   {elevator motion loop}
   FOR Step := 1 to NumFloors DO
      BEGIN {motion loop}
      FloorNum := FloorNum + Incr;
      DELAY (5000);
```

```
      WRITELN('At floor ', FloorNum);
      END; {motion loop}

   {Elevator has arrived at new floor}
   Up := FALSE; Down := FALSE; Stop := TRUE;
   WRITELN('The elevator has arrived.');
   WRITELN('Sending “stop” signal to hoist.');

   {warning of last trip}
   IF Cycle = Trips - 1
      THEN WRITELN('You have one trip left.');

   END; {of main loop}

END. {of program)
```

The addition of the promised outer loop caused a small ripple of change to spread through the program. A new index variable called *Cycle* had to be declared and a limit had to be put on the number of trips. Choosing a constant called *Trips* to hold this limit, I had to declare *Trips* equal to 10 (an arbitrary value) in a CONST statement.

It would be very foolish to make *NumFloors* the limit of the elevator motion loop if *NumFloors* happened to have a negative value. For this reason, I used the Turbo Pascal function ABS (short for "absolute value") to make *NumFloors* positive if it wasn't already. This is your second example of a Turbo Pascal function. The first was TRUNC. You may recall from the way this function was used in the graphics version of *RealInvest* that TRUNC chops off the decimal fraction part of any real number to which it is applied. As you will learn in Chapter 7, functions may be used in assignment statements, their values being assigned to a variable.

As a final flourish, I added a warning to the user; when the next to last trip has been completed, there will be just one trip left!

You can run this program as it stands if you have DOS- or OS/2-based Turbo Pascal. If you have Windows, merely add another USES statement to the program.

```
USES WinCrt;
```

The Gates of Computation

When a computer performs a computation by executing a program, thousands of tiny hardware decision makers called *gates* go into action. Etched into the silicon microprocessor chip by the millions, gates are the permanent hardware workers for temporary software bosses. Programs come and go, but the gates remain.

What is a "gate"? Generally speaking, it is any physical device that takes truth values as input and produces a truth value as output. The truth values could be electrical impulses, jets of water, streams of photons, or movements of ropes. Gates have been built or conceived for each of these kinds of inputs! (See the box on page 148.) In each case, the input encodes TRUE and FALSE in some manner. For example, the gates in a modern computer like the Simplex 2000 are fabricated out of silicon and other exotic materials. Their inputs are electrical voltages called Hi and Lo. The first voltage, somewhat higher than the second, stands for TRUE and the second voltage stands for FALSE.

Three Basic Gates

One could build a computer that uses just three kinds of gates called AND, OR, and NOT. If these names sound familiar, they should. They are the hardware embodiments of the Boolean operators that I discussed in the earlier section on Boolean logic. Because you will be drawing circuits that use these gates, you should know the symbols that computer designers use when laying out a circuit. The next figure shows three symbols: an elongated semicircle, a shield-shaped symbol and a triangle with a small circle attached. These symbols stand for the AND-gate, the OR-gate, and the NOT-gate, respectively.

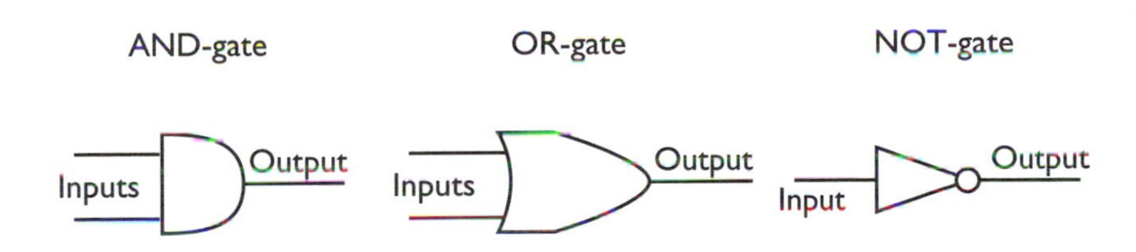

Three types of gates

A Rope-and-Pulley OR-gate

The accompanying diagram shows an OR-gate made from three pieces of rope, four pulleys, and one box. The operation is very simple. If you pull on either of the two input ropes (moving it from right to left in the diagram), the output rope also pulls (moving right to left). It makes no difference which input rope you pull, the output is the same. You could also pull both input ropes and the output rope would move by the same amount. Pull neither rope and, of course, you get no movement at all in the output rope.

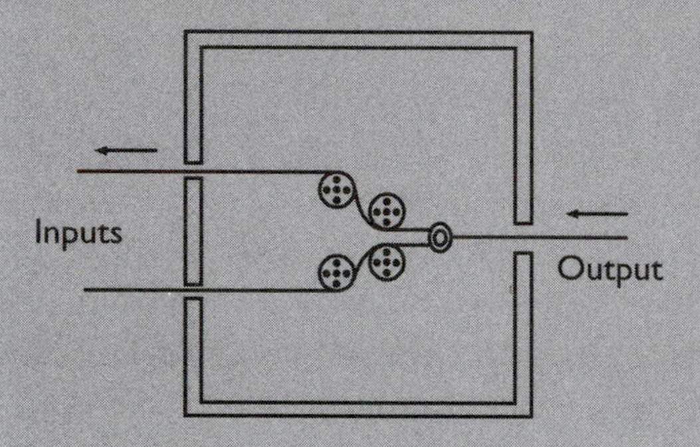

Logic gate made from ropes and pulleys

If you interpret a pulled-on rope as the value TRUE and the unpulled rope as FALSE, the rope-and-pulley gate has the same input/output relation as the OR function described earlier. Therefore, it is an OR-gate. In other words, if you substitute the symbol T for "rope is pulled" and F for "rope is not pulled," you can still interpret the rope-and-pulley gate as an OR-gate.

In an electronic OR-gate, input voltages being applied play the same role as input ropes being pulled. If at least one input voltage is Hi, so is the output, and not otherwise.

Each gate has one or two *input lines* entering it on the left and a single *output line* leaving it on the right. If you send any combination of truth values into the input lines, each gate will produce a corresponding truth value on its output line. Each gate type embodies the same truth table that belongs to its expressional counterpart. For example, in the

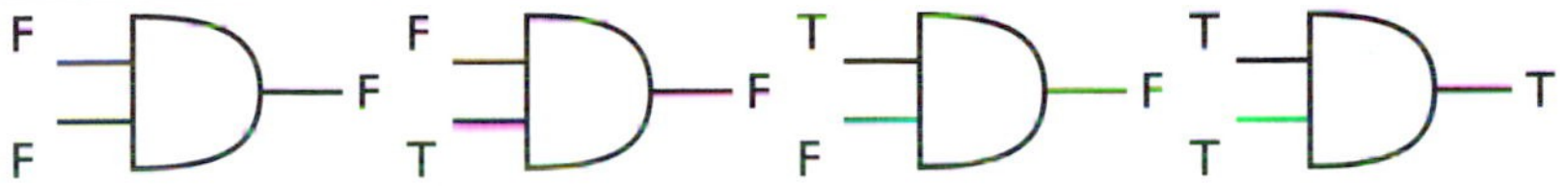

How the AND-gate works

above figure I have reproduced the AND-gate with four different combinations of input values. If you compare these values with the truth table for the AND operator on page 139, you will see that it has the same output in each case.

In other words, if *both* the inputs of an AND-gate are T, then so is the output; otherwise, the output is F. The OR-gate works differently. If *at least* one of the inputs is T, then so is the output; otherwise, the output is F. The NOT-gate simply reverses the input. If the input is T, the output is F. If the input is F, the output is T.

Now if input and output lines carry the same kinds of values, namely, T and F, shouldn't it be possible to take the output from one gate and make it the input of another? The whole field of logic design is based on this simple possibility. Let's go back to the elevator for inspiration.

Elevator Logic

In the basements of many buildings where elevators run, there are still control computers that do not run programs. Instead they contain special purpose circuits that control the elevators. These control circuits use logic gates to compute the control signals that operate the elevators.

Suppose you wanted to construct a circuit, instead of a program, to control your pretend elevator. You would have to connect various gates together in a way that produced control signals for the elevator hoist motor. The simplest circuit imaginable would accept two kinds of inputs and produce two kinds of output. It would accept the current floor number and the requested floor number as inputs. The circuit would then compare the two numbers and, depending on which was greater, issue either an up-signal or a down-signal as output.

Although you will not be asked to design such circuits as part of this course, you might enjoy looking over the shoulder of an engineer. There are many ways to design such a circuit. Sometimes when planning a

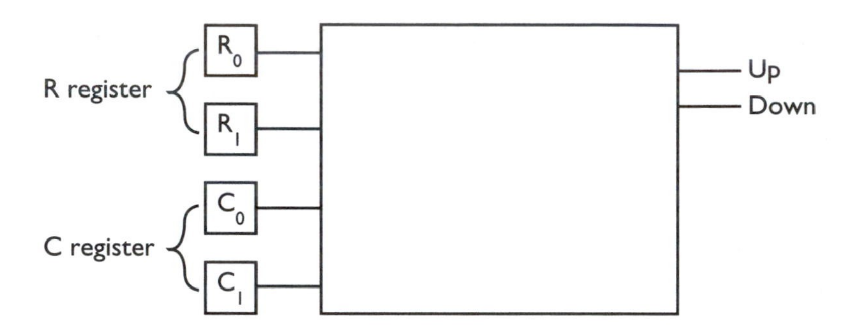

Elevator control circuit as a black box

design, engineers use the black-box symbolism to indicate a device whose contents they do not yet fully understand. Similarly, I will represent the elevator circuit by a black box, as shown in the accompanying figure. Outside the black box I have drawn two registers, each consisting of two single-bit memory elements. The two registers contain the current (C) and requested (R) floor numbers in binary form. Somehow, the black box must take the signals from these registers, as shown, and produce either an up-signal or a down-signal on one of the output lines.

Because the register represents numbers, it makes sense to switch the notation for the moment, from T and F to 1 and 0. Nothing has changed but the names. With the binary notation, it will be easier for you to translate the contents of the registers into numbers. For example, the next figure shows the four possibilities for the contents of the current floor register, C.

If you recall the excursion into binary numbers in Chapter 1 (page 21), then the corresponding decimal numbers—0, 1, 2, 3—will make sense to you. These represent the floor numbers in a humble four-story building. The same four possibilities exist for the register R. The circuit you are designing must compare the two numbers, decide which is greater, and produce a 1-signal on the appropriate output line.

C_1 C_0	C_1 C_0	C_1 C_0	C_1 C_0
0 0	0 1	1 0	1 1
[0]	[1]	[2]	[3]

Floor numbers in a four-story building

It's easiest to design the circuit in three stages. First to be constructed is a very simple circuit called a *disabler*. Next, the disabler will be employed to build a circuit that compares two bits and decides which is greater. Finally, two of these *one-bit comparators* will be wired together to make the elevator control circuit. The process of creating building blocks and assembling them into larger units is called the *modular approach* to circuit design. You may have noticed a certain parallel to the way a programmer constructs programs out of chunks or modules.

What is a disabling circuit? As the name implies, it disables a signal. The accompanying illustration shows a single AND-gate with two inputs. The upper input, labeled X, enters the AND-gate and the single output, Y, leaves it. The lower input, labeled C for "control," determines whether or not the AND-gate will pass the signal on line X through to line Y. If the signal on the control line happens to be 0 (that is, F), then, after it passes through the NOT-gate, it will be 1. In that case, whatever value—0 or 1—that enters the gate on line X will also leave it on line Y.

The control line resembles a guard, of sorts. As long as it has the value 0, the X signal is *enabled*, or allowed to pass through unchanged. But when the control line carries a 1 (that is, T), the input after the NOT-gate will be 0, and then it makes no difference what signal arrives on the X line, the output of the AND-gate will be 0. In this case, engineers say that the control signal has *disabled* the gate.

Next, I want to build a one-bit comparator. This circuit will have two inputs, one from C_0 and one from R_0, for example. The two outputs from the circuit represent two of the possibilities for the relative values of the bits. If the R-bit is greater than the C-bit, then the upper output line (labeled ">") will carry a 1 and the lower output line (labeled "<") will

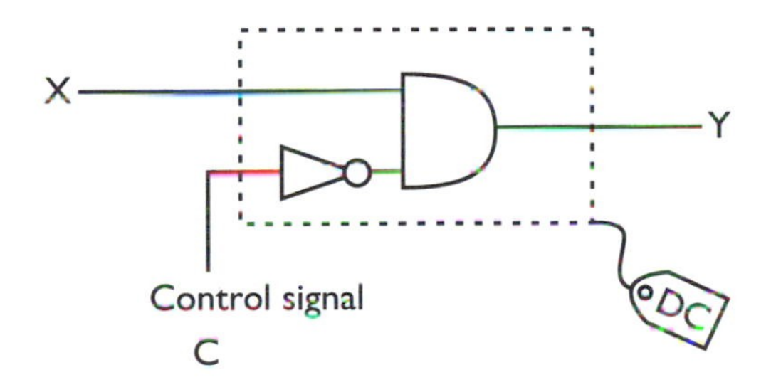

A disabling circuit

carry a 0. If the R-bit is less than the C-bit, however, the upper line will carry a 0 and the lower line will carry a 1.

The next figure shows the comparator circuit as a black box (left) and as a completed circuit (right). In the right-hand diagram, the boxes labeled "DC" represent copies of the disabling circuit that you just learned about. By replacing the actual circuits with such boxes, you get a cleaner diagram, but you have to remember how the DC module works, that is, how a 1 on the lower input disables a 1-signal on the upper input that would otherwise get through.

A 1 arriving on either input line to this circuit splits into two, one branch going to each of the DC modules. However, the branch that goes to the opposite module in each case becomes a disabling signal. A 1 arriving on either input will disable a 1 arriving on the other input line. This device works perfectly because if one of the inputs is 1 and the other is 0, the 0-input will not disable the 1-input and it will pass through the disabler and indicate to the world which input was greater. Conversely, if both inputs are 0 or both inputs are 1, either both inputs to the disabling circuits are 0 or both inputs are disabled. The end result is that the two output lines of the one-bit comparator will be 0. Having completed the one-bit comparator circuit, let's represent it from now on as a box labeled "COMP." To complete the control circuit for the elevator, you must install two one-bit comparators, one for each bit-pair, namely, C_1 and R_1, and C_0 and R_0.

Now you need another piece of background information. If you examine any binary number, you will notice that the bits at the left end

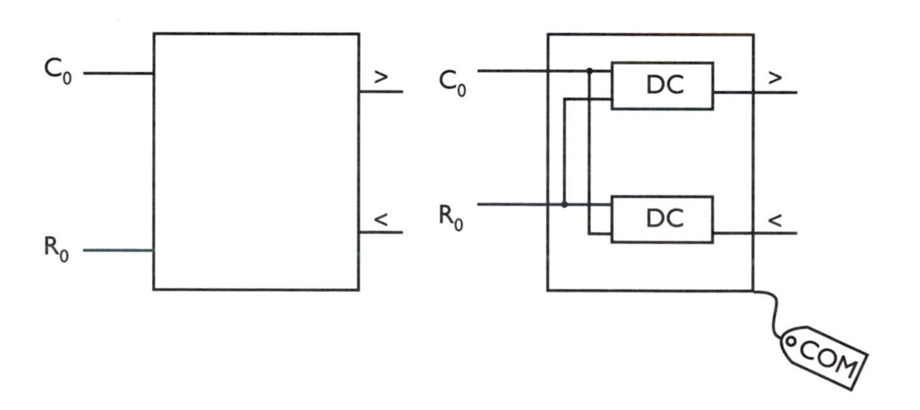

Birth of comparator circuit

carry more weight than those at the right end, just as the digits of a decimal number do. In other words, if you change a bit at the left end, called a *high-order bit*, the binary number will change much more dramatically than if you change a bit at the right end, a *low-order bit*. In the C and R registers, the bits with subscript 1 are high order and the bits with subscript 0 are low order. So, if $R_1 = 1$ and $C_1 = 0$, it makes no difference what values R_0 and C_0 have, the number in the R register will be larger than the number in the C register. For this reason, when you tie the outputs of the two comparators together, the outputs of the high-order comparator must disable the outputs of the low-order comparator.

Of course, it might happen that the high-order bits are equal. In such a case, the low-order bits will determine which number is larger. The next figure shows the values of the low-order bits arriving at a comparator at the bottom of the diagram. Meanwhile, the values of the high-order bits arrive at another comparator at the top of the figure. At this point, the outputs of the two comparators may have any combination of values at all. What happens to these outputs after they leave the comparator constitutes the rest of the design.

Suppose that the upper comparator happens to send a 1 out the line labeled < and the lower comparator sends a 1 out the line labelled >. Clearly, the signal from the upper comparator should prevail because it originates from the most significant bits; and, as you saw earlier, these determine the relative sizes of the two numbers.

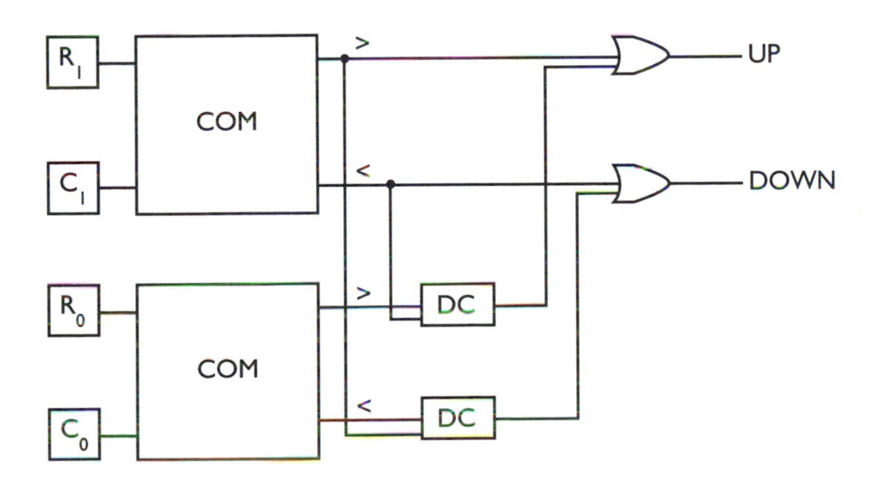

Control circuit in modular form

The output of the line labeled < from the upper comparator splits into two output lines at the black dot. The same signal then proceeds not only to an OR-gate on the right of the diagram but also down to a disabling circuit, which receives the > signal from the lower comparator as well. In other words, a 1 emanating from the < output of the upper comparator disables the > signal from the lower comparator. The same 1 also arrives at the OR-gate and passes through, no matter what the other input to the OR-gate happens to be. The output of that OR-gate, labeled *Down*, goes directly to the hoist motor, turning it on and sending the elevator down.

You should try this sort of analysis yourself for other combinations of outputs from the two comparator circuits. In particular, if the two outputs of the upper comparator are 0, then neither high-order bit is greater than the other. In this case, the less significant bits carry the day, because neither signal from the lower comparator will be disabled by the outputs of the upper one.

Although I have chosen to use logic gates to create a logical design for elevator control hardware, I could also have used logic gates to design a whole computer! In fact, I have already demonstrated that numbers can be compared by logic. Computers make extensive use of comparators in the chip known as the arithmetic logic unit. How could the computer evaluate a relational expression otherwise?

Expressions and Circuits

One role of computer science is to unify knowledge, to show how things that you might think of as very different are really the same. So far you have seen logic playing a role in both hardware and software. Is it possible to unify the two kinds of logic? The answer is "Yes." Boolean expressions and logic circuits turn out to be two ways of looking at the same thing. You will come to understand this identity as you follow the step-by-step process by which I construct either a Boolean expression or a circuit. In this process, I will compare logic gates in a circuit with the logic operators in a Boolean expression. I will also compare input and output lines in a circuit with Boolean variables in a Boolean expression. The following figure illustrates the correspondence.

To simplify matters, I'll speak only of Boolean variables with letter names such as A, B, C, and so on. The same letters also can be used to label the outputs and inputs of the gates. To begin, I will draw a little circuit on the left and post an equivalent Boolean expression on the right.

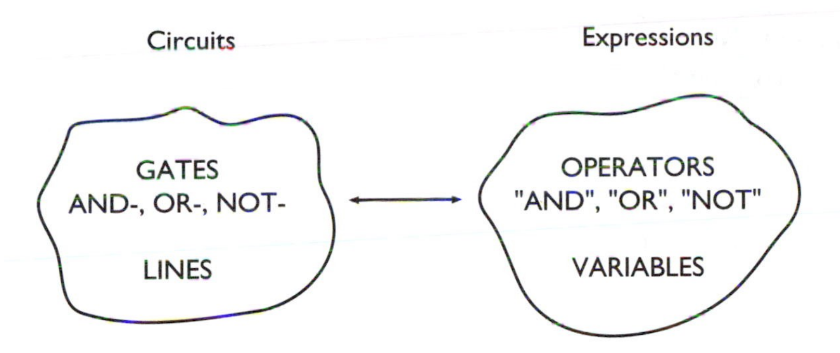

Are circuits and expressions the same thing?

When I say that the circuit on the left and the expression on the right (below) are "equivalent," I mean that they represent the same logical function. What happens, for example, if I set the three inputs to the logic circuit to T, F, and T, respectively? Tracing through the circuit, you will discover that the output of the AND-gate is T. This T value is enough to force an output of T from the right-hand OR-gate, because an OR-gate needs just one T input to produce a T output. To summarize, with inputs of T, F, and T, respectively, the circuit outputs a T.

Turning now to the Boolean expression, what value does it have if I set the variables A, B, and C, respectively, to T, F, and T? The answer is found by evaluating the expressions inside the parentheses, then combining the values according to the main operators. To discover the truth value of the first component, simply substitute the truth values for the variables in it:

T AND NOT F

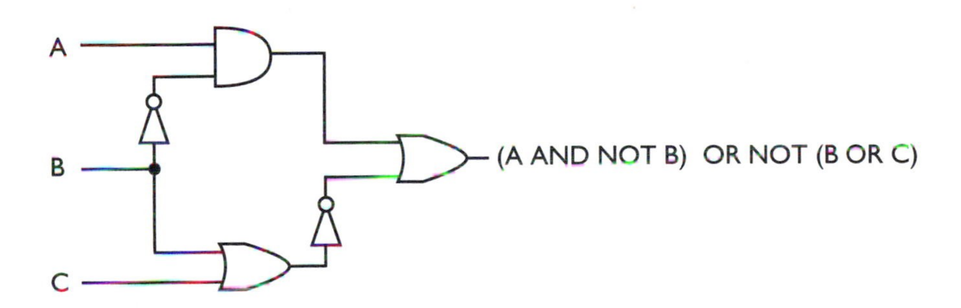

A logic circuit (left) and its equivalent expression (right)

As you know, NOT F is the same as T; so the expression boils down to T AND T. According to the truth table for the AND operator, the result is simply T. At this juncture, the OR operator makes the value of the other component expression irrelevant.

In the case considered, the circuit outputs the same value as the expression. You should try different truth values for the inputs to the circuit and then substitute the same values into the corresponding expression. The output of the circuit will always equal the truth value of the expression.

To see why every expression corresponds to a circuit and vice versa, let's revisit the construction process for Boolean expressions. I have not supplied a formal proof; instead I will illustrate the process with the example that I presented earlier. Beginning with the basic components of the expression, I will construct pieces of circuit that correspond to them because they compute exactly the same function. The next figure shows the two parenthetical components and their associated circuits.

Next, I negate the second component of the expression and, simultaneously, add a NOT-gate to the output line of the second circuit. Finally, I tie the two circuits together by feeding their outputs to a single OR-gate. You have already seen the resulting circuit in the figure on page 155.

At each stage of this construction and all similar ones, equivalent components are used in both the Boolean expression and the circuit. If at each stage the components compute the same logical values, then they will compute the same values at the final stage as well.

I have now demonstrated that for every Boolean expression there is a circuit that produces exactly the same truth values for every possible combination of input values. By setting up a stepwise procedure for constructing logic circuits, you could equally well demonstrate that for every circuit there

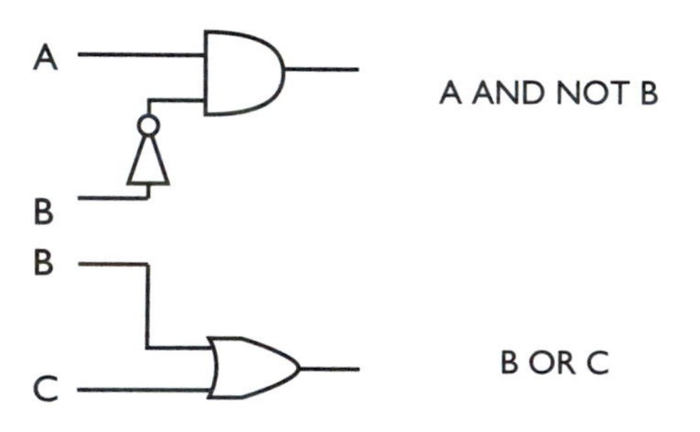

Correspondence of components

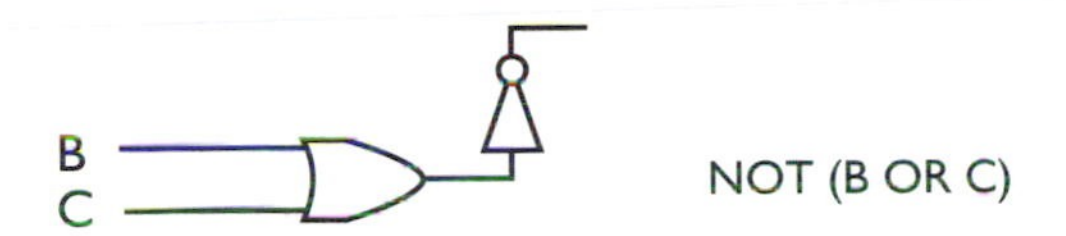

Negating the second component

is a Boolean expression that produces the same outputs. This equivalence amounts to a powerful tool. Engineers do not have to draw diagrams every time they want to design a new circuit. Working with Boolean expressions alone, they can design various logical functions by symbolic means, then translate the designs into working circuits just as I have done.

SUMMARY

Logic pervades computer software and hardware. Programs use logic to control the direction of execution. Under one set of conditions, a program may do one thing; under another set of conditions, something quite different. The elevator control program introduced you to Boolean variables and provided a jumping-off point for an excursion into Boolean expressions, a key element of any programming language.

To illustrate how logic pervades computing hardware, I went back to the elevator control problem and constructed a toy circuit that demonstrated the flexibility of the three standard gate types.

Computer science entered the picture during the discussion of how Boolean expressions and standard circuits are merely two ways of looking at the same thing.

EXPLORATIONS

1 Explain the result of executing the following IF–THEN–ELSE statement under the given conditions:

```
IF Wind <= 25 AND Go
   THEN Launch := TRUE
   ELSE WRITELN('Stand by for a countdown hold.');
```

a Wind = 22, Go = TRUE
b Wind = 35, Go = TRUE
c Wind = 14, Go = FALSE

2 Rewrite the *AddTutor* program of Chapter 2 by replacing the two consecutive IF statements by a single IF–THEN–ELSE statement, as outlined in this chapter (pages 142–143). Then run the program to confirm that it still works perfectly.

3 Which of the following are valid Boolean expressions?

a Roger < 40 OR Mary NOT > 30
b NOT(This AND That)
c AND (Arrive = 25) OR Alive

4 Run the elevator program by requesting ten consecutive floors that the elevator is not currently at. Next, run it again, requesting Floor 1 for the first ride. What happens?

5 Carry out *one* of the following modifications to the *Elevator* program:

a Add a message to the elevator program warning the user not to request a floor that matches the current elevator position. The warning should be inserted as part of one of the prompts.
b Fix the program so that it accepts requests for the floor the elevator is currently at.

6 Rewrite the *Elevator* program by incorporating new Boolean variables called *Open* and *Close*. These represent the opening and closing of the elevator doors. The revised program should set the variables and report on them, just as the current program does. To enhance the effect of the new variables, you can split the report into two parts and install a new DELAY statement between the parts. The effect would be as follows:

opening doors (pause)
doors open

7 The following program has a structure that is similar to that of the *Elevator* program. Examine it closely, then answer the questions below.

```
PROGRAM FitABox;
```

```
{declaration section}
VAR Index, Number, Size, Tries, Filling: INTEGER;
VAR Overflow: BOOLEAN;
CONST BoxSize = 56;

BEGIN

{main loop}
FOR Index := 1 TO 20 DO
   BEGIN
   WRITELN('Please enter the number of items');
   WRITE('you'd like to fit into the box: ');
   READLN(Number);
   WRITELN('Next, enter the size of the items.')
   READLN(Size);

   {initialization section}
   Overflow = FALSE;
   Filling := 0;

   FOR Tries = 1 to Number DO
      BEGIN
      Filling := Filling + Size;
      IF Filling > BoxSize
         THEN Overflow := TRUE;
      END;

   IF Overflow = TRUE
      THEN WRITELN('The items specified will not fit the box.')
      ELSE WRITELN('The box is full and ready to go.');

   END; {of main loop}

END. {of program}
```

a What Boolean variables does the program use?

b List the Boolean expressions and explain the role they play in the program.

c What is the main difference between the way *Elevator* and *Fitabox* use their constants?

d What does this program do and how does it do it?

8 Rewrite the program of Exploration 7 so that it does not use a loop but sets the value of *Overflow* on the basis of an arithmetic assignment statement and an accompanying Boolean assignment statement. You may have to introduce a new integer variable to accomplish this.

9 Draw up truth tables for the following simple Boolean expressions:

a A AND NOT B
b NOT A OR (X >= 17)
c B OR NOT(A AND B)

10 Refine the following algorithmic outline for a program called *TandF*. The program embodies a particular Boolean expression involving three logical variables. The user inputs the characters "T" and "F" to represent truth values for the three variables and the program reports on whether the expression is true for those values or not.

> Get three character values from the user.
> Translate these into truth values for A, B, and C.
> Evaluate the expression (A AND NOT B) OR NOT (B OR C).
> Report the value to the user as "true" or "false."

You will have to use some character variables and at least one Boolean variable to make this program work. You should also remember that Turbo Pascal automatically evaluates Boolean expressions.

11 Create a truth table for the Boolean expression of Exploration 10. You will need to consider eight possible combinations of T and F for the three variables. By listing them methodically, as in the two-variable tables, you can work out the values of the component expresssions, then the value of the expression itself.

12 Use the *TandF* program from Exploration 10 to create a truth table for the expression that appears in the program there. If you completed Exploration 11, you can compare the results with the table you have already derived. (The truth table of this exploration will not consider component expressions but dives straight to the truth values of the expression itself.)

13 Construct a truth table for the > output of the one-bit comparator that was designed in the section on logic circuits. To make matters simple, you can redraw the circuit, omitting all lines and gates that do not directly influence the > output decision.

14 Suppose the values residing in the R and C registers of the elevator control circuit are $R_0 = 0$, $R_1 = 1$, $C_0 = 1$, $C_1 = 0$. Trace through the circuit by hand, if possible, noting the truth value that each gate outputs, working through the circuit from left to right. Does it produce the correct output?

15 What Boolean expression does the following circuit represent?

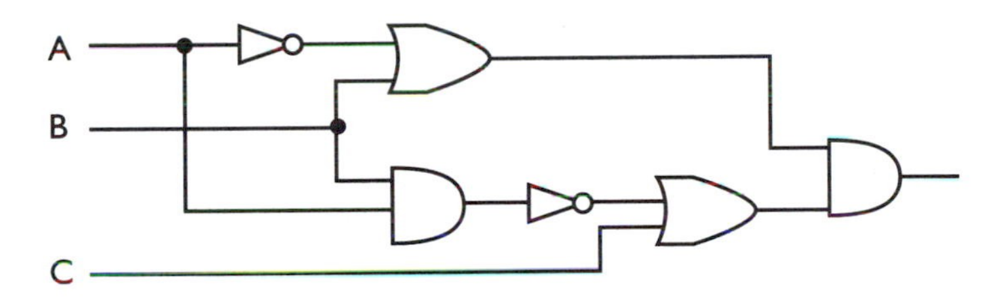

A logic circuit

16 Design a logic circuit that computes the same truth values as the expression below:

NOT(A AND NOT B) OR (NOT A AND B)

17 Just for fun, try to design an AND gate from ropes and pulleys. Enclose your design in a box, using the box to anchor or attach ropes, pulleys, or any other simple mechanism you can think of. Your completed design should pull on the output rope only when *both* input ropes are pulled.

6 Piling up Data

Arrays and Loops

Until now, the programs you have been studying and writing had only a few variables and so used very little data. The arrays introduced in this chapter allow programs to use very large amounts of data because an array contains a large number of variables. With arrays, for example, it becomes possible to expand your computing horizon and write a genuinely useful program that piles up data in the form of a histogram, which is a widely used form of statistical chart. The FOR-loop is the natural companion of the array. With it, you can scan and manipulate arrays for a huge variety of purposes.

But other, more useful kinds of loops wait in the wings. The WHILE- and REPEAT-loops give you a chance to return to earlier projects and upgrade them into more elegant vehicles for teaching arithmetic, forecasting investment values, and controlling elevators.

Computer science enters the picture when you see other ways of storing data besides arrays. The tree theme of Chapter 4 is reintroduced, not just to store pictures, but to save any kind of information.

Data in Arrays

The most common tool of those who explore data, in every field from physics to market research, is the histogram. Consisting of data piled up into columns, the histogram enables you to visualize how data is distributed. Often, construction of a histogram is the first step in detailed statistical analyses.

A biosurvey of a forest has revealed that some species are very rare, being found only a few times in the forest. Others, however, are very common, turning up at nearly all of the sample points. The histogram tells all. Each column represents a range of occurrence frequencies. Its height reflects the number of species occurring with those frequencies. For example, the spice bush, *Lindera benzoin*, was found at 36 of the 100 sample points and so gets counted in the column of frequencies from 30 to 39. That particular column is 14 units high because 14 of the species turned up between 30 and 39 times in the biosurvey.

Reviewing the shape of this distribution, a biologist would discover a curious and important fact. The rare species are common, so to speak, and the common species are rare! Histograms are useful for generating insight.

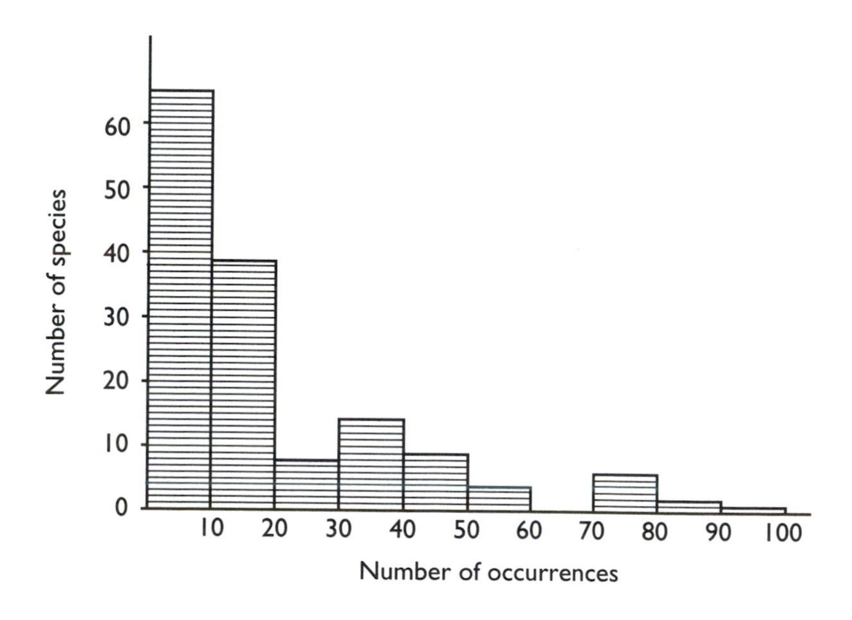

Distribution of plant species

The Histogram Project

Let's create a different histogram, not of plants, but of people. Specifically, let's make a histogram of their heights.

> *Given a number of heights from a population of people, write a program that will distribute these data into categories suitable for a histogram display. The program should also calculate the mean and standard deviation of the heights. Finally, it should report on these statistics and display the histogram for the user.*

The accompanying table displays the heights of 15 people. Each person has an identification number and a height, in centimeters:

Number	*Heights*
1	182
2	151
3	161
4	178
5	175
6	158
7	169
8	142
9	159
10	135
11	167
12	174
13	186
14	162
15	153

Population surveyed

To begin, you analyze the problem and decide that there are five main stages, not counting declarations and initializations:

Input the data.
Compute and output the mean.
Compute and output the standard deviation.
Build the histogram.
Display the histogram.

Whether these stages are in the right order or not is anyone's guess at the moment. You will discover the correct order as you proceed.

I could use computer graphics to display the result, but for some purposes computer graphics are not always necessary. In this case, for example, I will use not screen graphics but *text graphics*. In other words, I will use characters instead of pixels as the basic elements of a display of visual information. As you have seen, a histogram is like a bar chart in which the height of each column is proportional to the number of observations that lie within a given range of values. For example, you could divide the heights in the sample on the previous page into six categories:

130–139 cm
140–149 cm
150–159 cm
160–169 cm
170–179 cm
180–189 cm

If you actually count up the number of heights in the sample that fall within each of these categories, you end up with the following counts:

Height range (cm)	*Count*
130–139	1
140–149	1
150–159	4
160–169	4
170–179	3
180–189	2

The right-hand column of numerical counts is hardly a graphic display, but you can make one quickly and cheaply by using horizontal rows of characters, such as asterisks, instead of vertical bars. Who says the columns of a histogram have to be vertical? Here is the same data you just looked at in the form of a histogram on its side:

```
130–139 cm    *
140–149 cm    *
150–159 cm    ****
160–169 cm    ****
170–179 cm    ***
180–189 cm    **
```

Now it's time to get algorithmic. My first conclusion is that the program will have to use and reuse the 15 heights. This fact means that the program will need at least 15 variables, just to store the heights. It will need another six variables to store the counts for each of the six categories. In all, a total of 21 variables, not counting loop indexes, will be required. Using so many variables would call for some lengthy declaration statements, not to mention a great many assignment statements. If I were crazy enough to try this approach, what would I call the variables? Sooner or later I would stumble on a simple numbering scheme like the following one for the height variables: Height01, Height02, Height03, and so on. Wouldn't it be nice if Turbo Pascal did this for me automatically? In fact, it does.

Arrays of Data

In Chapter 3 you learned that a variable can be visualized as a kind of cubbyhole. As it runs, a program using that variable can insert new data in the cubbyhole. An array is like a series of cubbyholes, with each cubbyhole holding a different value. In the adjacent figure I have shown a single variable called *Money* and, beside it, an array variable called *Money[k]*. The number *k* is called an *array index* because it provides a means of locating each component of the array. You can imagine how such an array would come in handy in a version of the *RealInvest* program where you might want to save the annual investment values for analysis.

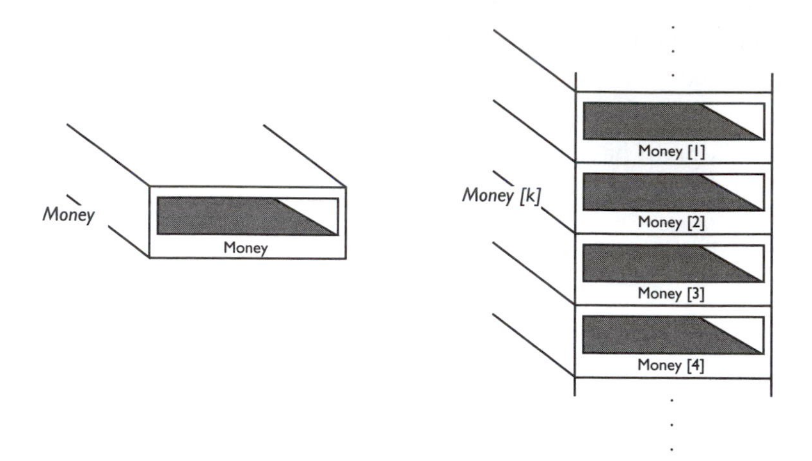

Single variable (*left*) and array variable (*right*)

All the cubbyholes shown in the illustration can each hold only one number at a time. The cubbyholes for the array variable are called *elements* of the array. Considered in isolation, each element of an array is like the single variable *Money*. Considered as a unit, however, the array *Money* can hold many numbers at a time. Using a loop, you can perform the same operation on all the variables that make up the array. For example, you can write out the values of a 10-element *Money* array with the following statement:

```
FOR Ind := 1 TO 10 DO
   WRITELN(Money[Ind]);
```

For each value of the loop index from 1 to 10, the program will print out the value stored in each cubbyhole. For example, on the third iteration of this loop, the program would write out the value of the variable *Money*[3].

A program could also read in values of this array:

```
FOR Ind := 1 TO 10 DO
   READLN(Money[Ind]);
```

On the third iteration of this loop, the program would wait until the user entered a value to be stored in the variable *Money*[3].

A program can perform arithmetic and other operations on an array if you place an assignment statement inside a FOR-loop. Suppose, for example, that you want to convert the currency of the amounts stored in the array *Money* by multiplying all the entries by an exchange rate of 0.764:

```
FOR Ind := 1 TO 10 DO
   Money[Ind] := Amount[Ind]*0.764;
```

It is important, when working with arrays, to realize that not one but two variables are usually involved. The array name, such as *Money*, must be distinguished from an index variable such as *Ind*. In the example above, the value of the first variable will be a dollar amount and the value of the second variable will be an integer.

As you just saw, a program can make a general reference to any or all of the variables in an array by the simple expedient of replacing a specific index value by the name of an index variable like *Ind*. Notice also that the index of an array variable is enclosed in square brackets and not in parentheses.

Declaring Arrays

A program that uses an array can declare it by making two statements, a TYPE statement and a VAR statement. The TYPE statement, intended to give programmers flexibility in defining new types of data, simply defines the kind of array your program will use. The accompanying VAR statement then uses the type that you have just defined. The syntax for the TYPE and VAR statements are straightforward. Instead of the usual term "identifier," however, I have used words like "name," "start," "stop," and "datatype" in some of the slots. These words indicate the roles of the various variables in the two kinds of statements.

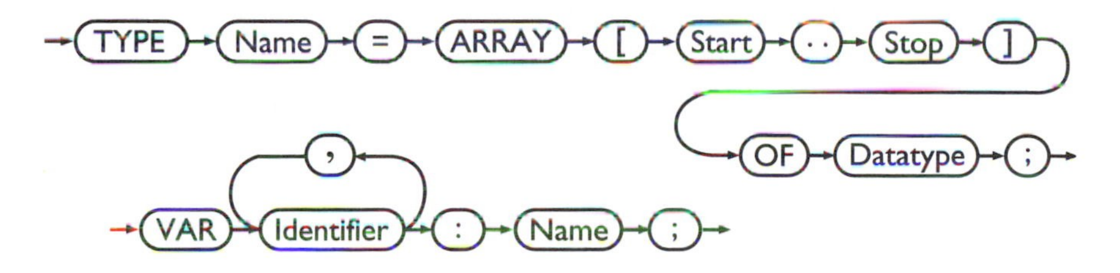

Declaring an array

Following the Turbo Pascal key word TYPE, the word "name" will be what the programmer decides to call the *type* of the array (not the array itself). For example, an array type that consisted of 31 integers to be used in a calendar might be called *Month*. As with variable names, the name of the type should reflect something about the structure or ultimate use of the array so that the type name is easy to remember.

The Turbo Pascal word ARRAY follows the type identifier and indicates to the compiler that it must set aside a whole block of memory locations for the datatype being defined. Between the square brackets that follow, the words "start" and "stop" refer to the values at which array indexes for this type will begin and end. For example, the values could start at 1 and end at 100. It depends on how large arrays of this type must be. The two values are separated by an ellipsis of two periods (with no intervening blank spaces).

Following the Turbo Pascal word OF comes the "datatype" of the individual array elements. If the array consists of integers, for example, you would place the Turbo Pascal word INTEGER here. If it consists of characters, on the other hand, you would put the Turbo Pascal word CHAR here. In addition, arrays can be BOOLEAN or REAL.

After declaring an array type with a TYPE statement, you must then declare the array itself by referring to the TYPE just defined. The declaration follows the usual syntax for declarations except that it uses the word you just gave to the type defined, not the usual Turbo Pascal words like INTEGER or CHAR.

According to the two syntax diagrams, you could define an array type of ten real numbers called *Moneytype*, then declare an array called *Money*.

```
TYPE Moneytype = ARRAY[1..10] OF REAL;
VAR Money: Moneytype;
```

This way of declaring arrays comes in handy when there are several arrays of the same type. For example, if my histogram program were to handle both heights *and* weights of people, I could use the following suite of statements:

```
TYPE BodyStat = ARRAY[1..15] OF REAL;
VAR Height, Weight: BodyStat;
```

It so happens that I will use these very statements, but with the array name *Weight* removed. Earlier, you saw an example of how a single FOR-statement would suffice to read in the values contained in an array. I can use the same structure to enter the values of the array called *Height*.

```
FOR Ind := 1 TO 10 DO
   READLN(Height[Ind]);
```

When the computer executes this loop, it will wait for the user to input each of ten numbers, one at a time.

You can assign values to an array element in Turbo Pascal, just as you can for any other variable. For example, if the value to be placed in the third element of an array called *Histogram* were to be incremented by 1, you could use an assignment statement like this one:

```
Histogram[3] := Histogram[3] + 1;
```

Thus, an array can participate in arithmetic assignment statements on either side of the assignment operator. As you have already seen, such assignment statements also can be executed with an index variable in place of the integer 3 shown above.

The Histogram Algorithm

The program I will call *Histogram* will accept data entered by keyboard. When all the data has been entered, the program may as well generate the histogram first. Then it can calculate the mean and standard deviation, and display them below the histogram. Therefore I will shuffle the previous crude algorithm into the following one:

Input the data.
Build the histogram.
Display the histogram.
Compute and output the mean.
Compute and output the standard deviation.

Inputting the data will require a loop within which the data entered by the user from the keyboard will be assigned to the array *Height*. I will use the name *Person* for the index variable:

```
{input section}
For each value of index Person from 1 to 15
   enter a height in Height[Person]
```

Building the histogram is a little more complicated. First, I'll need a new array to hold the counts, say, *HtCount*. Within a loop, the program must scan the input array *Height* one element at a time. For each element, the program must (a) determine which category the value of that element belongs to and (b) increment the appropriate element of the *HtCount* array. Once the histogram array *HtCount* has been constructed in this way, outputting it is simply a matter of printing out the correct numbers of asterisks for each index value of the array. Let's call the index value *Cat*, reflecting its origin as a category. While we're at it, let's call the index value that counts off the asterisks *Stars*.

```
{histogram section}
For each value of index Person from 1 to 15
   calculate category for Height[Person]
   convert category to a value of index Cat
   increment HtCount at Cat
For each value of index Cat from 1 to 6
   for each value of index Stars from 1 to HtCount[Cat]
      output an asterisk on the same line
```

Incidentally, to "output an asterisk on the same line," I will have to use the WRITE statement.

With this major section of the algorithm refined, I am ready to tackle the somewhat simpler job of calculating the mean and standard deviation. The box on page 188 provides some additional background on these all-important statistical measures.

To calculate the mean height, the program must add up all the entered heights inside a loop, then divide by 15 (the total number of entries). A variable called *HtSum* can hold the accumulated heights. After initializing *HtSum* to 0, the program can enter this loop. The variable *HtMean* will hold the value of the mean height after it is calculated by this section of the program.

```
{mean section}
Initialize HtSum to 0
For each value of index Person
   add Height[Person] to HtSum
HtMean := HtSum/15
Output HtMean
```

The standard deviation is more complicated than the mean. Here, the program must calculate the difference between each entry of *Height* and the mean *HtMean*. Then it must square this difference, add it to an ongoing sum of squared differences, and, finally, take the square root of the sum. To save on variables, I will reuse *HtSum* to add up the squared differences. The variable *HtSD* (short for height standard deviation) will hold the standard deviation.

```
{standard deviation section}
Initialize HtSum to 0
For each value of index Person
   set HtDiff to Height[Person] – HtMean
   square HtDiff as HtDiff
   add HtDiff to HtSum
Set HtSD to square root of HtSum
Output HtSD
```

Before translating the foregoing sections into Turbo Pascal, I must first address an unresolved problem. The histogram construction section was not very explicit about two of its steps (in bold below):

For each value of index *Person* from 1 to 15
   calculate category for *Height[Person]*
   convert category to a value of index *Cat*
   increment *HtCount* at *Cat*
For each value of index *Cat* from 1 to 6
   for each value of index *Stars* from 1 to *HtCount[Cat]*
      output an asterisk on the same line

How will I get the computer to recognize which range a particular number lies in? At first sight, you might think that a height of 178 centimeters, for example, must be converted somehow to the whole range 170–179. But it doesn't. Each height must be reduced to the appropriate index value of Cat. In short, the height of 178 centimeters must be reduced to the index value 5, as spelled out in the following table.

Category	*Cat value*
130–139	1
140–149	2
150–159	3
160–169	4
170–179	5
180–189	6

Let's tackle the reduction problem in steps. It is easy, for example, to go from 178 to the number 17. Simply divide 178 by 10 and truncate the result to an integer. Now 17 −12 = 5, the index value I am aiming for. It would be nice if this were a general rule. Is it? Let's try it on another height, say, 152:

1. 152/10 = 15.2
2. truncate 15.2 to 15
3. 15 − 12 = 3

Obviously, 3 is the right index value for this category. If you enjoy little puzzles, you might want to satisfy yourself that these steps always result in the right index value. This section of the algorithm can now receive its final refinement:

```
For each value of index Person from 1 to 15
   Temp := Height[Person]/10
   Cat := TRUNC(Temp) − 12
   increment HtCount[Cat] by 1
```

and so on. I used the real variable Temp to hold temporarily the result of the division by 10. In the very next step, the computer will truncate the result to an integer and subtract the magic number, 12.

You should try to write out your own version of a Turbo Pascal program based on this algorithm before reading the program I have listed below.

The Histogram Program

To build the declaration section of the *Histogram* program, it is only necessary to go through the foregoing algorithm and list all the variables. You have already seen how to declare the *Height* array. The array *HtCount* is declared in a very similar fashion, with the typename *Hist*.

The input section has been further refined by the addition of a prompt for the data. It includes a brief explanation to the user about the order in which the program expects the data. Everything else in the program is merely the Turbo Pascal version of the preceding, much-discussed algorithm. I have nevertheless added various comments to statements that are not immediately obvious.

```
PROGRAM Histogram;
{Displays a histogram of 15 heights, as input by the user.}
{Calculates and displays the mean and standard deviation.}

{declarations}
VAR Person, Cat, Stars: INTEGER;
VAR Temp, HtSum, HtMean, HtDiff, HtSD: REAL;

TYPE BodyStats = ARRAY[1..15] OF REAL;
TYPE Hist = ARRAY[1..6] OF INTEGER;
VAR Height: BodyStats;
VAR HtCount: Hist;

BEGIN {program}

{input section: Prompts user for the heights}
WRITELN('Please enter the height of the person indexed by');
WRITELN{'the number that appears on the left of screen.');
WRITELN{'only enter heights between 130 and 189 centimeters.'}
FOR Person := 1 TO 15 DO
   BEGIN
   WRITE('Person ', Person, ': ');
   {e.g., "Person 3:" when Person = 3}
   READLN(Height[Person]);
   END;
```

```
{histogram section}
FOR Cat := 1 TO 6 DO
   HtCount[Cat] := 0;
FOR Person := 1 TO 15 DO
   BEGIN
   Temp := Height[Person]/10;
   Cat := TRUNC(Temp)-12;
   HtCount[Cat] := HtCount[Cat]+1; {increment a height count}
   END;

{histogram display section}
WRITELN('Histogram of heights:');
FOR Cat := 1 TO 6 DO
   BEGIN
   WRITE(Cat, ' '); {print a blank after index value}
   FOR Stars := 1 TO HtCount[Cat] DO
      WRITE('*');
      {WRITE ensures that asterisks appear on same line}
   WRITELN; {moves the cursor to the next line}
   END;

{mean section}
HtSum := 0;
FOR Person := 1 TO 15 DO
   HtSum := HtSum + Height[Person];
HtMean := HtSum/15;
WRITELN('The mean height is ', HtMean:5:1);

{standard deviation section}
HtSum := 0;
FOR Person := 1 TO 15 DO
   BEGIN
   HtDiff := Height[Person] - HtMean;
   HtDiff := HtDiff*HtDiff;
   HtSum := HtSum + HtDiff;
   END;
HtSD := SQRT(HtSum);
WRITELN('The standard deviation of heights is ', HtSD:4:1);

END {of program}
```

You may notice two items in this program that I did not plan during the algorithmic design process. It was necessary to format the WRITELN statements that announce the mean and standard deviation to the user.

Without formatting, these (REAL) values would be displayed in floating point format with its huge raft of digits. The format for the mean, HtMean:5:1, allows for five (the 5) characters: three digits, a decimal point, and one digit (the 1) beyond the decimal point.

The built-in function SQRT in the third statement from the end of the program calculates the square root of any number or variable to which it is applied. This statement brings to four the total number of built-in functions that you have seen so far in this course. For the curious, I have included a box on page 178 that summarizes these functions. The value of *SQRT(HtSum)* is assigned to the variable *HtSD*.

Finally, you may have noticed that the FOR-loop in the mean-calculating section did not use BEGIN or END. You may omit these words when the body of a FOR-loop consists of a single statement.

A Sample Run

The *Histogram* program can be run as it stands in a DOS or OS/2 environment. Under Windows, you must add the usual

```
USES WinCrt;
```

statement to make it work. In case you were curious, the *Histogram* program produces the following output with the example of 15 heights at the beginning of this project:

```
Histogram of heights:
1 *
2 *
3 ****
4 ****
5 ***
6 **
The mean height is 163.5
The standard deviation of the height is 54.3
```

Once you have run this program, you might examine it a little more closely and receive a sudden inspiration for making it shorter (see Exploration 11).

Four Functions

Turbo Pascal comes equipped with a great variety of *built-in functions*. These special procedures reside in the Turbo Pascal system, ready to spring into action when a program calls for them. All built-in functions work in much the same way. They consist of a name (capitalized in this text's style) applied to a *parameter*, the part in parentheses. To make the value of a built-in function available to the program that uses it, you can assign the function to a program variable. So far, you have seen the following built-in functions in action:

```
Height := TRUNC(Money*0.04);

NumFloors := ABS(NumFloors);

HtSD := SQRT(HtSum);

FirstNum := RANDOM(100);
```

The TRUNC function was needed in the RealInvest_Graph program (Chapter 4) to convert the REAL value of *Money**0.04 to an integer

The Art of Upgrading

You have already seen it happen. You just finish a program and an improvement of one sort or another suggests itself. For example, Exploration 11 in Chapter 3 suggested making the *AddTutor* program restartable by enclosing it in a FOR-loop. In other words, the student using the program would be able to run it many times before quitting. Although this change improved the program somewhat, the student still had to decide in advance how many times he or she wanted to run the program, because the number of iterations in a FOR-loop is always predetermined. You encountered the same limitation when the FOR-loop was used to offer multiple rides to users of the elevator control program in Chapter 5.

The introduction of two new types of loops, the WHILE-loop and the REPEAT-loop, will make it possible to improve both programs so that the user can rerun them until the desire to do so vanishes. The user can then simply type a letter to quit. I will upgrade *AddTutor* by ripping out the old FOR-loop and installing a shiny new WHILE-loop.

value suitable for use by the bar-drawing statement. The TRUNC function evaluates the parameter and strips away the fractional part to produce an integer. The statement above assigns the integer to the variable *Height*.

The ABS function, which converts a negative integer or real number into a positive one, came in handy in the *Elevator* program (Chapter 5). Because the variable *NumFloors* might just have a negative value, it was necessary to make it positive before employing it as the limit in a FOR-loop. The ABS function does this by either leaving the number alone if it happens to be positive or changing the sign if it happens to be negative.

The SQRT function does something more complicated than chopping off a fraction or changing a sign. It takes the square root of whatever (positive) number appears as its parameter. In the *Histogram* program (this chapter), the final step in calculating the variance involved taking the square root of the value of *HtSum*.

One version of the RANDOM function has no parameter. It produces random numbers between 0 and 1. Soon you will see a new version that takes an integer such as 53 as its parameter and produces random integers between 0 and 52.

Two New Loops

Whereas FOR-loops go through a preset number of iterations, WHILE- and REPEAT-loops do not. The computer will iterate them until some condition is met. Mention of the word "condition" should remind you of Boolean expressions (Chapter 5). By controlling the iterations of the new loop types, Boolean expressions play a key role.

WHILE- and REPEAT-loops have the same overall structure as FOR-loops. In other words, both new types of loops have a control section and a body. In fact, you normally can't distinguish the body of a WHILE-loop or of a REPEAT-loop, out of context, from the body of a FOR-loop. The real difference lies in the control section, where a Boolean expression resides.

WHILE-loops. A WHILE-loop uses the Turbo Pascal word WHILE to help you remember that it is only "while" the Boolean expression remains true that the computer will continue to execute the body of the loop. A WHILE-loop consists of a loop control part followed by a loop body. Like the body of a FOR-loop, the body of a WHILE-loop is enclosed by a BEGIN and END if it happens to consist of more than one simple statement. The syntax of a WHILE-loop is straightforward:

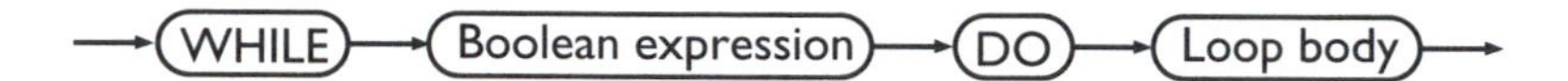

I can recast the syntax diagram to reflect the actual layout of a WHILE-loop as they are normally used in programs:

WHILE Boolean expression DO
  BODY of loop

As you learned in the previous chapter, a Boolean expression consists of Boolean constants (TRUE and FALSE), a relational expression, a Boolean variable, or any legal combination of these ingredients involving the logical operators such as AND, OR, and NOT. The computer will execute the loop body over and over again WHILE the logical expression has the value TRUE.

If the Boolean expression happens to be TRUE when the computer first enters the WHILE-loop, it will execute the body, then return to the control statement and evaluate the Boolean expression again. As long as the expression remains TRUE, the computer will execute the loop body over and over. It may happen, however, that the computation inside the loop body changes the value of the Boolean expression from TRUE to FALSE. As soon as the expression becomes FALSE, the computer will complete the current iteration of the loop body. When it returns to the head of the loop and evaluates the Boolean expression again, it will discover that it has become false. At his point, it will skip around the loop body and go on to the next executable statement.

I will illustrate the use of the WHILE-loop by examining a program that assists in the assembly of trains in a rail yard. The program adds together the tonnages of loaded boxcars, data that are contained in an array by the same name. It continues to add new boxcars to the train "while" the total tonnage remains less than the limit of 1800 tons. The loop is preceded by statements that set the variable *Next* to 1 and the variable *TotalTons* to 0.

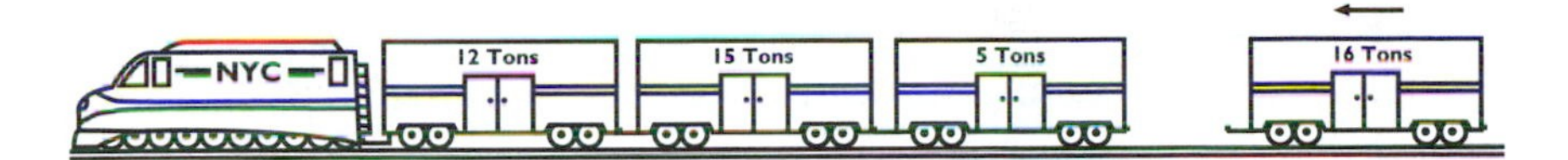

Assembling a train

```
WHILE TotalTons < 1800 DO
   BEGIN
   TotalTons := TotalTons + BoxCar[Next];
   Next := Next + 1;
   END;
```

Here, the Boolean expression

TotalTons < 1800

controls the iteration of the loop. As long as the steadily increasing value of *TotalTons* remains less than 1800, the computer will continue to execute the loop body. As soon as the accumulated weight exceeds the limit of 1800, however, the iterations will cease.

As you may already have realized, it is possible for this particular program to overload the train slightly by adding one boxcar too many. The program should therefore reduce the value of *Next* by 1 in an assignment statement that follows the WHILE-loop.

REPEAT-loops. Like its colleagues, the REPEAT-loop consists of a control section and a loop body. The control section, however, is divided into two parts. The first part, the Turbo Pascal word REPEAT, comes at the beginning of the loop, and the second part, the Turbo Pascal word UNTIL, comes at the end. Because the control section already sandwiches the loop body, there is no need for a BEGIN and END when the body consists of more than one Pascal statement. REPEAT loops follow this general syntax:

As I did with the WHILE-loop syntax, I can depict the layout of a REPEAT-loop with a somewhat more relaxed sort of diagram:

REPEAT
  BODY of loop
UNTIL Boolean expression

This kind of loop will execute its body over and over again UNTIL the Boolean expression has the value TRUE. The control over the iteration of a REPEAT-loop is nearly identical to that of a WHILE-loop. If the Boolean expression changes its value at any point in the execution of the loop body, the computer will not execute the body again.

Two important differences distinguish WHILE-loops from REPEAT-loops, however. First, as long as the Boolean expression in a WHILE-loop remains TRUE, the computer will continue to execute it. By contrast, the Boolean expression in a REPEAT-loop must remain FALSE for the computer to continue executing the loop. The second difference appears during the first iteration of either type of loop. The computer will not execute a WHILE-loop even once if the Boolean expression already has the "wrong" value—in this case, FALSE. But the computer *will* execute the body of a REPEAT-loop once if the Boolean expression already has the wrong value—in this case, TRUE.

Let's revisit the train example to see how a REPEAT-loop might handle the problem of accumulating tonnages.

```
REPEAT
   TotalTons := TotalTons + BoxCar[Next];
   Next := Next + 1;
UNTIL TotalTons >= 1800
```

Notice that the REPEAT-loop does not use BEGIN and END, even when the body consists of a compound statement. The opposite relational expression must be used for the loop condition, because, to be equivalent, it must be TRUE whenever the other expression is TRUE. In other words,

```
WHILE TotalTons < 1800
```

you want the WHILE-loop to keep going. By the same token, you want the REPEAT loop to keep going

```
UNTIL TotalTons >= 1800
```

As in the earlier version of this program, you would add the same statement decrementing *Next* following the REPEAT-loop.

AddTutor Revisited

In Chapter 2 you saw a simple computer-aided instruction program to help elementary school children learn addition. The *AddTutor* program, while effective up to a point, suffered from a rather severe disadvantage, namely, if the child wanted to practice on more than one example, he or she had to turn the computer off and restart the program. Exploration 11 of Chapter 3 suggested that you overcome this defect by making the program restartable, placing its main body inside a FOR-loop, but this solution also had some problems. WHILE- and REPEAT-loops make such problems a thing of the past. With the flexibility these loops offer, a program like *AddTutor* will continue to run as long as the student wishes to keep practicing.

Upgrading a program

I will use this upgrade as the excuse to add one small but significant change to the way *AddTutor* operates. Rather than have the student choose the addition problems, let the program do it. The Turbo Pascal built-in function called RANDOM is ideal for this purpose. Like other such functions (see the box on page 178), RANDOM operates on a parameter enclosed in parentheses following the function. With a parameter of 100, for example, it produces random numbers between 0 and 99. The assignment statement below illustrates how RANDOM works:

```
FirstNum := RANDOM(100);
```

When the computer executes this statement, it selects a random number between 0 and 99, then assigns it to the variable *FirstNum*. When both variables, *FirstNum* and *SecondNum*, have been assigned random integers in this manner, the program proceeds just as it did before.

```
PROGRAM AddTutor;

VAR FirstNum, SecondNum, Sum, Answer: INTEGER;

BEGIN

{problem selection}
FirstNum := RANDOM(100);
SecondNum := RANDOM(100);

{prompts and reply}
WRITE('Add these numbers and enter your answer: ');
WRITELN(FirstNum, ' and ', SecondNum);
WRITE('Your answer is: ');
READLN(Answer);

Sum := FirstNum + SecondNum;

{correct or not?}
IF (Answer = Sum)
   THEN WRITELN('Congratulations! You got the right answer!')
   ELSE WRITELN('Oops! You made a mistake. Can you find it?');

END.
```

I can now upgrade *AddTutor* by making it restartable at the student's option. At the end of each problem, the program will ask the student if he or she wishes to continue. If the student types "y" for "yes" and the program stores this character in a variable called *Response*, then I can form a Boolean expression that will determine whether or not the body of a WHILE-loop gets iterated one more time:

```
Response = 'y'
```

You will readily recognize the program on the previous page tucked away inside a WHILE-loop that keeps the program below going as long as the student wishes. To distinguish the new program from the old, I have given it a version number:

```
PROGRAM AddTutor2;
{This program drills people learning simple addition by}
{supplying them with a succession of problems to solve.}

{declarations}
VAR FirstNum, SecondNum, Sum, Answer: INTEGER;
VAR Response: CHAR;
VAR Continue: BOOLEAN;

BEGIN {program}

{initialize variables}
Continue := TRUE;
WHILE Continue = TRUE DO
   BEGIN

   {problem selection}
   FirstNum := RANDOM(100);
   SecondNum := RANDOM(100);

   {prompts and reply}
   WRITE('Add these numbers and enter your answer: ');
   WRITELN(FirstNum, ' and ', SecondNum);
   WRITE('Your answer is: ');
   READLN(Answer);
   WRITELN; {moves cursor to next line}
```

```
   Sum := FirstNum + SecondNum;

   {correct or not?}
   IF (Answer = Sum)
      THEN WRITELN('Congratulations! You got the right answer!')
      ELSE WRITELN('Oops! You made a mistake. Can you find it?');

   {continue session?}
   WRITELN('Want to try another problem?');
   WRITELN('If so, enter  "y" for "yes," ');
   WRITELN('Any other key will end the session.');
   READLN(Response);
   Continue := (Response = 'y');
   END; {of WHILE-loop}

END. {of program}
```

What happens when a student uses this program? Entering the main body of the program, the computer executes the first statement, which simply sets *Continue* to TRUE. Because WHILE-loops test their Boolean condition before execution, this variable needs to have a value going in, and the Boolean expression must be true for the computer to execute the loop at least once.

Inside the WHILE-loop, things go much as they did in the earlier version of the program until the first bit of drill is done and execution passes on to the section called {continue session?}. There, a prompt tells the student to enter “y” if he or she wishes to continue. If the student enters “y,” the Boolean expression

```
Response = 'y'
```

will be true. The assignment statement will set the Boolean variable *Continue* to the value of this expression, in any case. If the student enters some other character to end the session, the expression will have the value FALSE because *Response* no longer equals ‘y.’ Now, the assignment statement will give the value FALSE to the Boolean variable *Continue* and the program will exit the WHILE-loop.

As you may already suspect, it is possible to use a REPEAT-loop instead of a WHILE-loop to make the *AddTutor* program restartable. In fact, you might replace the control section of the WHILE-loop by the control section of the REPEAT loop, bearing in mind three things:

1. The second part of the control section of the REPEAT-loop must follow the body of the loop.
2. There will be no BEGIN or END sandwiching the loop body.
3. You must use the opposite Boolean expression, namely,

```
Response <> 'y'
```

4. following the word UNTIL.

What does this list suggest about the need to initialize the Boolean variable *Continue* before the loop?

Upgrading the Elevator

To upgrade the *Elevator* program to *Elevator2*, you can do exactly what I did with the *AddTutor* program. In fact, you can use the same variable (*Response*), the same WHILE-loop control, the same Boolean variable (*Continue*), and the same prompt to the user about continuing the session. If you do this now, you will already have completed Exploration 10 at the end of this chapter.

Some people might wonder why I bothered to use a Boolean variable in either program when, by simply inserting the Boolean expression

```
Response = 'y'
```

directly into the WHILE-loop, for example, the same effect would be achieved. The answer lies partly in my eagerness to demonstrate the further use of Boolean variables and Boolean assignment statements. But it is also a good idea to make programs as clear as possible to read. The appearance of the word "Continue" in the control part of the WHILE statement makes the program somewhat more transparent.

Mean and Standard Deviation

The two statistical measures mean and standard deviation summarize most of the distributions that statisticians, scientists, and engineers encounter in daily practice. The distribution of heights in any population of people, for example, always has a mean, or average height, which is calculated by adding together all the heights in the population and dividing the sum by the total number of people in the population. The mean height tells you something about the population as a whole. You can compare two different populations, for example, by comparing their means.

Distributions also always have a standard deviation. This statistic has a somewhat more complicated calculation:

1. Calculate the mean and call it M.
2. For each height in the population,
   form all the differences (height – M).
3. Square them: $(\text{height} - M)^2$.
4. Add all the squared terms together.

The sum of all the squared differences is technically known as the "variance" of the distribution. The final step in the calculation involves finding a square root:

5. Take the square root of the variance.

The result is the standard deviation of the distribution. The standard deviation measures the spread of a distribution. If there is a great deal of variation in heights, for example, the standard deviation will be large. But if all the heights are clustered closely around the mean, the standard deviation will be small.

Carmanian Licenses Computer scientists have devised many special structures for holding data in a computer memory, some of which are in common use today. The field known as *data structures* offers a great many challenging and fascinating research problems.

421	668	291	450	959	926	378	220	859	182	491	667	370	878	364

How many elements appear before element 370?

The data structure that computer scientists call an array is very convenient for holding large amounts of data, but it has some disadvantages. For example, if you wish to find an item in an array, you may have to scan most of it, element by element, to locate the item. In fact, you may have to scan all of it, only to discover that the item is not even there! This scanning process is not speedy or efficient. Because arrays can be very large, any program that has to search them frequently might run very slowly. Is there a better data structure for this purpose?

The data structure called a tree does not suffer from this problem. You can pile up just as much data as before, but you can retrieve data much more quickly from a tree than from an array. You have already used trees to store image data in Chapter 4. The quad-trees you used there had four branches at each node. In this chapter, I will use *binary trees*, ones with just two branches at each node.

In what sort of application area might one want to store numbers that can be retrieved quickly? One such area is the licensing bureau of a state or country. I will demonstrate the principles of binary tree structures with the federal licensing bureau of Carmania, a country too small to be found on any map. Everybody has a car in Carmania, but there are only 15 citizens. The computer program that keeps track of everybody's license number (and driving record) uses a tree structure. In a country of Carmania's size, this is hardly necessary; but should the population expand into the millions, the Carmanian licensing bureau will be ready. Currently, the tree is a pathetic affair.

Except for the bottom level, each node is linked to two other nodes lower down in the tree, one on the right and one on the left. The license number stored to the lower right, however, is always greater than the license number stored at the node. In fact, *all* the nodes on the right branch contain numbers that are larger than the one stored at the prior node. Similarly, all the numbers stored in the lower left branch are smaller.

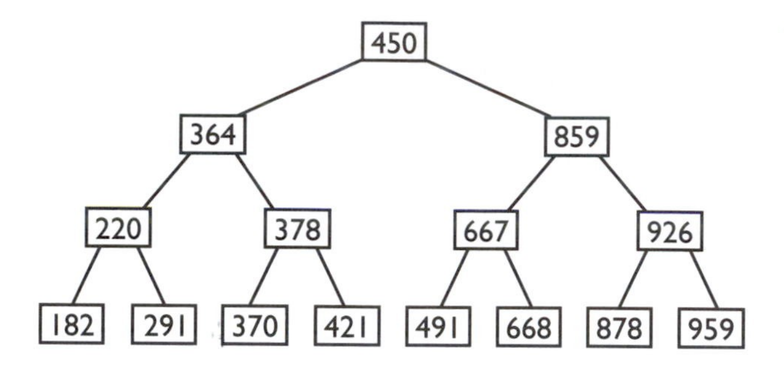

Binary tree of Carmanian driving licenses

To discover whether a particular item is in the tree, the search program must start at the top node of the tree, the one containing license number 450. As it goes, the program exploits the special numbering property. Suppose it happens to be searching for license number 370. At the very top node, the program discovers that 370 is smaller than 450, so it takes the left-hand branch of the tree. At the next level, it encounters the node containing 364. Because 370 is larger than 364, the program continues its search down and to the right. Finally, at the third level, it compares 378 with 370 and, discovering that 370 is smaller, takes the left branch down to find the sought-after item at the bottom level of the tree.

Computer scientists often write down such procedures in the form of algorithmic outlines. The algorithm is all they need to communicate the basic idea to any other computer scientist. Moreover, anyone who wants to write a program that uses such a procedure would translate the algorithm into the programming language of his or her choice. Note that the algorithm below employs an informal WHILE-loop:

```
Go to top node

While item not found
   if Item = value at node
      then found
   if Item < value at node
      then go down to left node
   if Item > value at node
      then go down to right node
```

This is just the bare-bones algorithm. It communicates the essential idea of the search through the tree without being very explicit about what variables to use or even what "go down to left node" means from a programming point of view. As I explained in the section on quad-trees in Chapter 4, however, all nodes of a binary tree are stored as addresses in memory, so "going" anywhere in the tree means looking up one of the two addresses stored at each node.

The most important ideas connected with binary trees concern their depth and the number of nodes in them. Such numbers give a direct clue to their usefulness in storing large amounts of data and, simultaneously, in getting at the data quickly. The accompanying illustration shows four binary trees as abstract structures. The trees have, respectively, 3, 7, 15, and 31 nodes.

It would not take you long to discover that the number of nodes in these trees appears to be increasing according to powers of 2. The number of nodes in each tree is one less than a power of 2:

$$3 = 2^2-1 \quad 7 = 2^3-1 \quad 15 = 2^4-1 \quad 31 = 2^5-1$$

As you can also see, the exponent, or power, is simply the number of levels in the tree. As you know, powers of two multiply explosively as the power increases. This growth rule is called *exponential*. For example, a tree with a mere 20 levels will have $2^{20} - 1 = 1{,}048{,}575$ nodes and be able to store this many items of data. Add one more level and you double the number to over 2 million! Binary trees have no lack of capacity when it comes to piling up data.

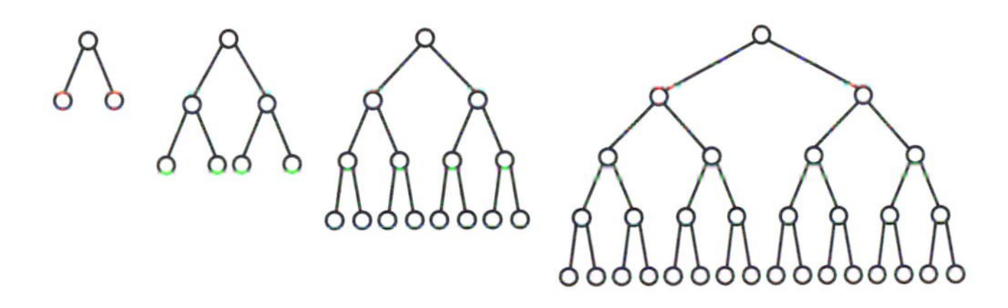

Binary trees with two, three, four, and five levels

To see how quickly binary trees can be searched, you must turn the mathematical telescope around and stare into the other end, so to speak. Given a lot of data items to be stored in a binary tree, how quickly can it be searched? In short, how many levels does it have? To answer this question, I will play a little mathematical game, doing a calculation that is routine in computer science:

If an n-level binary tree can hold 2^n items,
how many levels does a tree with m items have?

The answer lies in logarithms. For my purposes, the *logarithm* of a number m is the power to which I must raise 2 to equal m. To keep things simple, I will assume that m is already a power of 2. The question then is merely which power. The logarithm, which I write as log(m), is just the shorthand for this power.

A tree with m items will have log(m) levels. As m gets large, the logarithm log(m) grows v-e-r-y slowly. As you already know, the logarithm of 1,048,575 is 20. It takes only 20 iterations of the search loop, in the worst case, to find any of 1,048,575 items stored in a binary tree.

A program that searched an array would follow a much simpler algorithm:

For each index value
  check if item = element of array

To be sure, this loop has a "body" that consists of only one step. How many steps would it take such a program to find the item in an array of 1,048,575 elements? Obviously, it could take up to 1,048,575 steps. Even if you take into account the fact that the binary tree-searching algorithm has three times as many steps in its loop, it still takes the array-searching algorithm 18,000 times as many steps, in the worst case, to find the item.

Binary trees have other advantages over arrays. A program that needs to delete an item from an array may have to rearrange all the remaining entries after the deletion. As you already know, any kind of systematic array processing can run into millions of steps, and shifting all the elements to the right of the deleted element one position to the left can take a long time, relatively speaking. But to delete an item from a binary tree does not take long at all. A program to do this could move one of the pendant nodes up into the same position as the node being deleted, rearranging the pointers in the process.

SUMMARY

A program to construct a histogram required a new type of data structures called an array. After discovering how to declare and use arrays, you saw them used in two different ways in the *Histogram* program. In the process you learned to construct an invaluable statistical tool that is used in virtually every scientific and industrial field.

Arrays work naturally with loops, especially FOR-loops. But Turbo Pascal offers two other types of loops. After learning about WHILE-loops and REPEAT-loops, you got a chance to upgrade a program that badly needed it. Thanks to the WHILE-loop, the new version of the tutoring program, *AddTutor2*, now enables a student to work on addition problems exactly as long as he or she wishes. Advice was also given on upgrading the *Elevator* program.

The computer science component of this chapter returned to the theme of data structures, explaining how binary trees can store almost any amount of data, yet enable a program to retrieve it much more quickly than data from an array.

EXPLORATIONS

1 How would you declare an array called *July* that must hold 31 integers? Make up your own name for the type.

2 Given the FOR-loop below, construct a WHILE-loop that does exactly the same thing:

```
FOR Index := 1 TO 15 DO
   Sum := Sum + Weight[Index];
```

You may have to add one statement before the WHILE-loop and another within it. Now, replace the WHILE-loop by a REPEAT-loop.

3 Can you replace the rail yard WHILE-loop on page 181 by a FOR-loop? If not, why not?

4 In what two main ways do WHILE- and REPEAT-loops differ?

5 Explain why the Boolean expression in the control section of the WHILE-loop example on page 181 could be replaced with

```
WHILE NOT(TotalTons >= 1800) DO
```

6 Enter the *Histogram* program in your Turbo Pascal system and run it with heights of your own choosing. You might even get your lecturer or lab demonstrator to organize a height-measuring session with other students. If you can get your hands on about 40 real heights and don't mind entering them, you should discover a very interesting pattern in the resulting histogram. Do you know the name of that pattern?

7 Modify the *Histogram* program so that it no longer applies to heights alone. To make the program more general, you will have to change the messages to the user, the comments, and, most important, the names of many of the variables. You can even make the program more flexible in the amount of data it will handle by declaring the arrays to be much larger, say, 1000 elements. This does not mean that the user must enter this many elements, but for the program to know what limits to put on its FOR-loops, the program must ask the user to enter the amount of data to expect.

8 Write and test the *AddTutor2* program. Change any of the prompts that you think do not explain as fully as they should what the program expects the elementary school pupil to do.

9 Improve the *RealInvest* program by introducing an array to hold the computed values of the variable called *Money*. To do this, add the following type declaration, then declare the array:

```
TYPE Scenario = ARRAY[0..100] OF INTEGER;
```

Since it is unlikely that anyone will want to track an investment for 100 years, this seems a safe dimension for the array. Use the new array to hold the newly computed values of the investment, year by year. You can then make a separate section of program that reports on the amounts.

10 Rewrite the elevator control program of the previous chapter so that it uses a more convenient loop, such as a WHILE- or REPEAT-loop. You can employ the same method that I used in *AddTutor2* to get the user to control the number of iterations.

11 In the program called *Histogram*, is there any good reason why there have to be four separate FOR-loops, all with the same range of values and the same index? Why not use just one loop? If this is possible, you will be able to shorten *Histogram* by about nine lines of code. You might have to move the histogram-calculating section to the very end of the program to achieve this goal, however.

12 Rewrite the text graphics portion of the *Histogram* program so that it displays vertical columns of asterisks, instead of horizontal rows. [Hint: Under what conditions should there be an asterisk in column C? To decide whether the Kth row above the base of the histogram should contain an asterisk in column C, the following Boolean expression might be useful:

$$HtCount[C] = K$$

13 Rewrite *Histogram* as a Turbo Pascal graphics program that uses vertical bars (as *RealInvest_Graph* did) to display the histogram in its traditional orientation.

14 The following program has a structure somewhat like *Histogram*, but a very different mission. You may assume that the array *TotalPoints* has been initialized. Naturally, I have stripped away all comments from the program.

```
PROGRAM Points;

VAR Customer, Points: INTEGER;
CONST NumCust = 24915;
TYPE CustArray = ARRAY[1 . . 30000] OF INTEGER;
VAR TotalPoints: CustArray;

BEGIN

FOR Customer := 1 to NumCust DO
```

```
    BEGIN
    WRITELN('Enter month's points for customer ', Customer);
    READLN(Points);
    TotalPoints[Customer] := TotalPoints[Customer] + Points;
    END;

FOR Customer := 1 TO NumCust DO
    IF TotalPoints[Customer] >= 100
        THEN BEGIN
            WRITELN('Award customer ', Customer, ' 500 free miles.');
            TotalPoints[Customer] := 0;
            END;

END. {of program}
```

a Based on certain name clues in the program, what role does it play in the world of commerce?

b Explain what happens if Customer 3,459 had previously accumulated 82 points and, in the current month had accumulated another 41.

c It seems unfair to wipe out *all* the points of a customer simply because he or she has reached the magic number of 100. Replace the assignment statement inside the second loop by one that preserves a customer's excess points.

15 Here are some further items to search for in the tree shown on page 190 (reproduced below). For each item, count the number of iterations it takes the search algorithm to find (or not find) it.

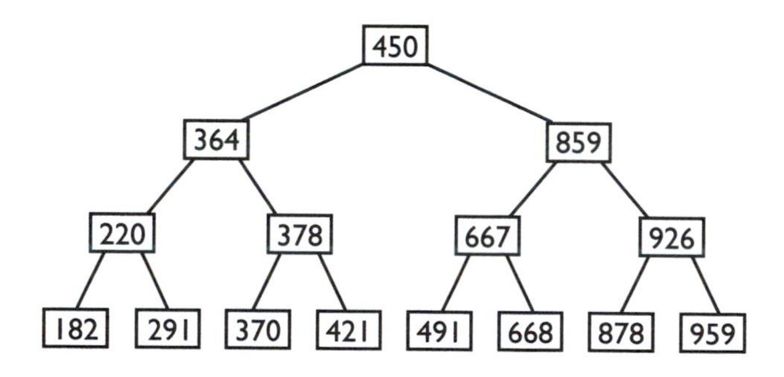

a. 667 **b.** 364 **c.** 385 **d.** 878 **e.** 450

16 A binary tree does not have to be full. A tree on n levels may have fewer than $2^n - 1$ nodes, but no more. How many levels must there be, at a minimum, in binary trees with 100, 10,000, 10,000,000,000 items stored in them. How many items can you store in a binary tree with 30 levels? If the latter number seems too large to write in decimal form, don't be afraid to use power notation to express it.

7 Simulating the Information Highway

Functions and Procedures

A program that simulates message processing on the Internet makes a launching pad for a new Turbo Pascal concept, the subprogram. The simulation program imitates the arrival of computer messages at a network computer, which must send them along to another site. If the messages come in too fast, however, the computer may not be able to keep up. Unacceptable delays on the information highway occur when this happens. The simulation program gives you an idea why this happens.

The program uses two kinds of subprograms, namely, a function and a procedure. These act like miniature programs in their own right, programs that the main program can "run": The function creates new messages for the simulation and the procedure sends them out to the network as fast as it can.

The introduction of subprograms reinforces a practice I have followed almost from the beginning of this book. Programs that are divided into modules are easier to write, read, and maintain than are programs put together willy-nilly. Subprograms are the ultimate modules.

Computer graphics enables you to watch the messages lining up for processing in the network computer. A horizontal red bar will show the messages queueing like cars at a freeway on-ramp. The graphics program is served up in two flavors, one for DOS- and OS/2-based Turbo Pascal, the other for Windows-based systems. Because Windows-based Turbo Pascal makes heavy use of modules called objects, the graphics portion of the chapter introduces both kinds of computer users to this fast-growing form of modularity. Objects extend the usefulness of subprograms by making them reusable.

At the end of the chapter, I delve into the theory of queues to see if there is any truth to the rumor that queues can get arbitrarily long, even when people (or messages) get served as fast as they arrive.

The Module Is the Message

People who write programs for a living usually find themselves involved with immense amounts of code. The word processing software that enables me to write this book, for example, has hundreds of thousands of lines of code. To write very long programs, or even to understand them, it becomes essential to work in modules. Every separate computational mission within a program has its own module or section. You could say that *subprograms* are the ultimate module. Miniature programs in their own right, subprograms can even be run by other modules. The fruitfulness of this idea is astounding. It brings new flexibility into the life of the programmer and heralds the rise of another kind of module, the object, which is described later in this chapter.

You have been writing modular programs for several chapters now. I assume that when you divided a program up into sections, you found it easier to understand. You will find it easier to understand a year from now, as well. With a quick scan through the program, the section of interest leaps to your eye. Soon modules will have modules, and this will make the reading even easier. Programs that are easy to read are also easy to modify, a desirable property in this age of continual change.

Programming Roger

Where are the robots the media have been promising us for years? While waiting for these computational and mechanical marvels to show up, I can illustrate the advantages of modular programming by pretending that I already have a robot. Its name is Roger. When complete, Roger's software will run into thousands of lines of code. To make programming Roger easy, I would not only work in modules, I would also use a lot of subprograms. Naturally, I would first design this huge program entirely at the algorithmic level.

I want Roger to act as human as possible. Here is my attempt at a design for the software that handles Roger's wake-up process:

```
{wake-up module}
repeat
  make snoring noise
```

Roger Butler, a fully programmable personal service robot

until alarm goes off
shut off alarm
get out of bed
put on bathrobe
go to bathroom

Being crude, the algorithm does not explain how Roger's control computer will carry out each of these steps. In fact, a subsequent design would break many of these steps up into modules of their own. Consider what happens when Roger returns from the bathroom:

remove bathrobe and pajamas
put on underwear
put on shirt
put on slacks
put on socks
put on shoes
tie shoelaces

Now, tying shoelaces is something that Roger, like you, may have to do more than once a day, and it happens to be a complex operation. Roger not only ties his shoes in the morning, he may find it necessary to tie them at odd moments throughout the day. The laces may come undone, Roger may put on new shoes, and so on. I wouldn't want to make my robot program unnecessarily long by repeating the shoelace-tying module in every circumstance that Roger might need to tie his shoelaces. Instead, I can make a subprogram out of it, amending the algorithm as follows:

.
.
.
put on socks
put on shoes
run shoelace-tying subprogram

Somewhere, my ultimate robot program will contain a listing of the actual shoelace-tying subprogram. (In Turbo Pascal, all subprograms must be listed at the beginning of the program.) Algorithmically, the subprogram might look something like this:

Subprogram: Shoelace
from bottom of shoe to top
  pull laces tight
cross free ends
tie half-hitch
double each free end over
tie half-hitch with doubled free ends
pull tight

Every time Roger needs to tie his shoelaces, the program will run the shoelace-tying subprogram. No matter what part of the program it happens to be executing, when the robot computer sees the order, or *call*, to run a subprogram, it will leave that part of the program, look up the subprogram, and execute it as though it were a program all by itself. When the robot computer has finished executing the subprogram, it will return to the part of the program that it had previously been executing without even pausing for a breath.

It is time to leave the science fiction world of robots and enter the real world of the Internet, a place where programs abound, even programs that simulate the Internet.

Waiting on the Internet

The Internet, subject of much public attention in recent years, consists of a network of computers called *servers* that send messages to other computers in the network. Most servers accept messages from local users. The messages have a variety of destinations, from one end of the network to the other. One message may be destined for another user in Omaha, another for a home page in Japan. The servers have the job of passing messages along so that they arrive at their destinations with reasonable speed. As you can see in the adjacent network diagram, a message may pass through many servers before it reaches its final destination.

I will focus on one server in the Internet. Like many servers, it happens to be connected to just one other server in the Internet. It sends all of its messages on a single cable to the other server, and from there the messages fan out to sites all over the world. The cable can handle a certain amount of information per second, and no more.

The Network Manager's Nightmare

In an era of greatly increased Internet activity, this particular server is getting close to capacity. What will happen when interactive users find the response to their queries and keystrokes slowing down? The network manager who is responsible for this particular server worries often about the problem. The server and user diagram on the next page illustrates the

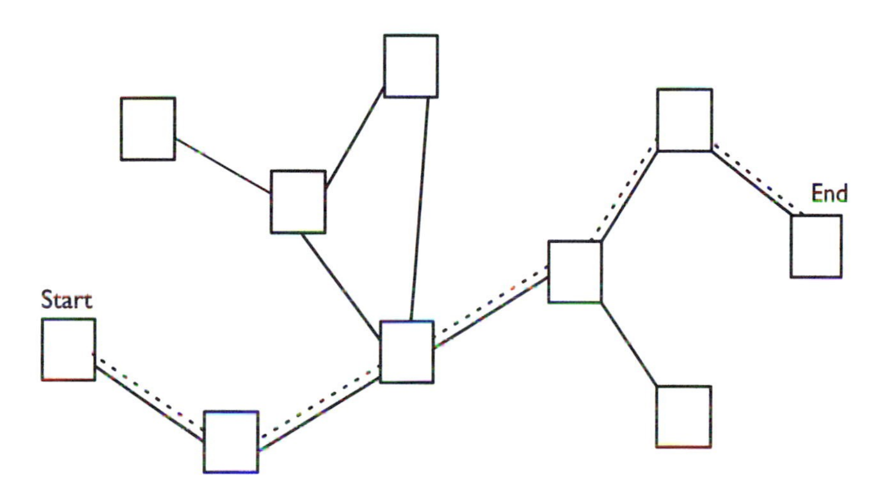

A message travels the network

layout schematically. The big square with the circles attached is the server, the other square is the distant server. The circles represent individual users connected to the server.

Two kinds of users share the server. Some users send e-mail, messages to which a reply is not expected immediately. Other users interact with another computer in the Internet. For example, an interactive user might read a home page and enter a keystroke or two to indicate which feature of the home page to explore next. Such users expect an instant response, perhaps the gratifying display of a color image or a page of text. A wait of mere seconds can undermine the experience to the point where the user throws up his or her hands in helpless frustration. As you are about to see, if the server gets too busy, the messages can pile up to the point where the waits become intolerable, minutes in fact.

Both kinds of users send their messages to the local server, where a program assembles them into one large file, then systematically divides them into *packets*. Each packet contains 1000 characters of text. The server processes the messages in serial order, gobbling up characters until the packet is full and can be sent to the other server. If a message has more than 1000 characters, it may have to be sent in two or more packets. A packet may also consist of several short messages and part of a longer one.

A message consists of not only user keystrokes but also a message header that contains the network address of the target and the address of the user. On the basis of this information, messages can be routed from server to

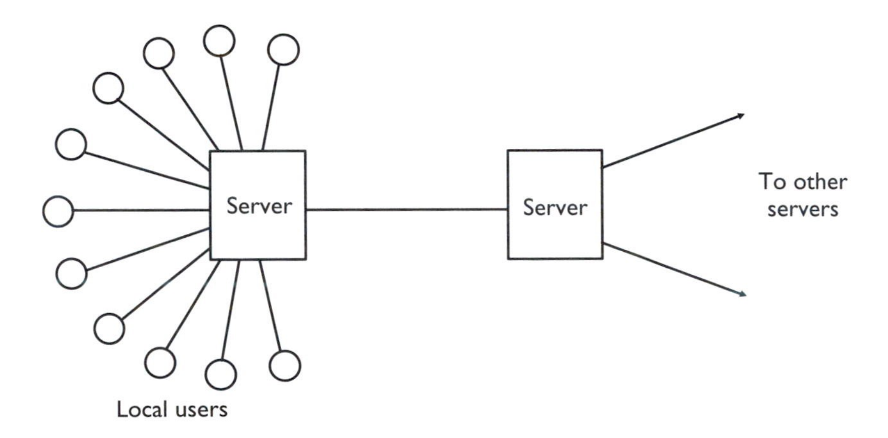

A server, local users, and another server on the Internet

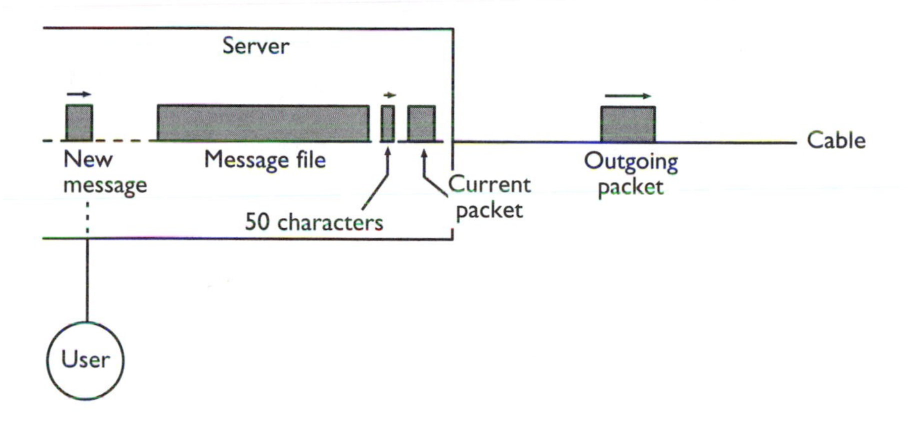

The server divides messages into packets

server until they reach their destination. A message, even a single keystroke, rarely contains fewer than 50 characters. In the simulation to follow, I will take 50 characters as a fundamental unit. Without invalidating the simulation, I will assume that all messages consist of multiples of 50 characters. In other words, they contain 50, 100, 150, or even 1650 characters.

The server sends all of its outgoing messages through a special cable that runs to the other server. It can send 5600 characters every second, a rate that the manager cannot improve. A little arithmetic reveals that the server takes about 9 milliseconds (thousandths of a second) to send the 50 characters of the fundamental unit.

Project: A Server Simulation

I will use some of the foregoing information to construct a program that simulates the server as it processes messages for the cable. In particular, I will follow these specifications:

> *Write a program that simulates a local Internet server by creating user messages at random times with random lengths. The server lumps the simulated messages together into a file as they arrive. It then divides the messages into packets of 1000 characters each for transmission. The program processes the messages in 9-millisecond time steps, keeps track of the maximum size of the message file, and produces a report on the longest delay experienced by any user at the end of its run. The program should operate in simulated time steps of 9 milliseconds, the time it takes to process 50 characters of text.*

According to the specifications, I should structure the program around a repeating cycle that embraces 9 milliseconds of operation. This design concept suggests the use of a loop. Within the loop, the cycle might consist of four steps that accomplish what I have already discussed:

For 10,000 time steps:

user messages coming in:
1. See if a (simulated) local user has just sent in a message.
2. If a message has arrived, add it to the message file.

packets going out:
3. If the current packet is full, send it.
4. If the packet is not full,
add another 50 characters of the message file to it.

As you can see, the 9-milliseconds requirement is something of a red herring. Although each time step represents this very short period of time, only the 50-character unit plays a direct role in the simulation.

When the loop has finished and the simulation is over, the program must still generate a report to the manager. The report must tell the manager the largest size ever reached by the message file. If I can get the program to compute this information, a simple further calculation will reveal the longest wait that any user would have had to endure while using the server under those conditions.

If the assumptions behind the simulation are reasonably accurate, the simulation will make reliable predictions about what to expect as the server reaches saturation, which occurs when the average rate of incoming messages just equals the rate at which the server can divide them into packets and transmit them to the network. You might think that the server could keep up, but you won't know until you run the program.

Once they have been translated into Turbo Pascal, three of the steps inside the loop will use subprograms. Step 1 will become a user-defined function, and steps 3 and 4 will become a procedure. I will outline both subprograms in algorithmic form, then translate them into Turbo Pascal.

A Function Called *Message*

You have already seen examples of built-in functions such as TRUNC, ABS, and RANDOM, functions explained in the box on pages 178 and 179. This chapter deals with a very different kind of function called a *user-defined function*. This works like a built-in function except that the programmer defines it within a program.

It is mildly ironic that the user-defined function I need will require the assistance of the built-in function called RANDOM. The function I am about to define must simulate users by imitating the tendency of incoming messages to arrive randomly. More than this, the function must also determine the length of each user's message (in units of 50 characters), also on a random basis. I will call this function *Message* and define it tentatively as follows:

Function: Message
decide whether or not a message will arrive in this time cycle
assign a random length to this message

As I will shortly explain in more detail, a user-defined function sits aside from the main program but can be called into action by the main program whenever that program uses the function name in statements such as assignment statements. When the simulation program calls my function, it will swing into action by first deciding whether a message has arrived and, if so, what the length of the message is. As I have already made clear, random numbers will play a central role in this particular function.

Random Numbers. What is a random number? Computers, which seem to represent the essence of nonrandomness, are incapable of generating truly random numbers. Yet, they can generate numbers that look random, numbers that almost no amount of analysis can discover to be nonrandom. Such numbers are so close to being truly random that they can be safely used in simulation programs.

As you already know, Turbo Pascal has a built-in function called RANDOM (see page 178) that generates such random numbers. When used with a number parameter such as 1000, say, the function

```
RANDOM(1000)
```

will generate a random number between 0 and 999. You may recall that when used with no parameter at all, the function RANDOM will produce no integer, but a real number between 0 and 1, that is, RANDOM will produce a real number somewhere between 0.000 and 0.999. It shows no preference for any part of this range, producing every number within this range with equal probability. Such a function can be very useful in generating events according to certain probabilities.

Suppose, for example, that the manager of the server decides that a new message should arrive at intervals that have an average length of 180 milliseconds. This specification does not mean that every 180 milliseconds, exactly, the program will generate a new message, only that the long-term average should have this value. To arrange such events is far simpler than you might think. During the 9 milliseconds that each iteration of the main loop represents, there is a probability of 9/180 that a message will arrive. Simplified, this probability becomes 1/20 or 0.05.

When I roll a die with the expectation of a specific number such as a 3, that number comes up about one-sixth of the time. Can I invent a new kind of die that, when rolled, comes up "message" 1/20 of the time? The answer lies in the RANDOM function that selects random numbers between 0 and 1. Why not let RANDOM determine the event just as a die does? If the number happens to be less than or equal to 0.05, for example, then I will take this value as a signal that a message has arrived. After all, a random number selected from the range 0 to 1, will fall between 0 and 0.05 about 1/20 of the time.

In algorithmic terms, the test could use a variable called *Event* to hold the RANDOM number and test it:

```
Function: Message
set Event equal to RANDOM
if Event <= 0.05
   then a message has just been received
```

If a message has just been received, the work of my user-defined function is not over. It must now assign a random length between 50 and 2000 characters to the message. This range of lengths reflects a reasonable sample of user messages. I therefore refine the function to include this additional task:

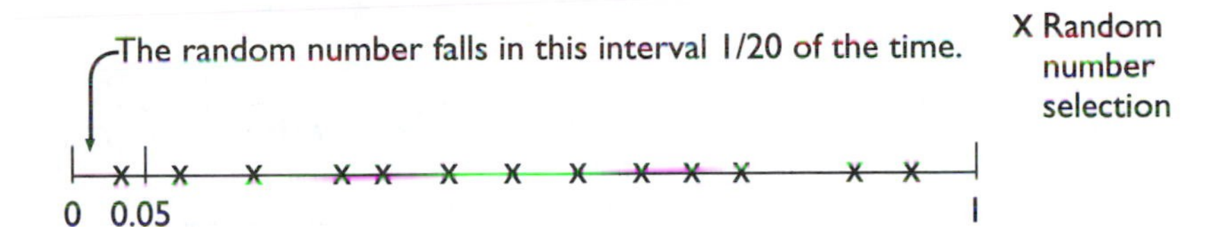
The random number falls in this interval 1/20 of the time.
X Random number selection
0
0.05
1

Choosing a random number is like rolling a die

```
Function: Message
set Event equal to RANDOM
if Event <= 0.05
   then set Message to 50*(RANDOM(40) + 1)
```

The function RANDOM(40) will select a random integer between 0 and 39. To convert this number into an equally random number between 1 and 40, I simply add 1. The formula then calls for multiplication by 50, the fundamental unit of my program. To see that this expression produces the right message lengths, look at the extremes: If RANDOM(40) comes up with a 0, the expression will equal 50*1 = 50, the shortest possible message that the server will have to deal with. If, on the other hand, RANDOM produces a 39, the expression will boil down to 50*40 = 2000, the maximum message length.

User-Defined Functions. The design of my message generator seems good, but in translating this task into a Turbo Pascal function, how will you know what to aim for? What does a Turbo Pascal user-defined function look like and how does it work in general?

User-defined functions resemble built-in functions in one key respect. The value of a function is carried in the name of the function. As the term "user-defined" implies, however, such functions must be declared. The syntax diagram on the following page is general enough, for my purposes, to use as a guide in forming the function header.

Function declarations always include the Pascal word FUNCTION, followed by the name of the function and, in parentheses, the name of any parameter that will contain the data to be operated on by the function. The type of the parameter appears after a colon and within the parentheses. The type of the function, however, which does not need to be the same as that of its parameter, appears outside the parentheses. Although the syntax

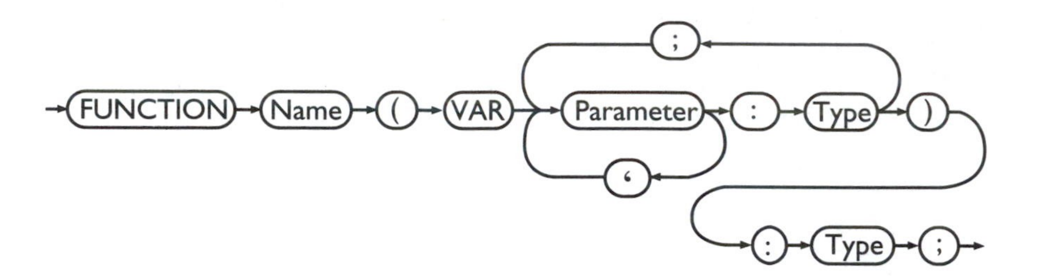

Declaring a user-defined function

diagram does not reflect this possibility, a function need have no parameters at all. The function we are about to define, for example, has no parameters.

As I mentioned earlier, a function is like a miniature program in its own right. Like a program, It has not only a header but also declarations and a body. I will follow the layout below in defining functions:

function header
declarations
BODY

The body will consist of a compound statement containing a BEGIN and an END. But, unlike a program, a function ends not with a period, but with a semicolon.

Now that the syntax has been defined, I can convert the algorithmic function into a real one:

```
FUNCTION Message: INTEGER;
VAR Event: REAL;
BEGIN
Message := 0;
Event := RANDOM;
IF Event <= 0.05
   THEN Message := 50*(RANDOM(40)+1);{up to 2000 characters/message}
END;
```

The function header follows the syntax diagram shown earlier. It has no parameters, so there are no parentheses, just a colon and the key word INTEGER, which defines the type of the function. This type designation means that the values carried in the function name (which acts like a variable) will be integers.

Later, when I write the server-simulating program, I will add this function to the declaration section, just below the part where variables and constants are declared. The function *Message* will be called from the main program by the simple act of having its name mentioned in the program. The adjacent illustration shows the function *Message* sitting up in the declaration section. Meanwhile, down in the body of the main program, its name appears in an assignment statement.

When the computer executes the body of the program, it comes, eventually, to the assignment statement that contains the name of the function. As soon as it sees the function name *Message*, the computer stops executing the assignment statement and jumps, instead, up to the function

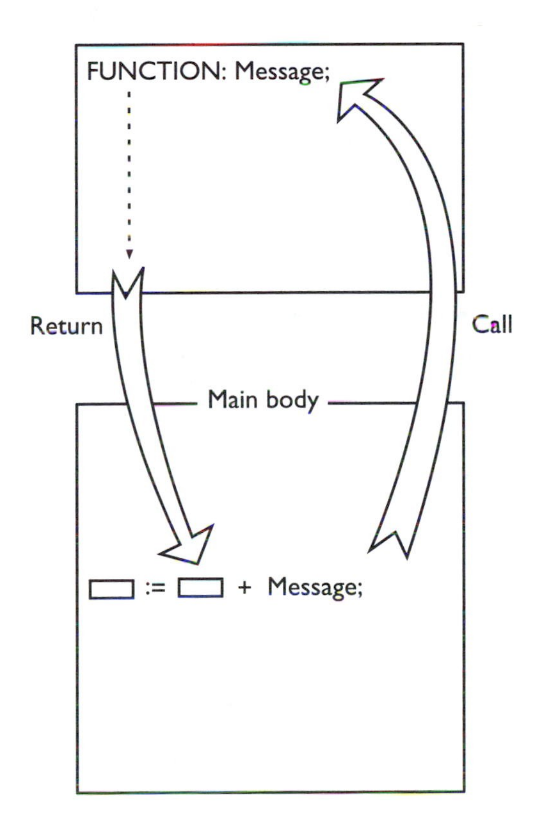

How a function functions

itself and begins to execute *Message*. As soon as it has finished executing *Message*, it jumps back to the main program, back to the very assignment statement it was called from in the first place. But now it has in hand a new value for the function *Message*, carried in the very name, just like a variable. It substitutes this value into the expression on the right-hand side of the assignment statement, finishes executing it, then moves on to the next statement. The arrows in the illustration tell the whole story.

Suppose, for example, that when the computer moves its execution up to the Message function, it produces a value of 350. The computer uses this value in place of Message, just as it would for a variable of the same name. As a miniature program in its own right, a user-defined function can have its own variables, ones that appear only inside the function. These are called local variables. Such variables must themselves be declared inside the function. In the user-defined function Message, for example, the variable Event must be of type REAL. The declaration of such local variables has exactly the same syntax pattern as variables in any program;

```
VAR Event: REAL;
```

In general, you will find no statement in the declarations or body of a subprogram that could not appear in a program.

A Procedure Called *Server*

The most useful type of subprograms in Turbo Pascal is the procedure. Like functions, procedures have names, but the value (or values) returned by a procedure does not reside in the name. Like functions, procedures usually have *parameters* associated with them. You have already seen parameters in action. For example, the parameter 40 in the built-in function

```
RANDOM(40);
```

is used by the function to determine its output. The number 100 in the built-in function

```
SQRT(100)
```

is also a parameter. It determines the output or value of the square root function, in this case, 10.

Parameters themselves, whether in functions or procedures, can also be variables. In procedures, it is the parameters that carry information to the procedure and back from it to the main program. I will use a particular kind of parameter called a *variable*, or *VAR*, *parameter*. Such parameters are capable of carrying information both ways. As soon as I have outlined the procedure to be used in the simulation program, I will demonstrate exactly how such parameters work.

An Algorithm for the Server. As you may recall, I had already decided to turn the following steps of my crude simulation algorithm into a procedure:

> packets going out:
> 3. If the current packet is full, send it.
> 4. If the packet is not full,
>   add another 50 characters of the message file to it.

In a subprogram, these steps must be supplied with certain information. In order to add 50 characters of the message file to the current packet or to subtract the same 50 characters from the current message file, the subprogram must have access to the appropriate variables. The time has come to name names.

Let's call the message file *MessFile*, a memorable name and useful to the procedure. Similarly, I'll use the name *Packet* for the size of the packet about to be sent off. Even without knowing a thing about how procedures are defined, I could still lay out the algorithm in a way that anticipates almost any form:

```
Procedure: Server
(will need access to the variables MessFile and Packet)
if Packet = 1000
   then reset Packet to 0
   else increment Packet by 50
      decrement MessFile by 50
```

The procedure to be called *Server* will first check the size of the current packet. If it has already reached its limit of 1000 characters, the packet is ready to be sent. This simulation does not actually send packets. It only cares about the size of what's left after a packet is sent. In this case, it merely resets the *Packet* variable to 0. In the next time cycle of the simulation, this procedure will begin to fill the new packet by adding 50 characters, the very option it takes when the packet is not full to begin with. In this other branch of the conditional statement, it not only adds 50 characters to the packet, it subtracts (the same) 50 characters from the messagefile.

Now that I have outlined the operation of the *Server* procedure, let's move on to procedures in general, examining how they are defined and how they operate in the context of a program.

Procedures. Procedures can be described as the subprogram workhorses of Turbo Pascal. Although functions have a secure place within the language, a procedure can do anything a function can do and more. Yet a procedure must be defined just as completely as a function is, with a similar syntax. The diagram for the procedure header has been specialized to just those kinds of procedures that I use in this book. As you can see, the VAR word may be bypassed. The parameter defined without the VAR key word would be a *value parameter*, a concept I shall introduce in the very next chapter.

The most important difference between procedures and functions is found at the end of the header diagram. Because a procedure carries values in its parameters rather than in its name, you do not need to give a type to the procedure itself as you do to a function.

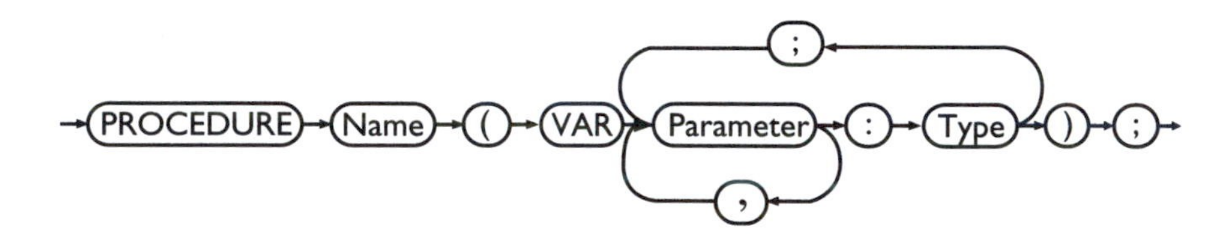

Syntax for a procedure

As a subprogram, a procedure has a header, declarations, and a body of its own. I will follow the layout below in defining procedures:

procedure header
declarations
BODY

The body will consist of a compound statement, namely, a statement or statements sandwiched between a BEGIN and an END. Like functions, procedures end in a semicolon.

Procedure headers always contain the Pascal word PROCEDURE followed by the name of the PROCEDURE and, in parentheses, the names of parameters that will carry information back and forth between the procedure and the main program that calls it.

But what is the function of the word VAR inside the parentheses in the procedure header? The procedure I use in this project has *VAR*, or *variable, parameters*. Such parameters carry information in two directions. They carry information from the program to the procedure and, when the procedure has been executed, they carry information back again. The word VAR indicates to the computer that the parameters are variable parameters. Each VAR parameter must correspond with a variable (or value) in the program, but the variable parameter in the procedure should not use the same name as its corresponding variable in the program. Even though it will carry the same information, a VAR parameter must have a different name. Thus, I must change the refined algorithm for the procedure by replacing the names *Packet* and *MessFile* by other names such as *PSize* and *MSize*, respectively. They are simply other names for the same variables.

```
PROCEDURE Server(VAR PSize, MSize: INTEGER);
BEGIN
IF PSize = 1000
   THEN PSize := 0
   ELSE BEGIN
      PSize := PSize + 50;
      MSize := MSize - 50;
      END;
END;
```

This particular procedure has no declarations, as such. The two variables that appear in it are declared as VAR parameters. Apart from its lack of normal declarations, the procedure looks just like the program that it is.

The body of the procedure contains all the steps of the refined algorithm and carries out those steps exactly the way you would expect. The important thing to grasp about this procedure, and about procedures in general, is how information passes back and forth between the program and the procedure. The accompanying diagram shows the program *ServerSim* laid out in blocks. It includes the program header, the procedure *Server* (shown as a rectangle), and the main body of the program (shown as another, larger rectangle). It omits the declarations and the function *Message,* because these are not relevant to the action.

The procedure name *Server* appears twice in this figure, once in the procedure definition, upstairs, and once in the main body, downstairs. The statement

```
Server(Packet, MessFile);
```

in the main program is a *procedure call*. It contains the variables *Packet* and *MessFile*. When used in a procedure call in this manner, such variables are known as *actual parameters*. Meanwhile, the two variable parameters in the procedure definition upstairs are known as *formal parameters*. The cardinal

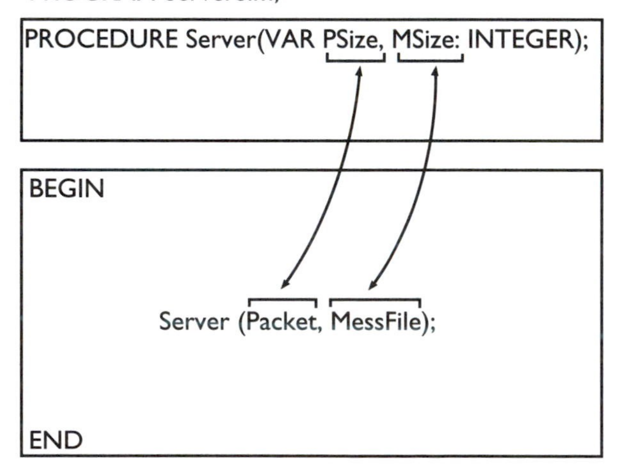

How a procedure proceeds

rule of parameters in procedures is that formal parameters must correspond in number, type, and position with the actual parameters. Here there are two formal parameters and two actual parameters. All parameters happen to be of type INTEGER. Thus the two kinds of parameters correspond in number and type. These two sets of parameters also obey the positional rule. The formal parameter *PSize* corresponds to the actual parameter *Packet* because both occupy the first position in their respective parentheses. Similarly, the formal parameter *MSize* corresponds to the actual parameter *MessFile*, because both parameters occupy the second position in their respective parentheses.

In the earlier figure, two arrows connect the actual parameters in the procedure call to the formal parameters in the procedure definition near the head of the program. To see how values flow back and forth between the main program and the procedure, let's focus on the actual parameters, *Packet* and *MessFile*. Being variables, *Packet* and *MessFile* will already have values when the computer encounters the call to the procedure and begins to execute it. Suppose, for example, that *Packet* happens to equal 850 and *MessFile* equals 1200.

The computer scans the values of the two actual parameters, finds the value 850 for *Packet* and immediately makes that number the value of the formal parameter *PSize* in the procedure. Similarly, it finds that *MessFile* has the value 1200 and makes this the value of the formal parameter *MSize*. I have reproduced the procedure *Server* below with one little alteration. I have replaced the names of the formal parameters by their values as the computer begins to execute the subprogram. Within the subprogram, the formal parameters become variables in their own right:

Beginning the execution

```
                        PSize  MSize
                          ↓      ↓
PROCEDURE Server(VAR 850, 1200: INTEGER);
BEGIN
IF PSize = 1000
   THEN PSize := 0
   ELSE BEGIN
      PSize := PSize + 50;
      MSize := MSize - 50;
      END;
END;
```

If you were the computer executing this procedure, you'd immediately determine that 850 is not equal to 1000, so you would not reset the variable *PSize* to 0. Instead, you would execute the ELSE branch of the conditional statement. Here, you would change the values *PSize* and *MSize* to 900 and 1150, respectively. At this juncture, you, the computer, will have new values for the formal parameters *PSize* and *MSize*. Now you follow the double-headed arrows from the procedure back down to the main program. In doing so, you carry the values 900 and 1150 with you. At the procedure call in the main program, you give these new values to the corresponding actual parameters, *Packet* and *MessFile*.

When you go on to execute the rest of the main program, the variables *Packet* and *MessFile* have acquired a new life. *Packet* now has the value 900 and *MessFile* has the value 1150. In other words, thanks to the procedure, two major operations of the simulation program have been achieved: The packet size has increased by 50 and the size of the message file has decreased by the same amount.

One of the advantages of having these things happen in a procedure would become apparent should you ever decide to change the way the simulation operates. You might be able to confine your repairs to the procedure alone, like taking your carburetor indoors to fix it.

The Algorithm Again. Before rushing off to write the Turbo Pascal program called *ServerSim*, it makes sense to finish the algorithm. Apart from initializing the key variables to 0, the remaining unfinished business is the report to the manager. What was the maximum time users had to wait during the simulation run? One way to find out is to keep track of the maximum size of the message file. For this reason, I must create a new variable, say, *MessMax*. At the end of the main loop, the computer will use the number contained in this variable to figure out how long someone may have had to wait. The variable *Wait* will hold the result of multiplying the number of characters in the message file (when it peaked in size) by the number of milliseconds it takes to process one character. Divided by 1000, the result of this multiplication will yield the number of seconds it would take the server to process a message file that large.

If runs of this simulation program consistently reported times of 2 to 3 seconds, the manager might worry. An interactive user who had entered a single keystroke at the unfortunate moment when the message file had grown to maximum size, would have to wait at *least* 2 or 3 seconds for a response from a distant computer. Only by this time, will the message be on its way to other adventures in the Internet. It might take another second beyond this before the user gets a response.

The algorithm below does not spell out the function or the procedure, because you have already seen these.

ServerSim algorithm

Program name: *ServerSim*

variables:
MessFile: holds the sum of individual messages in bytes
MessMax: largest value of *MessFile*
Tick: a counting variable
Packet: number of bytes in the current packet
Wait: maximum wait for a user

Message: {a function}
Server(*PSize*, *MSize*): {a procedure}

algorithm:
{initialize variables}
set *Packet* to 0
set *MessFile* to 0
set *MessMax* to 0

{main loop represents 10,000 × 0.009 = 90 seconds of time}
for *Tick* := 1 to 10000 {each tick represents 9 milliseconds}

{new message from a user?}
call *Message* function
increment *MessFile* by *Message*

if *MessFile* > *MessMax*
then replace *MessMax* by *MessFile*

{packet assembly section}
call *Server* procedure with parameters (*Packet*, *MessFile*)

{report to manager}
set *Wait* to (9/50)∗*MessMax*/1000
output: "The maximum delay was ", *Wait*, " seconds."

Note the step that changes *MessMax* whenever a higher value of *MessFile* is encountered. This kind of calculation can be adapted to any situation where a maximum or (for that matter) a minimum value is required.

Have I missed anything? Hmmm. What happens if the program calls the *Server* procedure when *MessFile* happens to be 0? The procedure will subtract 50 from *MessFile*, giving it a negative value. If this should go on for a few cycles during which no new messages came in, the behavior of the simulation program would diverge markedly from reality. The first few messages might not even be enough to bring the size of the message file back to 0!

To avoid this fault in the logic of the program to come, I insert a conditional statement in front of the procedure call:

if *MessFile* > 0
then call *Server* procedure with parameters (*Packet*, *MessFile*)

The program *ServerSim* is now within grasp.

The Simulation Program

With a well-refined algorithm on hand, the process of translation to a Turbo Pascal program usually proceeds smoothly. There is the program header with a brief statement of mission below it. To reflect the modular approach, I renamed the major "sections" as "modules."

In name only, I have split the subprograms away from the declaration module into a module of their own. As the first subprograms you have encountered, they deserve it. Look through them briefly before you go on to the main program. You will find them easy to understand because you watched them grow from vague ideas to definite statements.

```
PROGRAM ServerSim;
{Simulates an Internet server}
{processing outgoing messages.}

{declaration module}
VAR MessFile, MessMax, Tick, Packet: INTEGER;
VAR Wait: REAL;
```

```
{subprogram module}
FUNCTION Message: INTEGER;
VAR Event: REAL;
BEGIN
Message := 0;
Event := RANDOM;
IF Event <= 0.05
   THEN Message := 50*(RANDOM(40) + 1);
   {up to 2000 characters/message}
END;

PROCEDURE Server(VAR PSize, MSize: INTEGER);
BEGIN
IF PSize = 1000
   THEN PSize := 0
   ELSE BEGIN
      PSize := PSize + 50;
      MSize := MSize - 50;
      END;
END;

BEGIN {main program module}

RANDOMIZE; {so that each run will be different}

{variable initialization module}
Packet := 0;
MessFile := 0;
MessMax := 0;

{main loop: simulates 90 seconds of real time}
FOR Tick := 1 TO 10000 DO

   BEGIN {main loop}

   {new message module}
   MessFile := MessFile + Message;
   IF MessFile > MessMax
      THEN MessMax := MessFile;

   {packet assembly module}
   IF MessFile > 0
      THEN Server(Packet, MessFile);

   END; {main loop}
```

```
{report module}
Wait := (9/50)*MessMax/1000;
{i.e., byte-time * maximum message size, in seconds}
WRITELN('The maximum delay was ', Wait:3:1, 'seconds.');

END. {program}
```

The main program also follows the algorithmic outline. Before the variables are initialized, however, you saw the following statement:

```
RANDOMIZE;
```

Without this statement, every run of the *ServerSim* program would be the same. The RANDOM function would choose exactly the same "random" numbers it did before. With RANDOMIZE, every time you run *ServerSim*, you will get a different maximum waiting time. This variation is natural, because every 90 seconds, the real-world server experiences a similar variation in its own maximum waiting time.

In the main loop, you will find the new message module that calls the function *Message*. With a roll of the RANDOM die, a message appears—or doesn't. Following the new message module, the packet assembly module calls the procedure *Server*, handles the bookkeeping for packet and file sizes.

You can run this program under DOS or OS/2 as it stands. With Windows, you must add the usual statement below the program header:

```
USES WinCrt;
```

When you run *ServerSim*, you may get a shock—actually, two shocks. The probability of 0.05 selected by the network manager reflects the situation in which messages are coming in, on average, at exactly the rate the server can handle them. If every twentieth message has non-zero length, you can take an average over all lengths and arrive at 1000 characters as a reasonable estimate. In other words, the manager has chosen the probability so that, on average, 1000 characters arrive every $20 \times 9 = 180$ milliseconds. This boils down to 50 characters every 9 milliseconds, the rate at which the server assembles packets.

Your first shock comes when you run the program a few times and notice that the maximum waiting time is invariably several seconds. This is an intolerable waiting time on the Internet. To see how such backlogs develop when the server rate equals the average message rate, you might consult the final section of this chapter, where computer science explains the anomaly.

Your second shock comes when you notice that many of the maximum waiting times cluster around the values 5.8 and 5.9 seconds. This is due to a subtle bug in the program as it stands. You may recall that in Chapter 3 I mentioned that the largest value that an integer variable can hold is 32,767. The value of *MessFile* has actually exceeded this amount and overflow has occurred. Adding more to *MessFile* does nothing to change the value!

To remedy this situation, you can take advantage of a special Turbo Pascal data type called LONGINT, short for "long integer." Instead of being composed of a single 16-bit word, a LONGINT integer is composed of two. This gives a vastly increased range to *MessFile* and the other integer variables in the program when you re-declare them. Simply replace the word INTEGER by LONGINT. In fact, to avoid assignment compatibility problems, carry out the replacement in a wholesale manner. This includes not only the declarations proper, but the parameter declarations in the Procedure *Server*, as well as the type declaration for the function called *Message*.

Now, when you run the simulation program, you get a new version of the first shock; the waiting times frequently involve two digits. Imagine a 24-second wait on the Internet! You not only rush to change the format for the variable *Wait* from :3:1 to :4:1, you also rush off to the final section of this chapter (page 239) to find out how such immense queues can develop in such reasonable-looking situations.

Animating the Server

Your second excursion into computer graphics will provide a window into the workings of the Internet server. You have already seen a program that computes all the numbers of interest, including the times and sizes of incoming messages and the message-file sizes these messages produce. Shouldn't it be possible, by representing these variables on the screen somehow, to make the operation of the server visible? If you can do this, the resulting program will show you the server in action, almost like watching an animated short. You will get new insights into how the parts of the program work together, as well as a new appreciation of how graphics can make some programs fulfill their mission even better.

Designing the Screen

To make a new version called *ServerSim2*, I only need to add some Turbo Pascal graphics statements. First, however, I must decide what sort of display will best show the operation of the server. There are endless possibilities for such a design, but the watchword is "simplicity."

The simplest way to display three variables in the act of varying is to use bars, as I did in *RealInvest_Graph* (see Chapter 4). If a bar can show a static value, as it did for the variable called *Money*, it might work equally well for dynamic values, numbers that change from one iteration of the simulation loop to the next. I might have to add a delay statement, as I did in the *Elevator* program. This addition will slow the program down to a point where you can appreciate what the server is actually doing.

The accompanying illustration shows a VGA screen with the positions of three rectangles plotted on it. I have labeled each rectangle with its purpose. No labels will appear in the graphics program, but it takes little time to remember that the long bar represents the message queue, the short bar on the right represents packets as they build up, and the short bar below the message file represents an incoming message. For each

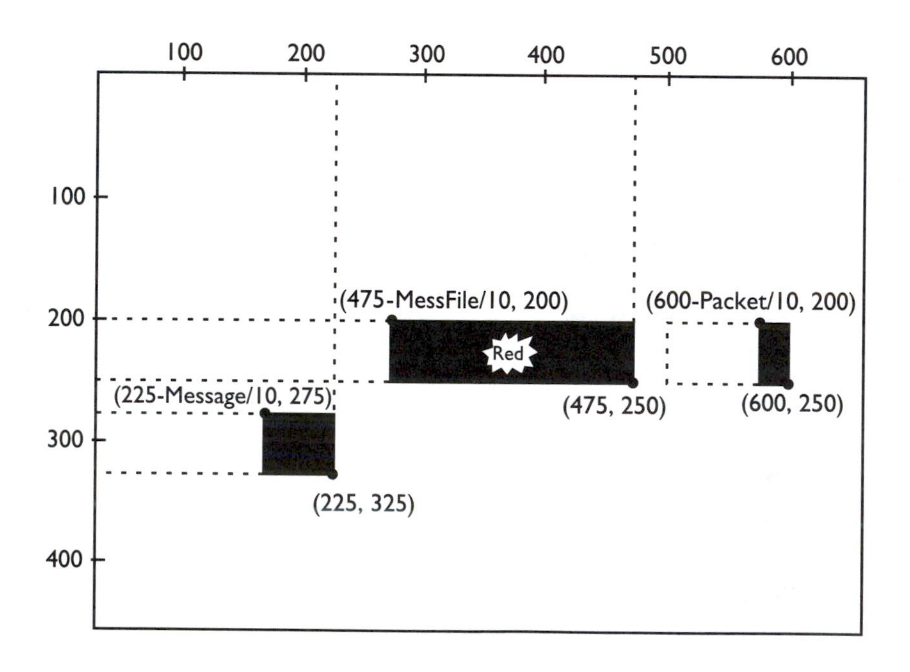

Graphics layout on a map of the VGA screen

rectangle, there is just one coordinate that is not a fixed constant. In each case, the x-coordinate of the upper left corner of the rectangle is given as a formula. To get this formula, I divided the variable by 10 to scale it down for the screen and subtracted the result from the x-coordinate of the right side of the rectangle. Each of these formulas will appear on the right-hand side of assignment statements in both graphics modules. The values of these formulas will be assigned to three new variables to contain this coordinate information.

Designing the Program

I have outlined the *ServerSim* program below, reducing modules to their titles alone and adding some graphics commands at the end of the main loop. I have omitted the report to the manager, because the display will tell the whole story.

```
PROGRAM ServerSim2;

declaration module

subprogram module

BEGIN

variable initialization module

FOR Tick := 1 TO 1000 DO

   new message module

   packet assembly module

   draw three horizontal rectangles,
   one for each of the three variables,
   Message, MessFile, and Packet

   delay

   erase the three horizontal rectangles
```

The first new module will draw the three horizontal rectangles that will represent the key simulation variables. If I neglected to add a delay command, the next iteration of the loop would be upon me before I could even begin to appreciate how the rectangles are behaving. A brief delay of half a second, however, will make the whole show much easier to follow. After the delay, a second graphics module must erase the rectangle drawn a half second earlier. This action will prevent early, large rectangles from obscuring later, smaller ones. Execution of the program is so quick that the computer will draw the next set of rectangles immediately.

The Animation in DOS

Here I come to a fork in the road. In this section, I will design *ServerSim2* for DOS- and OS/2-based Turbo Pascal. In a subsequent section, I will design *ServerSim2* all over again for Windows-based Turbo Pascal. Between the two sections, I introduce a third kind of modules—objects—that extends the subprogram concept still further.

If I can write a program that displays the server and its variables in computer graphics form, you will be able to view the simulation as though it were a movie, an animated movie. You will be able to see the message file grow when incoming messages arrive and shrink as a new packet is assembled. Watching this movie will provide you with a new and simultaneous appreciation of the power of simulation and the power of computer graphics.

After the addition of graphics statements and their accompanying procedure, the *ServerSim2* program will have become the longest program that you have encountered up to this point. Specifically, I will add the following items:

1. The *Graph* unit will be added to the USES statement at the beginning of the program.
2. The *SetGraph* procedure will be included in the subprogram module.
3. A graphics initialization module will be included inside the main program. This module clears the screen and calls the *SetGraph* procedure.
4. Six BAR statements and their accompanying coordinate calculations will be inserted at the end of the main loop, with a DELAY statement between them. These statements follow exactly the algorithmic plan that I laid down in the previous section.

To accompany all BAR statements, the programmer must include a SETFILLSTYLE statement that specifies what texture to use on the bars and what color to make them. I used the *SolidFill* option and two colors. This option gives the bars a solid color. The bars that display the three variables are drawn in red (color 4), and the bars that erase these bars are drawn in black (color 0).

The calculations that accompany the BAR statements must have access to the size of the current message. Unfortunately, with the way *ServerSim* was designed, there was no way to get this access without calling the *Message* function a second time. This would of course produce a different value for the function and the bar that appeared on the screen would not represent the value of *Message* used by the simulation. To circumvent this problem, I incorporated a new variable into the program. The LONGINT variable *LastMess* saves the value returned by *Message* so that it can be used in the display portion of the program, as well as the numerical simulation part.

```
PROGRAM ServerSim2;
{Simulates an Internet server processing outgoing messages.}
{This version uses graphics bars to display key server variables.}

USES CRT, Graph;

{declaration module}
VAR MessFile, MessMax, Tick, Packet: LONGINT;
VAR LastMess, MessFileX, PacketX, MessageX: LONGINT;

{subprogram module}
FUNCTION Message: LONGINT;
VAR Event: REAL;
BEGIN
Message := 0;
Event := RANDOM;
IF Event < 0.05
   THEN Message := 50*(RANDOM(40) + 1);
   {maximum message has 2000 chars}
END;

PROCEDURE Server(VAR PSize, MSize: LONGINT);
BEGIN
```

```
IF PSize = 1000
   THEN PSize := 0
   ELSE BEGIN
      PSize := PSize + 50;
      MSize := MSize - 50;
      END;
END;

PROCEDURE SetGraph;
VAR GraphDriver, GraphMode: INTEGER;
BEGIN
GraphDriver := Detect;
InitGraph(GraphDriver, GraphMode, '\tp\bgi');
END;

BEGIN {main program}

{graphics initialization module}
SetGraph;
ClrScr;

RANDOMIZE; {so that each run will be different}

{variable initialization section}
Packet := 0;
MessFile := 0;
MessMax := 0;

{main loop}
{Each iteration simulates 9 seconds of real time.}
FOR Tick := 1 TO 1000 DO {Each tick represents 9 milliseconds.}

   BEGIN {main loop}

   {new message module}
   LastMess := Message;
   MessFile := MessFile + LastMess;
   IF MessFile > MessMax
      THEN MessMax := MessFile;

   {packet assembly module}
   IF MessFile > 0
      THEN Server(Packet, MessFile);
```

```
    {display module}
    SETFILLSTYLE(SolidFill, 4);
    MessFileX := TRUNC(475 - MessFile/10);
    PacketX := TRUNC(600 - Packet/10);
    MessageX := TRUNC(225 - LastMess/10);
    BAR(MessFileX, 200, 475, 250);
    BAR(PacketX, 200, 600, 250);
    BAR(MessageX, 275, 225, 325);

    DELAY(500); {Hold display for a half-second.}

    {erase module}
    SETFILLSTYLE(SolidFill, 0);
    BAR(MessFileX, 200, 475, 250);
    BAR(PacketX, 200, 600, 250);
    BAR(MessageX, 275, 225, 325);

    END; {main loop}

END. {program}
```

Adapting a program that runs in one milieu to another can produce surprises. For example, without thinking too much about it, I added the half-second DELAY statement between the display and erasure modules. The main loop still had an iteration limit of 10,000. When I ran the program, everything seemed to work quite well and I was pleased. I waited for the program to end. And I waited. Presently, I began to wonder how long it would take and suddenly remembered the 10,000 iterations. At a half-second per iteration, this came to 5000 seconds, or 1 hour and 24 minutes! This is yet another example of how a simple change in one line of code can cause changes elsewhere in a program. So I cut the limit from 10,000 to 1000. Now the program will run for 10 minutes, long enough for anyone to fully appreciate the animation. You can reduce it further, later on.

Another result of modifying programs is the fortuitous bug. This kind of event is far rarer, but it happened with *ServerSim2*. I had forgotten that if the programmer does not specify a background color for the screen, Turbo Pascal will assume you want white. Meanwhile, *ServerSim2* merrily displayed red bars and erased these with black bars. Like prints in the snow, the black bars showed the sizes the red bars had been. This annoyed me until I realized that this bug was actually what programmers call a "feature." Within each run, the black bar that erased the red bar for the *MessFile* variable would thereafter always show the maximum size ever reached by this variable. By sheer accident, the black bar that was intended only to erase now filled the additional function of representing the variable *MessMax*! When you run the program, you'll see what I mean.

Object Lessons

The third kind of modules introduced in this chapter—the object—extends the idea of a subprogram by incorporating not only program code, but data as well. An *object* consists of two components, a *data* component and a *method* component. The data can be something as simple as an integer or as complex as an array. The method is usually a function or a procedure.

Consider the case of a small, high-security company that has ten rooms on the mysterious ninth floor. Here, every door has a special keypad. When an employee enters the top-secret door code on this pad, it opens the door. The security chief is currently writing a Turbo Pascal program that will enable her to enter and change the door codes at will. It's been slow going because programming is not her normal line of work. But she just doesn't trust anyone in the Information Systems Department. She has decided to use objects because she has heard that this approach will give her great flexibility later on when she expands the program in various ways.

Currently, she has written a program that will accept a list of ten door codes. The program also enables her to easily change any of the codes. Here, without any further introduction, is the object that she has declared in a program called *DoorCodes*.

```
TYPE Codes = ARRAY[1 . . 10] OF INTEGER;
   SafeDoor = OBJECT
   Code: Codes;
   PROCEDURE ChangeCode(DoorNum, NewCode: INTEGER);
   PROCEDURE ReadCodes;
   END; {SafeDoor}
```

This object, called *SafeDoor*, consists of both data and methods. The data is an array that contains the door codes. The methods consist of two procedures, one to change a code, the other to read in codes. Notice that the array *Code*, which will contain the data associated with the object, uses the same kind of TYPE statement that you encountered in the previous chapter. An object declaration is terminated by the word END, no BEGIN being required.

The *DoorCodes* program will take advantage of this object by using its methods to access its data (the array of secret door codes) and change that data. While she could easily write a program that did the same thing without objects, she has made a good decision. If she ever becomes a sophisticated programmer (assuming she still doesn't trust the Information Systems Department), she will find herself able to create a whole security system that embraces not only door codes but also employee clearances, staff numbers, workplaces, movement patterns, and a host of other things that only a security chief would ever worry about.

In the next chapter, you will revisit objects and learn the syntax for declaring them. The purpose of this section is to introduce you to the main ideas and to pave the way for the following section where, in your excursion into Windows Turbo Pascal, objects will abound.

The following program uses the object *SafeDoor*. The methods associated with the object, namely, the procedures *ChangeCode* and *ReadCodes*, are declared, not inside the object, but immediately following it.

```
PROGRAM DoorCodes;
{This program reads in the high-security door}
{codes and enables the user to change a code.}

VAR Ind, DNum, DCode: INTEGER;

{declaration of object SafeDoor}
TYPE Codes = ARRAY[1 . . 10] OF INTEGER;
   SafeDoor = OBJECT
   Code: Codes;
   PROCEDURE ChangeCode(DoorNum, NewCode: INTEGER);
   PROCEDURE ReadCodes;
   END; {SafeDoor}

{a procedure to change a door code}
PROCEDURE SafeDoor.ChangeCode(DoorNum, NewCode: INTEGER);
BEGIN
Code[DoorNum] := NewCode;
END;
```

```
{a procedure to read in door codes}
PROCEDURE SafeDoor.ReadCodes;
BEGIN
WRITELN('Please enter the door codes.');
FOR Ind := 1 TO 10 DO
   READLN(Code[Ind]);
END;

{making an instance}
VAR S: SafeDoor;

BEGIN {program}

S.ReadCodes;
WRITELN('Enter number of door and the new code');
READLN(DNum, DCode);
S.ChangeCode(DNum, DCode);

END. {program}
```

The procedures associated with the object *SafeDoor* have curious double titles that consist of the object name and the procedure name separated by a period. This notation indicates that the procedures both belong to the object in question. It makes object-oriented programs easy to read (and write) among other things. Thus the name *SafeDoor.ChangeCode* indicates that the procedure *ChangeCode* belongs to the object *SafeDoor*.

These particular procedures have value parameters, which carry information into the procedure, but not back out again. In other respects, the procedures resemble the ones you have already seen. To review the difference between value parameters and VAR parameters, refer to page 265.

The first procedure alters the data associated with the object by changing one of the entries in the *Code* array. The second procedure will read in a whole array of door codes. It prompts the security chief for the codes, then enters them, in a loop, one by one into the array. On the basis of what you have already encountered, you should be able to read these procedures and understand them completely. The order in which you declare procedures as part of an object is immaterial. It's how the program uses them that counts.

To understand how the object really works, however, I must focus your attention on the program itself, a miserable little fragment of code at the bottom:

```
VAR S: SafeDoor;

BEGIN {program}

S.ReadCodes;
WRITELN('Enter number of door and the new code');
READLN(DNum, DCode);
S.ChangeCode(DNum, DCode);

END. {program}
```

After an object has been declared, an instance must be created. That's the purpose of the VAR statement just before the program. The object, being declared as a TYPE, cannot be referred to directly by the program. An instance must therefore be created in order for the program to use the data and methods associated with the object. The situation parallels that of arrays. A TYPE statement for arrays is useless until an array instance is named which has that type. The letter S stands for the instance of the object that will be created when the program runs. The two statements

```
S.ReadCodes;
```

and

```
S.ChangeCode(DNum, DCode);
```

both use the dot notation, with S replacing the object name *SafeDoor*. Apart from such niceties, notice how the second method amounts to a procedure call in which the actual parameters differ from the formal parameters as declared in the object *SafeDoor*. When the computer executes these statements, it not only executes the procedures, it also uses the data array associated with the object. But neither procedure makes the slightest reference to the array. The action is hidden and the program, as a result, is simpler.

The presence of so many declarations and so little body gives *DoorCodes* a somewhat lopsided appearance. Ninety percent of it seems to consist of declarations. The program proper has shrunk almost into insignificance at the bottom. As object-oriented programmers know, however, this appearance is only temporary. When the security chief becomes thoroughly saturated with the subject, she will keep her objects hidden away in *units*, which are large collections of objects and can be used by a variety of programs for a variety of purposes. Only the programs, short and sweet (relatively speaking), will show.

For the time being, the security chief realizes that *DoorCodes* has not yet reached the level of a usable program, but she is nearly there. (You may be able to help her by adding one more method in the Explorations at the end of this chapter.)

Despite this limited background discussion about objects, you should now be able to follow the next program, a Windows incarnation of *ServerSim2*.

Server Animation Revisited, in Windows

The time has come for Windows-based students to explore a major part of their system, its object-oriented environment. Up to now, you have not had to use objects; you have merely added the USES WinCrt; statement at the head of your programs.

Computer graphics in the Windows-based programming environment requires the use of objects. Using the discussion of the previous section as a guide, you should be able to (1) identify all objects and name them and (2) state what data and what methods are associated with each. If you look closely, you will find a slightly different incarnation of the program *ServerSim2* lurking in one of the procedures. To see which one, look for the word PROCEDURE in bold type. I have also put the BEGIN and END of this procedure in bold type so that you can quickly trace its full extent. In recasting *ServerSim2* as a Windows-based Turbo Pascal program, I needed two objects. I will begin with the object that houses the relevant procedure:

```
TYPE PservWin = TServWin;
   TServWin = OBJECT(TWindow)
   PROCEDURE WMLButtonDown(VAR Msg: TMessage);
   Virtual WM_First + WM_LButtonDown;
   END;
```

The object *TServWin* uses a procedure called *WMLButtonDown*. This name refers to the Windows left mouse button, which initiates the action. The next statement specifies that when the cursor is on the window for this object and the left mouse button is depressed, the procedure will be called. Its full name is

```
TServWin.WMLButtonDown
```

This name follows the syntax that I outlined in the previous section. The first part is the object name; the second part, the procedure name. In the parentheses following the key word OBJECT, you will find the name *TWindow*. This is a predefined Windows Turbo Pascal object with many capabilities that have to do with windows. Through this generic object, a program is able to open windows, close them, access mouse data, and so on. The word “Virtual” indicates an address (the following sum) to be used by the Turbo Pascal mouse unit.

The next object, *TServApp*, is declared to be an instance of the generic object called *TApplication*. Every Turbo Pascal application program using graphics will need this object.

```
TYPE TServApp = OBJECT(TApplication)
   PROCEDURE InitMainWindow; Virtual;
   END;
```

The procedure *InitMainWindow* sets up the window in which you will view the simulation.

Without further ado, I will now display the entire Windows version of *ServerSim2*. Look through it, noting not only the two objects I have discussed but also the graphics commands in Windows Turbo Pascal that differ from their DOS counterparts. I’ll meet you at the bottom.

```
PROGRAM ServerSim2;
{A graphics program that simulates an Internet server processing}
{outgoing messages. This version runs on Turbo Pascal for Windows.}

{predefined Windows units needed by program}
USES WObjects, WinTypes, WinProcs;

{TApplication objects create and display the main window.}
```

```
TYPE TServApp = OBJECT(TApplication)
   PROCEDURE InitMainWindow; Virtual;
   END;

{PServWin defines the main window.}
TYPE PservWin = ^TServWin;
   TServWin = OBJECT(TWindow)
   PROCEDURE WMLButtonDown(VAR Msg: TMessage);
   Virtual WM_First + WM_LButtonDown;
   END;

{Initializes main window of this application.}
PROCEDURE TServApp.InitMainWindow;
BEGIN
MainWindow := NEW(PServWin, Init(nil, 'ServerSim'));
END;

{Left mouse button activates this procedure.}
PROCEDURE TServWin.WMLButtonDown;
{This procedure contains the earlier ServerSim program.}

{declaration module}
VAR DC: HDC;
VAR RedBrush, BlkBrush: HBrush;
VAR MessFile, MessMax, Tick, Packet: LONGINT;
VAR LastMess, MessFileX, PacketX, MessageX: LONGINT;

{subprogram section}
FUNCTION Message: LONGINT;
VAR Event: REAL;
BEGIN
Message := 0;
Event := RANDOM;
IF Event < 0.05
   THEN Message := 50*(RANDOM(40) + 1);
END;

PROCEDURE Server(VAR PSize, MSize: LONGINT);
BEGIN
IF PSize = 1000
   THEN PSize := 0
   ELSE BEGIN
      PSize := PSize + 50;
      MSize := MSize - 50;
      END;
END;
```

```
{DELAY procedure not available in Windows.}
PROCEDURE Delay(VAR Time: LONGINT);
VAR Counter1, Counter2, Temp: LONGINT;
BEGIN
FOR Counter1 := 1 TO Time DO
   FOR Counter2 := 1 TO 300 DO
      Temp := Counter1*Counter2;
END;

BEGIN {procedure TServWin}

{graphics initialization module}
RedBrush := CreateSolidBrush(RGB(255, 0, 0));
BlkBrush := CreateSolidBrush(RGB(0, 0, 0));

RANDOMIZE; {so that each run will be different}

{variable initialization section}
Packet := 0;
MessFile := 0;
MessMax := 0;

{The main loop simulates 9 seconds of real time.}
FOR Tick := 1 TO 1000 DO {Each tick represents 9 milliseconds.}

   BEGIN {main loop}

   {new message module}
   LastMess := Message;
   MessFile := MessFile + LastMess;
   IF MessFile > MessMax
      THEN MessMax := MessFile;

   {packet assembly module}
   IF MessFile > 0
      THEN Server(Packet, MessFile);

   {display module}
   MessFileX := TRUNC(475 - MessFile/10);
   PacketX := TRUNC(600 - Packet/10);
   MessageX := TRUNC(225 - LastMess/10);
   DC := GetDC(HWindow);
   SELECTOBJECT(DC, RedBrush);
   RECTANGLE(DC, MessFileX, 200, 475, 250);
   RECTANGLE(DC, PacketX, 200, 600, 250);
   RECTANGLE(DC, MessageX, 275, 225, 325);
```

```
  RELEASEDC(HWindow, DC);

  Delay(500); {holds display for a half-second.}
  {erase module}
  DC := GetDC(HWindow);
  SELECTOBJECT(DC, BlkBrush);
  RECTANGLE(DC, MessFileX, 200, 475, 250);
  RECTANGLE(DC, PacketX, 200, 600, 250);
  RECTANGLE(DC, MessageX, 275, 225, 325);
  RELEASEDC(HWindow, DC);

  END; {main loop}

{delete the brushes.}
DELETEOBJECT(RedBrush);
DELETEOBJECT(BlkBrush);

END; {procedure TServWin}

{create an instance of TServApp.}
VAR ServAp: TServApp;

BEGIN {main program}

ServAp.Init('ServerSim2');
ServAp.Run;
ServAp.Done;

END. {main program}
```

The declaration module of the main procedure contains the variables you are already familiar with, along with some new ones:

```
VAR DC: HDC;
VAR RedBrush, BlkBrush: HBrush;
```

The variable *DC*, which stands for display context, is declared to be of type *HDC*, which belongs to a Windows unit that handles Windows displays. *RedBrush* and *BlkBrush* are both declared to be instances of a generic brush handle called *HBrush*. Right after the BEGIN for the procedure, you may have noticed the following statement:

```
RedBrush := CreateSolidBrush(RGB(225, 0, 0));
```

This statement is equivalent to the one requiring a solid fill in the display bars that I used in the DOS version of *ServerSim2*. The red/blue/green (RGB) components of the color to be used are set to red = 225, whereas blue and green are both set to 0. These parameters specify the color red.

Further down in the *TServWin* procedure, you encountered the bar-drawing statements. Here I used the RECTANGLE statement, which is very similar to the DOS-based Pascal BAR statement except for the *DC* that appears just within the parentheses. This variable provides a display context for the rectangles.

In case you missed it, the program itself came at the very end. All Windows applications programs have three statements, a Turbo Pascal object that initializes programs, a Turbo Pascal object that runs programs, and a Turbo Pascal object that cleans up the system when it's all over. If you have Turbo Pascal for Windows, you should run this program and experiment with it in the ways suggested in the Explorations to come.

Waiting, in Theory

Since their inception in the 1940s, computers have been used to simulate many artificial and natural processes. By building the rules that govern such processes into a program, scientists and engineers can study the behavior of such a system without actually building one or, in the case of a natural system, bringing it into the lab. Computers have been used to simulate electrical circuits, weather systems, molecular interactions, assembly lines, forest growth, predator–prey relations, projectile behavior, and so on. I could easily extend the list to fill the rest of this book!

The important field of simulation illustrates how computer science draws on many different disciplines for its techniques. The subject called operations research, begun during the Second World War, has developed into an impressive edifice of useful theory. In this section I will show how a purely theoretical approach to a subject can produce insights obtainable in no other way. You will learn about a simple queue in which abstract entities called *tokens* line up for an abstract service that removes them from the head of the queue at regular intervals. In particular, you will examine what happens to this abstract queue when the average rate of random arrivals exactly equals the regular service intervals. As one instance of such a queue, you might imagine an Internet server in which all the messages are 50 characters long. The network manager's nightmare scenario prevails: The amount of text arriving at the server still equals the rate at which the server processes the messages. In other words, messages arrive at the average rate of one per time cycle. Such a change in the server's diet does not necessarily alter the conclusion of the simulation study. You have already seen the message-file grow arbitrarily long under these very conditions.

If you have run any of the server simulation programs, you already know that long waits plague the impatient interactive user. If you were to alter the function *Message* so that it produced 50-character messages at an average rate of one per cycle (probability 1/2), you would discover exactly the same behavior. In case you think these delays are accidental, you might want to compare your results with the predictions of theory.

Now let's look at the queue. Imagine abstract entities called tokens that line up for processing at an abstract server. The tokens arrive according to various patterns, and the server processes them by causing them to disappear from the head of the queue, also according to various patterns. The many combinations of patterns of arrival and of service lead to a host of problems for queueing theorists to solve. In general, they try to develop formulas for the average queue length and other important measures of queueing activity.

In the adjacent figure, circles represent tokens and the box represents the server. Time passes in regular units, just as it did in the Internet simulation. If the tokens arrive randomly, at an average rate of one per time unit and the server gobbles them up at exactly this rate, what happens to the length of the queue?

In a more general setting tokens would arrive, on average, every a time units and be served, on average, every b time units. Under these conditions, queuing theory has a formula for the average length of the resulting queue.

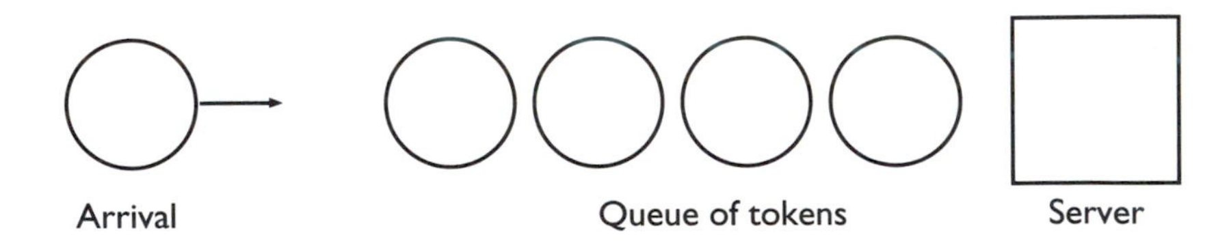

How long will the queue get?

$$\text{length} = \frac{1}{\frac{a}{b} - 1}$$

Since b, the average server-time, is fixed in the simulation program, we may regard the length of the queue as being a function of a alone. As you can see in the formula above, the length grows infinite as a approaches b in value.

From a simulation point of view, this simply means that when a equals b, there is no limit on how long the queue may grow! The curve in the next figure bears this observation out. The horizontal axis is marked off in b-units (whatever value the service time b happens to have). For example, at $a = 2b$, the formula predicts a long-term queue length of 1. At $a = 3b$, the formula predicts an average queue length of 0.5, and so on. But as a gets closer and closer to 1 from the right, the curve trends up

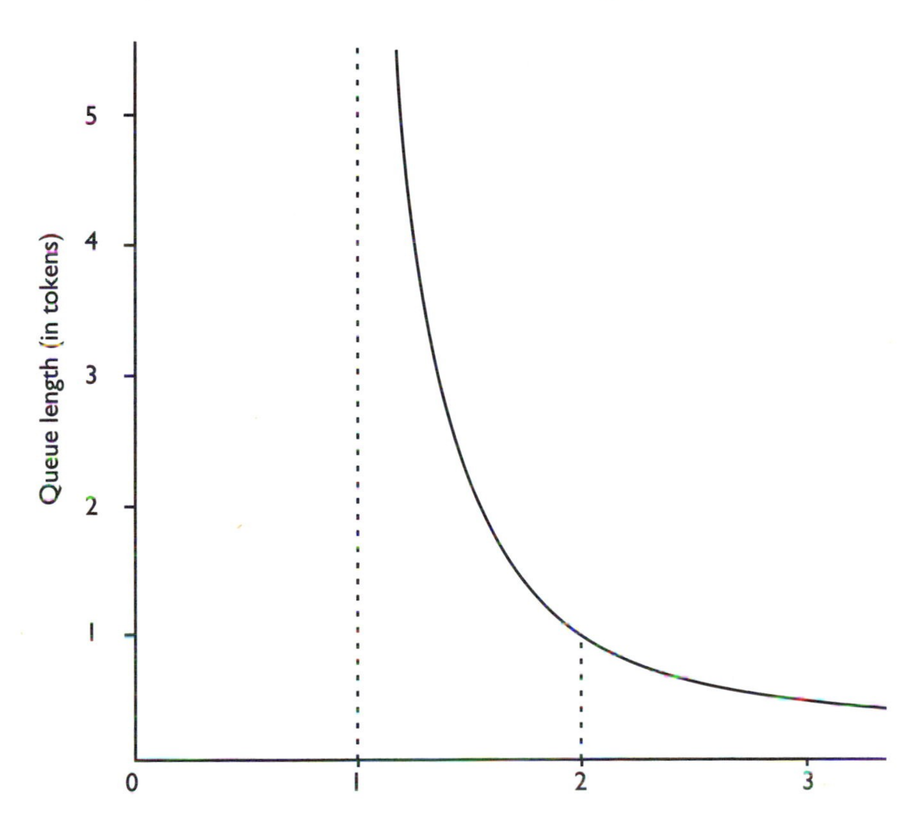

Queue lengths predicted by theory

without limit. The queues are getting impossibly long. Was the network manager's nightmare true?

Here comes a token. It could have come at any time, but here it is. The server will devour it in *b* time units no matter what happens. The question is, When will the next token come? Because tokens arrive every *b* time units only on average, nothing prevents them from being early or late. In fact, there is a 50:50 chance that the next token will arrive *after* the first token has disappeared.

In the following analysis, I will assume that $b = 1$. The conclusion I will reach will be true for all values of *b*, but the argument is simpler in this case.

If the first token disappears before the second token arrives, the server will be idle for a time. Let's call this time t_1. Following this, perhaps a bit of a queue builds up, then vanishes again. For another period of time, t_2, the server is idle again. Sooner or later, again and again, the server will be idle and new idle times, t_3, t_4, t_5, and so on, will occur.

The key question is this, "What is the real rate at which the server deals with tokens?" A bit of accounting provides the answer. If I take some long period of T time units that ends just as the server processes a token, I can produce a formula that tells me the average number of tokens processed per unit of time. To get this number, I must divide the total number of tokens processed, N, by T.

$$\frac{N}{T}$$

This formula will yield up its secrets if I divide the time T into two portions: the amount of time spent busily processing tokens and the idle time when the queue is empty. The idle time is the sum

$$t_1 + t_2 + t_3 + \ldots$$

If the server processes N tokens during time T, the busy time totals N time units and I can rewrite the formula as follows:

$$\frac{N}{N + t_1 + t_2 + t_3 + \ldots}$$

Now compare the numerator of the formula with the denominator. It is definitely smaller, so the actual rate at which the server processes the tokens is less than 1. In other words, the server processes tokens at an effective average rate of less than one token per time unit! The result can only be that the server gets further and further behind in its task of processing tokens, because idle time is lost forever and cannot be made up.

The behavior of the simulation program, in either graphics or non-graphics form, is fascinating to watch. Queues build up, then shrink to nothing. After shrinkages, when another bit of idle time occurs, the queues tend to become even longer. In the long run, the queues become arbitrarily long and the returns to idle time increasingly rare. Nevertheless, the occurrence of the idle times never wholly ceases, so the server just gets further and further behind. The formula, which predicts an infinite "long-term" average queue length, is quite correct!

SUMMARY

Your adventure on the Internet is over. You didn't surf, you simulated instead. In the course of writing the program ServerSim, the usefulness of subprograms like functions and procedures became apparent. You also learned something curious about what happens when messages queue up for processing. Even though the server can deal with them, character for character, at the same rate that they arrive in the average case, the server actually will get further and further behind because of the randomness of the interval between arrivals and the lost idle time. It wasn't until the final section of the chapter, when I probed the theory of queues, that the underlying reason for the problem was illuminated. Network managers beware! Keep a healthy margin between the arrival rate of text and the rate at which your server processes it into packets.

The ability of computer programmers to think in modules has progressed from dividing a program into neatly labeled sections to using subprograms and even objects. The latter modules are especially important to those who would use Windows-based Turbo Pascal for computer graphics.

EXPLORATIONS

1 Here is a function called *Length* that takes the parameter *A* and returns a value stored in the function name. For each value of *A* listed, state what value the function will return.

```
FUNCTION Length(A: REAL): REAL;
BEGIN
Length := 1/(A - 1);
END;
```

a $A = 2$; $A = 3$; $A = 3.5$

b Why does the keyword REAL appear twice in the function header?

c What value of *A* will cause a run-time error?

2 Write a function that takes two integer parameters, *This* and *That*, decides which of the two is larger, and carries this value in the function name.

3 Write a procedure that carries out the same calculation as the function in Exploration 1. It may use two VAR parameters, one to carry the value of *A* to the procedure, the other to carry the computed value back to the main program that calls it.

4 Run the program *ServerSim* and make a note of the maximum delay that it reports. Now repeat the experiment nine more times. What is the average maximum delay over the ten simulation runs? How much do the times vary over all the runs? Change the number 0.05 into a CONSTant called *Prob*. Set this constant to 0.01 and 0.02. What do you see happening to the waiting times?

5 Simplify the kind of queue that *ServerSim* simulates as suggested on page 240. Do this by changing the function *Message* as follows: Make the probability of the next message equal to 0.5 and do not use RANDOM to create new message lengths. Instead, set them all to 50.

6 Modify the *ServerSim* program so that it reports not only how large the message file got, but also the number of "ticks" into the simulation run at which the maximum size occurred.

7 What does the following program do? To save space, I have included only the relevant parts of the program. To answer this question fully, you should be familiar with the last section of this chapter.

```
PROGRAM PlotGraph;

VAR XCoord, YCoord: INTEGER;
VAR Token, QLength: REAL;

PROCEDURE Curve(VAR X, Y: REAL);
BEGIN
Y := 1/(X - 1);
END;

FOR Count := 1 TO 400 DO
   BEGIN
   XCoord := Count + 100;
   Token := 1 + (XCoord - 100)/400;
   Curve(Token, QLength);
   YCoord := TRUNC(QLength);
   PUTPIXEL(XCoord, YCoord, 4);
   END;

END.
```

8 Run the *ServerSim2* program and report on its behavior. How long did the message file get? In most runs, you should see it go off the screen.

9 Can you devise a ruler with which you can measure the horizontal bar that represents the variable *MessFile* on the screen? Your ruler should be marked off in tenths of a second. How can you be sure that the ruler works?

10 Write a graphics program that uses a function to draw squares on the display screen at random. The program must select random coordinates for the squares, random colors and random sizes (within limits) for the squares. The function must be called with four parameters, two for the position of the square, one for the color, and one for the size. It then draws the right kind of square on the screen.

11 A project for the ambitious: Write a program that does conversions between the English and metric system for at least three kinds of units: meters/feet; kilograms/pounds; degrees Celsius/degrees Fahrenheit. At the user's request, each conversion can go in either direction. Perhaps you can design a procedure that will work with all the conversions and in both directions. After all, each conversion involves the same basic formula, consisting of a multiplication and an addition.

12 Add a new method to the security director's program in the section on objects. The new method should write out the array called *Codes*. Modify the program by invoking this method to print out the array that the user inputs at the beginning. That way the security chief can confirm that the code was indeed changed.

13 In a simple queue like the one described in the last section of this chapter, what would be the expected, long-term queue size when the average number of tokens arriving per unit time (a) is a. 2; b. 3; c. 3.5?

14 Suppose the server has just disposed of the one token in a queue. What is the probability of a token arriving during the next time unit? What is the probability of no tokens arriving for three time units? [Hint: Multiply the probabilities of no token arriving in the next time unit.]

8 Public and Private Codes

Characters, Words, and Files

Mention the word "computers" and most people think of numbers. The fact that computers deal equally well with words mystifies more than a few people, even the ones who use word processing software on a regular basis. The secret is, of course, that even when computers seem to be processing words, they are actually working with numbers. The key to word processing (and all computer operations involving words) lies in a table that relates individual keyboard characters to numbers that represent them in the computer.

To provide a focus for your first view of a new world of words, let's simultaneously look at the cloak-and-dagger world of data security. The programs in this chapter will code and decode documents that include, for example, secret plans for a warp drive. A quick analysis reveals the need for some new Turbo Pascal tools. As it turns out, there are two built-in functions, one to turn characters into their corresponding numbers and one that goes the other way. I will introduce modular addition in order to build what spies call a polyalphabetic cipher. And I will talk about CASE statements to use with a procedure that enciphers individual characters.

Most programs, like the ones in this book, use words to interact with users. But some programs deal so extensively with words that they require a special memory medium to store them all. They use disks or diskettes to store *files*. Many of today's computers (like the Simplex 2000) use both a hard disk and floppy disks. Much of the information stored on disks takes the form of files. This chapter deals with the simplest kind of files, called *text files*. Four new Turbo Pascal statements enable the encryption program to read a file, encrypt it, then store it back in a file again, safe from invading hackers.

The computer science excursion looks at coding from a broader perspective, not security from prying eyes, but safety from the digital accidents that beset every transmitted message. Whether through wires, microwave beams, or radio transmission, binary messages lose bits or are otherwise altered. By padding your message with a few extra bits, you can protect it from errors.

The *CodeMaker* Project

Even before the time of the Romans, people used secret codes to send private information to other people. The idea was to scramble the message in a systematic way that nevertheless *looked* random to an interloper. The system that scrambled the message also had a reverse gear that enabled the recipient to unscramble it. It was hoped that spies would never discover the key to the code.

The Caesar Code

The famous Caesar cipher was simplicity itself. You can pick it up in a second. Simply arrange the alphabet in a circle and pick a number, say, 7. The *plaintext*, the message you want to encode, can be translated letter for letter into a new message by shifting each character around the circle by seven positions. For example, the adjacent figure shows what happens to the word SECRET when each letter is shifted seven positions clockwise. The new word, ZLJYLA, forms part of the *ciphertext*, the encoded message that now looks completely unreadable. Notice how every letter of the word SECRET gets shifted by the code exactly seven positions in the clockwise direction. The letter T, in fact, gets shifted just far enough to move it right off the end of the alphabet. However, because the end now joins the beginning, T merely becomes A.

The Caesar code encrypts the word SECRET

The Caesar code is easy to break, as you might suspect, but the *polyalphabetic cipher* is slightly more secure. In this code, the key is not a single shift number, like 7, but three of them. Suppose the key is the three-part number (5, 2, 8). The idea is to cycle through these numbers as you read the plaintext, character by character. Each character will be shifted by the amount of the current number. Here is what would happen to the word SECRET in this case.

S — +5 ⟶ X
E — +2 ⟶ G
C — +8 ⟶ K
R — +5 ⟶ W
E — +2 ⟶ G
T — +8 ⟶ B

SECRET ⟶ XGKWGB

I'm sure you could cheerfully design and write a program called *CodeMaker* if you only knew how to make a program count off letters! Of course, one way to count off letters is to number them from 1 to 26. To shift a letter, you simply shift its corresponding number by adding the shift to it. The new number represents a new character, the encrypted version of the one you started with.

As it happens, there is already a numbering system for letters, and it is already built into the computer. The system, called the *ASCII code*, extends to every character on the keyboard. Why bother reinventing the wheel? After I explain this public code, I will present two new Turbo Pascal functions that will turn characters into their ACSII code numbers and numbers back into characters. This public code will be the genesis of *CodeMaker*.

A Public Code

Most people who use computers don't need to know that all the characters they type on the keyboard are essentially numbers. But, in fact, whenever they press any key, it transmits a number to the microprocessor. When a character appears on the screen or on the page of the printer, the microprocessor has just transmitted a number to the device in question.

The key to characters and, consequently, to all character processing by computers, lies in the ASCII code. The acronym hints at the application: *American Standard Code for Information Interchange*. The interchange in question might take place between a user and a computer or between two computers. It might involve only the few feet of wire that connect a keyboard with the computer proper; or it might span a distance of thousands of miles, zipping along telephone wire or fiber optic cable, or through empty space to a communications satellite. In all cases, the "information" is essentially numbers—eight-bit binary numbers, in fact, the ones that most people call *bytes*.

How much information can you store in eight bits? One way to probe this question is to find out how many different items an eight-bit byte might represent. This probe raises a new question, How many bytes are there? You could systematically list the bytes, but a neater way is to use a little induction. How many one-bit "bytes" are there? Just two, 0 and 1. How many two-bit "bytes" are there? They are 00, 01, 10, 11—four of them. How many three-bit bytes are there? It didn't take you long to discover that there are exactly eight of them. The pattern 2-4-8 ought to remind you of those so-called IQ tests where you are asked to complete the sequence. Does it not proceed to 16-32-64 and so on? By the time you get out to eight bits per byte, you will have 256 different bytes.

Each of the 256 bytes can be used to represent something. For example, imagine a telephone keypad with just two digits, 0 and 1, on it. A small community of 256 people could use such binary telephones, and their numbers could be stored in a directory in which each of the 256 numbers would be listed. In this case each number would stand for a

Walter Aikenhead	10010111
Theresa Arkwright	00111001
Axel Balushi	10101011
Manfred Bachmann	00110101
Anita Bick	11011101
.	
.	
.	

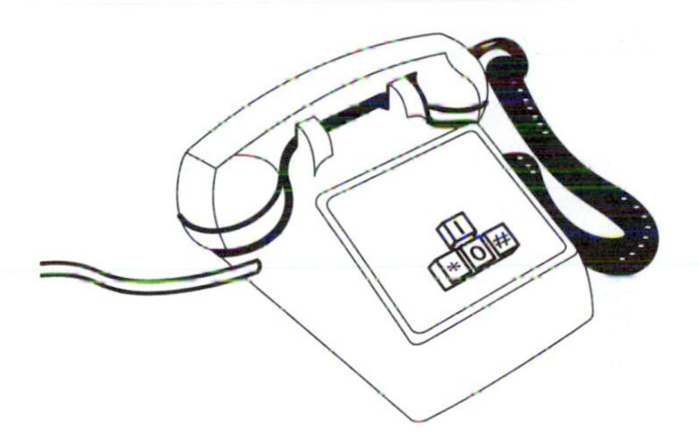

A binary telephone

different person. The switching equipment would translate each number into a ringing noise in the appropriate home.

In a similar manner, each of the 256 eight-bit bytes can be used to represent characters and symbols, one per combination, to communicate between machines.

Every character on a computer keyboard has a corresponding ASCII code number that ranges from 0 to 127. The table on page 252 shows the exact correspondence between code numbers and characters. The code numbers 0 to 31, as well as the very last code number, 127, correspond to nonprintable characters such as the carriage return (CR), end-of-transmission (EOT), or the escape key (ESC). The remaining numbers, 32 to 126, correspond to printable characters that you can easily find on your keyboard, characters that you have probably already typed many times before sitting down to a computer. In this chapter I use only the printable characters and their ASCII codes.

The digits 0 through 9 have code numbers 48 through 57. This correspondence illustrates the arbitrary nature of the ASCII code. Any matching between symbols and numbers is as good as any other. But as soon as a code is agreed upon, it must be adhered to rigidly if machines (and the people who use them) are to communicate with one another.

There are actually twice as many ASCII codes as are shown in the table on the next page. The other codes refer to specialized characters such as typographers' marks and other symbols that do not appear on standard keyboards.

Table of ASCII codes for keyboard characters

Code	*Character*	*Code*	*Character*	*Code*	*Character*	*Code*	*Character*
0	NUL	32	space	64	@	96	‘
1	SOH	33	!	65	A	97	a
2	STX	34	“	66	B	98	b
3	ETX	35	#	67	C	99	c
4	EOT	36	$	68	D	100	d
5	ENQ	37	%	69	E	101	e
6	ACK	38	&	70	F	102	f
7	BEL	39	’	71	G	103	g
8	BS	40	(	72	H	104	h
9	HT	41	)	73	I	105	i
10	LF	42	*	74	J	106	j
11	VT	43	+	75	K	107	k
12	FF	44	,	76	L	108	l
13	CR	45	-	77	M	109	m
14	SO	46	.	78	N	110	n
15	SI	47	/	79	O	111	o
16	DLE	48	0	80	P	112	p
17	DC1	49	1	81	Q	113	q
18	DC2	50	2	82	R	114	r
19	DC3	51	3	83	S	115	s
20	DC4	52	4	84	T	116	t
21	NAK	53	5	85	U	117	u
22	SYN	54	6	86	V	118	v
23	ETB	55	7	87	W	119	w
24	CAN	56	8	88	X	120	x
25	EM	57	9	89	Y	121	y
26	SUB	58	:	90	Z	122	z
27	ESC	59	;	91	[	123	{
28	FS	60	<	92	\	124	|
29	GS	61	=	93	]	125	}
30	RS	62	>	94	^	126	~
31	US	63	?	95	_	127	DEL

From Numbers to Characters and Back

Many programs that deal with characters require a way to go back and forth between a character and the ASCII code for the character. In Turbo Pascal, two functions accomplish these tasks. The ORD function returns the ASCII code number for the character that appears as the function's parameter. The CHR function does the reverse. With a number in the range from 32 to 126 as the parameter, this function produces the corresponding character.

If you look at the ASCII table on page 252, you will find that 'Y' has the code number 89 and ']' (right square bracket) has the code number 93. The value of ORD('Y') will therefore be 89, whereas the value of ORD(']') will be 93. You must remember, when using the ORD function, always to enclose the character parameter in single quotes. Let's move in the opposite direction, from numbers to characters. The value of CHR(89) will be 'Y' and the value of CHR(93) will be ']'.

Suppose you have the following assignment statement:

```
Letter := CHR(89);
```

The character that corresponds to the ordinal number 89—namely, 'Y'—will be assigned as the value of the (CHAR) variable *Letter*. But the following assignment statement is quite different:

```
NumCode := ORD('Y');
```

This statement will assign the integer 89 (the ASCII code for the character 'Y') to the (INTEGER) variable *NumCode*. In more general settings, assignments that involve ORD and CHR with variable parameters will work in essentially the same way, as the following example shows:

```
NumCode := ORD(Letter);
```

When the computer executes this statement, it will look up the value of the parameter *Letter*, convert that character to the corresponding ASCII code number, then assign it to the variable *NumCode*. The assignment statement

```
Letter := CHR(NumCode);
```

works the same way but in the opposite direction. Whatever numerical value *NumCode* has between 32 and 126 will be converted by the CHR function to the corresponding character and assigned to the variable *Letter*.

Naturally, any variable to which you assign the value of ORD must be declared as INTEGER. Any variable to which you assign the value of CHR must be declared CHAR.

Before returning to the encryption project, let's try a simple exercise involving case conversion. Suppose you needed a program that could read some text and convert lowercase letters to uppercase letters, or vice versa. A glance at the ASCII table will show that the letters 'a' to 'z' use the numbers 97 to 122, inclusive, and the letters 'A' to 'Z' use the numbers 65 to 90, inclusive. To convert from lowercase to uppercase, then, a program would only have to subtract 32 from the code for a lowercase letter to get the code for the corresponding uppercase letter.

An 'f', for example, has the ASCII code 102. Subtract 32 and you get 70, the ASCII code for 'F'. Here's a simple little program fragment that will carry out the conversion perfectly:

```
READ(Lttr);
Nmbr := ORD(Lttr);
Nmbr := Nmbr - 32;
Lttr := CHR(Nmbr);
WRITE(Lttr);
```

Whatever lowercase letter the user enters, the program will first apply the function ORD to that letter, obtaining its ASCII code. The same statement will assign that number to the variable *Nmbr*. The next statement will reduce the number by 32, converting it to the ASCII equivalent of an uppercase letter. The fourth statement uses the function CHR to change the number back into its corresponding letter, and the fifth statement then WRITEs this character.

Mention of the ASCII "code" may have made you wonder whether this table has any connection with international espionage. As it happens, the ASCII code has nothing to do with encryption or secret codes. But the ASCII code can be used to good advantage by a program that encrypts sensitive documents.

Project: Security by Encryption

Now that you know what a polyalphabetic cipher is, you will understand the following program specification. You will also have some ideas for the program, based on the discussion of the ASCII table and the twin functions ORD and CHR.

> Many individuals, companies, institutions, and governments routinely handle sensitive information and data. Often, they will encrypt the data so that, were a hostile agent to obtain sensitive information, he or she would not be able to read it. Write a program that employs a polyalphabetic cipher to encrypt user messages that are read into a character array. The program must output the encrypted file to enable the user to check the encryption process. After you have learned about files, rewrite the program so that it reads a file instead of typed input. This program must then encrypt the file and store it as ciphertext. A further development will enable your program to work in reverse, decrypting encrypted files.

The polyalphabetic cipher discussed earlier could be algorithmically summarized in four steps:

1. Convert the character to its ordinal number.
2. Cyclically add a certain constant to this number.
3. Convert the new number back to a character.
4. Store it in the array.

Let's worry later about the loop that will contain these steps. For the present, try to visualize the execution of these steps as the user inputs the characters. As they stand, the steps make sense. Step 1, for example, must use the ORD function to convert a character into its corresponding ASCII code. Step 2 demands that a "certain constant" must be added to the ASCII code number. This step thus contains the seeds of an important part of the program, the cyclic process by which one of three keys will be added to the current ASCII number. In step 3, the CHR function will convert the result of step 2 back into a character. Step 4 is certainly straightforward. You already know how to store things in arrays. The only new feature here is the use of arrays to hold characters, namely, arrays of type CHAR.

In step 2, the phrase "cyclically add" refers to the process I outlined earlier, with the three different shifts applied in cyclical succession. This time, I will not be shifting letters but the numbers that correspond to them. The process could be called "wraparound addition." It means adding a constant to any number from within the entire range of ASCII keyboard numbers, from 32 to 126, but in a way that "wraps" those numbers that fall beyond the range.

For example, if the program were to add the constant 22, say, to an ASCII code number in this range, the new number will then lie somewhere in the range from 54 to 148. This is fine for numbers that end up with values of 126 or less, but what happens to the numbers that "spill over" the end of the range beyond 126? *CodeMaker* must "wrap" these back into the first 22 numbers of the range: This way, 127 just makes it into the low end of the range at 32, whereas the largest number, 148, "wraps" back to 53. The adjacent diagram illustrates the process. The actual calculation is simplicity itself: Merely subtract the size of the whole range (126 – 31 =) 95 from the new number!

Let's work quickly through an example of what the process would do with a character from the following message:

"The secret device has been concealed in a laundry bag."

Take the letter "s" from the word "secret," for example. It has the ASCII code number 115. When you add 22 to 115, you get 137, which is outside the range of allowed characters. In this case, the wraparound

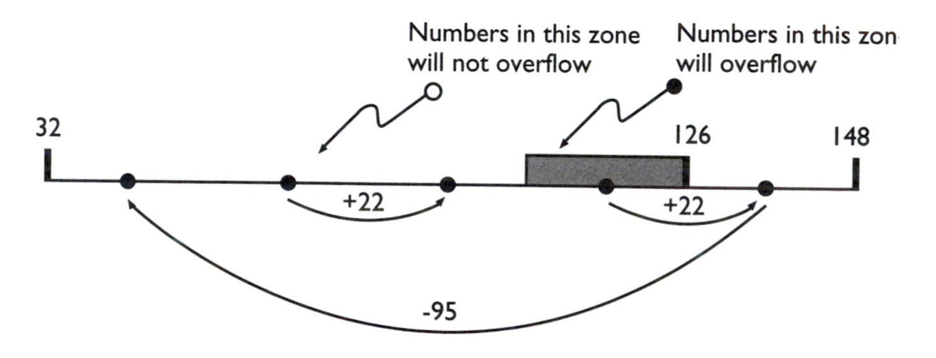

Wraparound addition

addition amounts to subtracting 95 from 137. The resulting number, 42, happens to be the ASCII code for the asterisk (*) character. *CodeMaker* would then use the CHR function to convert the number to its corresponding character, prior to storing it away in the array. Note in passing one advantage of the larger range of permitted characters; the resulting encrypted messages are more opaque when they end up with asterisks and other oddball symbols.

The first algorithm will use just four variables in addition to the loop indices: *Letter* will hold the input character; the array *Plain* will hold the complete message input by the user; the variable *Code* will hold the ASCII code for each input character; the array *Crypt* will hold the encrypted characters.

In all versions, I will use the key (6, 2, 38) in the *CodeMaker* program. This key consists of three numbers that the program will add cyclically to each character it processes.

Encryption Algorithm

```
{input section}
within a loop
   read characters into array Plain via the variable Letter
   (keep track of the number of characters)

{encryption section}
within a loop
   recall characters from Plain as the variable Letter
   depending on the value of the index K
      call procedure with a key value and Letter as parameters
   store Letter in array Crypt

{output section}
within a loop
   output (encrypted) letters on the screen
```

To make the whole program as simple as possible, I have separated the algorithm into three distinct modules, one for inputting the text to be encrypted, one to do the encryption, and one for outputting the encrypted text—to reassure the user that the encryption has taken place correctly. In the first module, the algorithm calls for a loop within which the user types characters at the keyboard. As each character enters the computer, it is stored in the character array *Plain* (short for plaintext). At the same time, the loop must count the number of characters entered. This first loop cannot be a FOR-loop because the number of characters cannot be known in advance. By counting the characters as they come in, however, this initial loop will make it possible for subsequent loops to be FOR-loops.

I will live with one limitation when it comes to character input. When the user comes to the end of a line, he or she might type a carriage return (the ENTER key) to get to the next line. The ASCII code for the carriage return (see CR in the table on page 252) is 13 and this will not be translated by the program into a character in the proper range from 32 to 126. For this reason, I will limit the program to the entry of a single line of text. Until I get to the next version of the program, which will read files, secrets will be short.

The second module is more complicated. Because the encryption process will use three different key values over and over again, it really should be made into a procedure. If it were not, you would have to repeat the encryption process three times within the program, once for each possible key value. Thus the second module calls for a FOR-loop within which each character is read from the plaintext array, *Plain*.

Having read the latest character into the variable called *Letter*, the algorithm next must use the index value of the FOR-loop to trigger the appropriate procedure call. Somehow the program must translate the successive values of the loop index, 1, 2, 3, 4, and so on, into a cyclic sequence of procedure calls that will use the key values 6, 2, 38, 6, 2, 38, over and over again, as long as the characters last. Enter the next Turbo Pascal tool, MOD.

Modular Division

Modular division is a very old mathematical operation. It is used whenever humans form teams for various projects by "telling off" candidates. Suppose you want seven teams or task forces. The first candidate goes to team 1, the second to team 2, and so on, until the seventh candidate goes to team 7. The modularity comes in with the eighth candidate, who goes into team 1. The ninth goes to team 2. In other words, the next group of seven candidates goes into the same seven teams that the first seven candidates went into.

Suppose now that the teams are called 0 through 6 instead of 1 through 7. This seems like a very small change, but it makes a big difference. It permits me to give a numerical definition to the telling-off process. Thus candidate 372, for example, will go to the team that you get by looking at the remainder of the division 372 /7. The remainder is 1, so the 372nd candidate goes to team 1. The 371st candidate, by the same token, must have gone to team 0. When you are only interested in the remainder after dividing one integer by another, you are doing modular division. The number you divide by is called the **modulus**. In this example, the modulus is the number 7.

In Turbo Pascal, the operator called MOD must appear in any arithmetic statement that does modular division. The syntax looks like this:

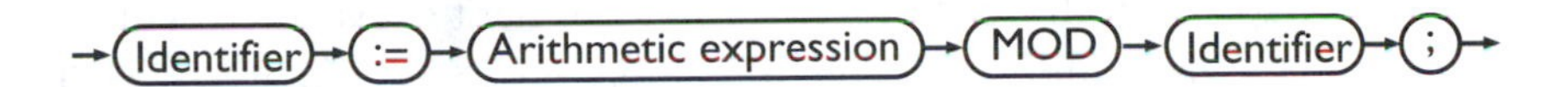

This is an arithmetic assignment statement to which the MOD operator has been added, along with an identifier that will act as the modulus, or number to divide by. The arithmetic expression must evaluate to an integer; so the identifiers must both be of type INTEGER.

Romans select teams

The computer will execute such a statement by first evaluating the arithmetic expression, then finding its value relative to the modulus. In other words, it divides the value of the expression by the modulus and assigns the remainder to the identifier on the left-hand side of the := sign.

Suppose the variable *Candidate* contains the number of the current candidate for team membership. Which team should he or she belong to? The following Turbo Pascal statement, which follows the MOD statement syntax, will do the calculation, placing the final result in the INTEGER variable *Team*.

```
Team := Candidate Mod 5;
```

Notice that the variable Candidate, all by itself, constitutes an example (albeit a humble one) of an arithmetic expression. Whatever value this expression happens to have at the time this statement is executed will be divided by the modulus (5). The remainder from that division will become the newly assigned value for the variable *Team*.

Within the *CodeMaker* program, I will use the MOD operator to convert the values of the index variable *K* into successive values 0, 1, 2, 0, 1, 2, and so on. Three separate IF–THEN statements could then serve to call the encryption procedures, which have the key values 6, 2, and 38, respectively. But I'm getting ahead of myself.

CodeMaker Refined

Now I'm ready to refine the basic algorithmic plan. I will start by writing the procedure in algorithmic form. The procedure itself simply implements the encryption process outlined earlier. It takes the value of the key into the formal parameter called *Shift* and the character value into the formal parameter called *Code*:

```
procedure name: Encrypt
parameters: Shift, Code

set NumCode to ordinal number of Code
if NumCode + Shift <= 126
   then set NumCode to NumCode + Shift
   else set NumCode to NumCode + Shift - 95

set Code to character for NumCode
```

The procedure is so close to a Turbo Pascal formulation that you could almost translate it immediately into a procedure. The procedure changes the character entered by the user into its ASCII number, then tests whether the shifted number will remain within the required range (up to character number 126). If the shifted number falls within the range, the procedure simply adds the value of *Shift* to the ASCII value in *NumCode*. But if the shifted number overflows, the procedure adds the shift, but subtracts 95, as I had already planned to do.

The procedure, when translated and installed in the program, will be called with three different values of the parameter *Shift*, namely, 6, 2, and 38, the three key values of my polyalphabetic cipher. In connection with this parameter, some additional information on parameters and procedures will come in handy.

The rest of the algorithm for *CodeMaker* refines what I have already laid out. I have added titles to the main modules, anticipating titles in the finished program. Let's examine the refined algorithm, module by module. I start with the header and input module.

```
program name: CodeMaker

variables used: Count, Letter, Index
arrays used: Plain, Crypt

{prompt module}
output: operating instructions to user

{input module}
set Count to 0
while Letter not equal to 126 (the tilde)
   input: Letter
   Count := Count + 1
   Plain[Count] := Letter
```

You may recall my earlier concern about how to count the number of characters in the message entered by the user. There's no problem incrementing a variable like *Count* every time through the loop, but how do you know when the user is done? One way is to use a special termination character. When the user enters this character, the program

Value Parameters

In the previous chapter, you learned about VAR parameters, which were capable of carrying information both *to* procedures and back *from* them. What shall I do with a parameter like *Shift*, which supplies vital information to the procedure but does not need to carry any information back from it. For such a purpose, Turbo Pascal has another kind of parameter. Called a *value parameter*, it carries information *to* the procedure only. Value parameters are declared exactly like VAR parameters, except the VAR key word in front of the parameter is omitted.

will consider the message to have ended. Naturally, you must use a character so unpopular that the user is unlikely to include it in a message. The tilde (~) character (ASCII code 126) should serve this purpose very nicely; and I have used a while-loop to test for this character on every iteration. The loop will exit as soon as it encounters a tilde in the stream of input characters entered by the user.

The encryption module will call the procedure *Encrypt* once it has figured out which key value to call it with:

```
{encryption module}
for Index running from 1 to Count
   set K to Index modulo 3
   set Letter to Plain[Index]
   if K = 0 then call Encrypt(6, Letter)
   if K = 1 then call Encrypt(2, Letter)
   if K = 2 then call Encrypt(38, Letter)
   set Crypt[Index] to Letter
```

To implement the step

```
set K to Index modulo 3,
```

the program will use the MOD function to convert the value of *Index* into one of the numbers 0, 1, or 2. On the basis of these values, three IF–THEN statements will call the procedure with the appropriate key value.

The final module is straightforward:

{output module}
output: "The encrypted text is: "
for *Index* running from 1 to *Count*
  set *Letter* to *Crypt*[*Index*]
  output: *Letter*

The *CodeMaker* Program

The program *CodeMaker* is listed below, minus its header and variable declarations. These elements appear in the Exploration section at the end of this chapter, along with a challenge to reconstruct them. In any event, you already know that a procedure must be declared at the head of a program. For obvious reasons, I include the procedure *Encrypt* and start the program there:

```
PROCEDURE Encrypt(Shift: INTEGER, VAR Code: CHAR);
VAR NumCode: INTEGER;
BEGIN
NumCode := ORD(Code);
IF NumCode + Shift <= 126
   THEN NumCode := NumCode + Shift
   ELSE NumCode := NumCode + Shift - 95;
Code := CHR(NumCode);
END;

BEGIN {program}

{prompt module}
WRITELN;
WRITELN('Enter your message on one line and terminate');
WRITELN('with a tilde (~). The program will display the');
WRITELN('encrypted text when you press the ENTER key.');

{input module}
Count := 0;
Letter := 'A'; {Letter must be initialized.}
WHILE ORD(Letter) <> 126 DO
   BEGIN
   Count := Count + 1;
   READ(Letter);
   Plain[Count] := Letter;
   END;
```

READ versus READLN

Note the READ statement in the input module. The *CodeMaker* program provides an ideal excuse to introduce you to that READ statement. It has the same syntax as the READLN statement and takes the same kinds of variables within its parentheses. However, it works a little differently.

A program that contains a READLN statement with a single variable, say, reads in the value typed by the user and ignores all other input until the screen cursor has advanced to the next line. The READ statement, on the other hand, can continue to read in values that the user enters on the same line.

Files also contain lines that are separated by invisible end-of-line markers. The execution of a READLN will cause the file cursor to jump to the next line of the file after it reads a single variable, so all the remaining data on the current line is ignored. I don't want this to happen with my text files, so I have used READ instead of READLN in the program.

```
{main loop: encryption module}
FOR Index := 1 TO Count DO
   BEGIN
   K := Index MOD 3;
   Letter := Plain[Index];
   IF K = 0 THEN Encrypt(6, Letter);
   IF K = 1 THEN Encrypt(2, Letter);
   IF K = 2 THEN Encrypt(38, Letter);
   Crypt[Index] := Letter;
   END;

{output module}
WRITELN;
WRITELN('The encrypted text is:');
FOR Index := 1 TO Count DO
   BEGIN
   Letter := Crypt[Index];
   WRITE(Letter);
   END;
END.
```

You will notice that I split the algorithm's input module into two parts, thereby forming a prompt module and an input module. The decision was as much aesthetic as practical, but it seems to make the *CodeMaker* program easier to read.

The *CodeMaker* program gives you an opportunity to review how procedures work. The procedure *Encrypt* has two formal parameters called *Shift* and *Code*. The first parameter is a value parameter. It is not preceded by the VAR word. It carries information in only one direction—to the procedure from its corresponding actual parameter, a number in the call to *Encrypt*. The accompanying figure illustrates the difference between these two types of parameters. Within the procedure, the parameters *Shift* and *Code* work just like ordinary variables, one of type INTEGER, the other of type CHAR.

Within the main program, the IF–THEN statements in the encryption module call the procedure, each time with actual parameters that consist of a constant (the key value) and the variable *Letter*. According to the rules for procedure calls, the values of the actual parameters are taken directly into the corresponding formal parameters. When the program executes the second IF–THEN statement, for example, it will place the value 2 in the formal parameter *Shift* and place the character stored in *Letter* in the formal parameter *Code*.

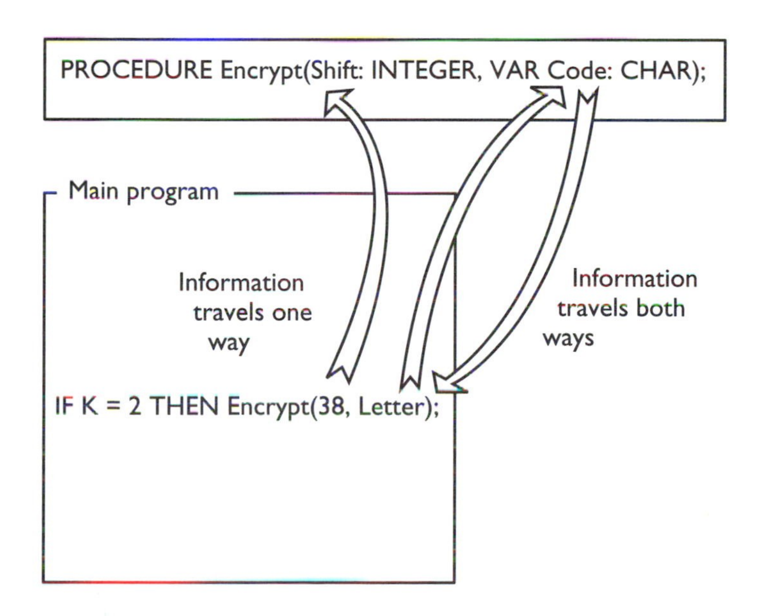

Difference between a value parameter and a VAR parameter

When the computer has finished executing the procedure *Encrypt*, it will have a new character stored in the formal parameter *Code*. The computer carries this character back to the main program and stores it in the actual parameter *Letter*. The computer ignores the value of the formal parameter *Shift* because it is a value parameter and not a VAR parameter. The computer does not carry that value back to the main program.

Just in CASE

I could improve the *CodeMaker* program by using a new Turbo Pascal statement type, CASE. It is sometimes possible to replace a whole series of IF–THEN statements by a single Turbo Pascal CASE statement. For example, here is a fragment from a program that builds a record of bird sightings. The section shown uses a character variable called *Bird* to decide which category of the histogram array to increment next.

```
IF Bird = 'R' THEN Robins := Robins + 1;
IF Bird = 'B' THEN Bluejays := Bluejays + 1;
IF Bird = 'C' THEN Cardinals := Cardinals + 1;
IF Bird = 'S' THEN Sparrows := Sparrows + 1;
```

This string of IF statements can be replaced by a single CASE statement, as follows:

```
CASE Bird OF
   'R': Robins := Robins + 1;
   'B': Bluejays := Bluejays + 1;
   'C': Cardinals := Cardinals + 1;
   'S': Sparrows := Sparrows + 1;
END;
```

Depending on the case or value of the variable *Bird*, the computer will execute only one of four assignment statements, just as the four IF–THEN statements collectively would have done. CASE statements are not used only to replace a series of IF–THEN statements. They come into play whenever the program has several alternatives to check and needs to take only one course of action as a result. A series of IF–THEN statements will all be executed and allow several courses of action to be followed.

The accompanying syntax diagram hints at the great flexibility that CASE statements can give to programs. Notice that any expression can

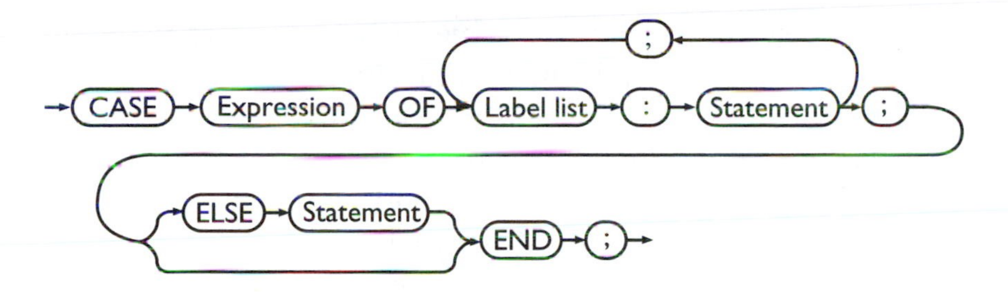

Syntax of the CASE statement

follow the Pascal word CASE and that any statement can be part of the action performed as a response to each case encountered. The diagram contains one term that will be new to you: A *label list* consists of a series of constants (either INTEGER or CHAR) separated by commas.

Following the Pascal word CASE, you may use any expression you like, provided it is *ordinal type*, that is, a type with values that have a predefined order. INTEGER and CHAR are ordinal types, for example, but REAL is not. When the computer executes the statement, it automatically evaluates the expression and then determines which category, if any, it falls under.

In the previous program, each category consisted of just one constant, but you may list as many constants as you like for a category, as long as you separate them by commas. As you can see from the lower part of the syntax diagram, one may add a catchall ELSE category to a CASE statement. There may be some action the program should take if none of the listed alternatives happens to prevail. This action is carried out by the "statement" following the ELSE. In all cases, the END statement needs no BEGIN to match it. The Pascal compiler will match the END with the Pascal word CASE instead. I am now ready to install the CASE statement in the next version of *CodeMaker*.

The *CodeMaker* File

As you already know, processing files via arrays of characters is a tedious business. First of all, the user must create whatever array he or she wishes to work with, and the array itself will vanish when the program has finished execution. Second, there is a limit to how large an array most Turbo Pascal systems will accommodate.

For large and permanent records, you need files. Although the main memory of your computer can hold portions of files at any one time, only disks and diskettes provide a proper home for them. The hard disk of any modern microcomputer has room for many, large files. The diskettes or floppy diskettes that you insert in the auxiliary drive(s) of your machine have room, collectively, for many more.

I will illustrate how Turbo Pascal files work by modifying the *CodeMaker* program to read from and write to files. First, however, you need to know more about how Turbo Pascal allows a programmer to give his or her own names to files that already have another name in the computer's filing system.

Filling Up Files

In either the DOS-based or Windows-based Turbo Pascal environment, all files have two names, an *external name* that identifies the file outside a program and an internal name, or *handle*, that identifies the file within a program. Whenever you examine your directory, you see the external names of files. These names have up to eight characters, followed by a special name called an *extension*. A period or dot separates the filename from its extension. For example, the file that contains the text of plans for a secret warp drive is called SECRETS.TXT. The extension TXT, as you might guess, means "text." There are many other kinds of extensions, including PAS for Pascal programs and BAK for back-up files. I will discuss only TXT files.

Turbo Pascal allows considerable latitude in giving files internal names or handles. Any valid Turbo Pascal identifier can become a handle. But a Turbo Pascal program in this environment must first declare the files:

```
VAR Plain: TEXT;
```

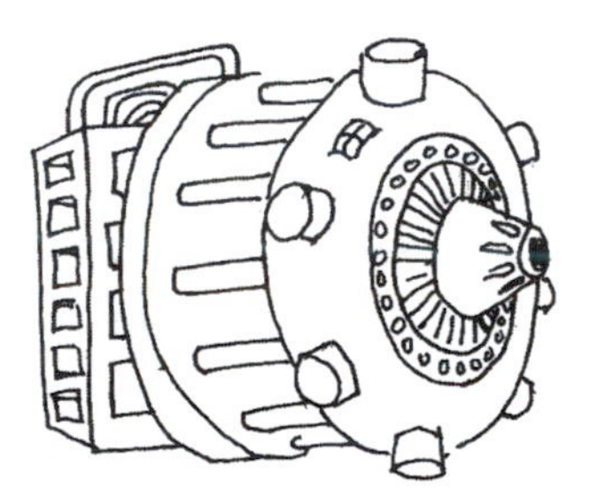

Details of the warp drive are contained in a file

This declaration statement follows the same basic syntax that other declarations use.

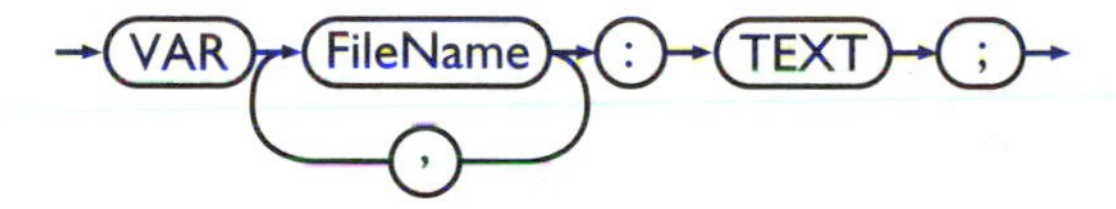

A file-based program must then create a link between the external name and its own two names by using an ASSIGN statement. This statement does not appear in the declarations but at some other point in the program. Before the program can READ from or WRITE to a file, it must ASSIGN the external file name to the program's handle for that file.

The new version of *CodeMaker* will read from a file with the external name SECRETS.TXT and write to a file called TRANSMIT.TXT. The ASSIGN statements used by this version of the program look like this:

```
ASSIGN(Plain, 'SECRETS.TXT');
ASSIGN(Crypt, 'TRANSMIT.TXT');
```

The program uses two handles for these files, *Plain* and *Crypt*. The file SECRETS.TXT contains a secret message that needs to be encrypted before it falls into the wrong hands. *CodeMaker* ASSIGNs this external name to its own file with the handle *Plain*, a name that helps the programmer remember that this file contains plaintext. The file TRANSMIT.TXT will contain the encrypted version of the message in SECRETS.TXT, the idea being that this file, once filled with encrypted text, will be safe to transmit. The program ASSIGNs the DOS name TRANSMIT.TXT to the file with the handle *Crypt*, a name that also reflects the idea of an encrypted text. By making such links, the program lets the Pascal programming system know which (external) file the program refers to when it calls for action on either *Plain* or *Crypt*.

To READ a file, a Pascal program must first open it for reading via the RESET statement. This instruction resets a variable called the *file cursor* back to the beginning of the corresponding external file. Thus, when the program reads the file, it will start at the very beginning. For example, *CodeMaker* RESETs the file SECRETS.TXT through its surrogate *Plain* as follows:

```
RESET(Plain);
```

The file *Plain* is now ready to read from the beginning. The computer knows that the name *Plain* refers to the external file SECRETS.TXT because the ASSIGN statement has already forged the link between the two names.

It will not surprise you to learn that Turbo Pascal also makes parallel provisions for WRITEing to a file. To reset the writing cursor to the beginning of a file to be written, Turbo Pascal provides the REWRITE statement. Here, for example, is how the new version of *CodeMaker* will use this command for the file called *Crypt*:

```
REWRITE(Crypt);
```

When the computer executes this statement, the file *Crypt* will be ready to write to. Moving the writing cursor back to the beginning of the file effectively erases whatever was there before. The computer knows that the name *Crypt* refers to the external file TRANSMIT.TXT, because this handle was already ASSIGNed to that file.

When the computer executes these new statements in the revised version of *CodeMaker*, the file *Plain* will be ready to read from and the file *Crypt* will be ready to write to. In the revised program, the READLN and WRITELN statements must now include an extra parameter, namely, the name of the file to be read from or written to. In the program to follow, you will find these two statements:

```
READ(Plain, Letter);

WRITE(Crypt, Letter);
```

Both statements function just like regular READ and WRITE statements except that only one of the parameters, the second, indicates ordinary variables. The first parameter in both cases is the name of a file. This name tells the computer where to find the value in question. The first statement reads a single character from the file called *Plain* and places that character in the CHAR variable *Letter*. In the second statement, just the reverse happens. It writes a single character from *Letter* to the file called *Crypt*.

Using Files in *CodeMaker2*

To illustrate these new file capabilities and to advance the art of encryption, all at one go, here is the new version of *CodeMaker*. Called *CodeMaker2*, it reads the *Plain* file one character at a time, encrypts that character by using the same procedure that appeared in *CodeMaker*. It then stores the character in *Crypt*.

The program *CodeMaker2* lacks a header and variable declarations, just as *CodeMaker* did (see Exploration 8 at the end of the chapter).

```
PROCEDURE Encrypt(Shift: INTEGER, VAR Code: CHAR);
VAR NumCode: INTEGER;
BEGIN
NumCode := ORD(Code);
IF NumCode + Shift <= 126
   THEN NumCode := NumCode + Shift
   ELSE NumCode := NumCode + Shift - 95;
Code := CHR(NumCode);
END;

BEGIN {program}

{file initializing module}
ASSIGN(Plain, 'SECRETS.TXT');
RESET(Plain);
ASSIGN(Crypt, 'TRANSMIT.TXT');
REWRITE(Crypt);

{Reading, encoding, and writing module}
Count := 0;
WHILE NOT EOF(Plain) DO
   BEGIN
   Count := Count + 1;
   READ(Plain, Letter);
   K := Count MOD 3;
   CASE K OF
      0: Encrypt(6, Letter);
      1: Encrypt(2, Letter);
      2: Encrypt(38, Letter);
      END; {case}
   WRITE(Crypt, Letter);
   END;
CLOSE(Plain);
```

```
CLOSE(Crypt); {NOTE: If you don't do this,}
              {the next WRITELN may malfunction.}

{output module}
RESET(Crypt);
WRITELN;
WRITELN('The encrypted text is:');
WHILE NOT EOF(Crypt) DO
   BEGIN
   READ(Crypt, Letter);
   WRITE(Letter);
   END;
CLOSE(Crypt);

END.
```

CodeMaker2 differs from its predecessor in a number of respects. Not only does it contain new file processing statements, but it has a different form, as a result of differences in the ways an encryption program deals with files and arrays. For one thing, the program no longer needs to ask the user for input to be read into an array. That section of the program has disappeared in the new version. I have also collapsed the reading and writing loops into one.

Following the general syntax for declarations, *CodeMaker2* declares its two files as follows:

```
VAR Plain, Crypt: TEXT;
```

Both files, naturally, are text files.

In its executable part, after the BEGIN, the program ASSIGNs external file names to the program file handles, *Plain* and *Crypt*. It opens *Plain* for reading via the RESET statement and opens *Crypt* for writing via the REWRITE statement.

The main loop, still a WHILE statement, now does everything. It reads the value stored at the current cursor position in *Plain* into the variable *Letter*. When it comes to calling *Encrypt*, however, it now does so from the midst of a CASE statement and not three IF–THEN statements. The program then writes the character now encrypted in *Letter* to the file *Crypt*. Unlike *CodeMaker*, however, *CodeMaker2* uses a different loop termination condition:

```
WHILE NOT EOF(Plain) DO
```

The built-in Pascal EOF (end-of-file) function returns a BOOLEAN value. During the execution of a program, it always is either TRUE or FALSE. As the program reads its way through a file, the EOF function remains FALSE. But as soon as the program arrives at the end of the file, EOF becomes true. Naturally, as long as EOF is FALSE, NOT EOF will be true, and the WHILE-loop will continue to execute. But the moment the program arrives at a special character called the *end-of-file marker*, EOF becomes true and NOT EOF becomes FALSE. Execution leaves the loop and passes on to the next instruction following it.

Because there is no need for a numerical loop control, the variable *Index* has disappeared from the program. The variable *Count* might seem to have replaced it, but *Count* has only one function, to provide a continuing flow of values 1, 2, 3, 4, and so on as inputs for the cyclic variable *K*.

When the WHILE-loop ceases executing, the program CLOSEs both files. All programs that use files must CLOSE them when they have finished with them. A program must even CLOSE a file after writing to it in order to read from it. In such a case, as in the present program, such a file must then be reopened.

The final module of the program reads the *Crypt* file and displays it for the user to see. This module uses the same kind of WHILE-loop that the previous module used, including the test for end of file (EOF). When it exits from the loop, it closes *Crypt*.

The development and discussion of *CodeMaker2* are complete now. But the Explorations at the end of this chapter contain a number of interesting ideas and projects related to the program.

Coding for Interference

Computer science has two branches that study codes. One branch, called cryptology, concerns the theory and development of ciphers, such as the one I have just implemented. The newest discoveries go well beyond this simple polyalphabetic cipher, however. Public key encryption, for example, is a scheme that conceals messages in hard-to-solve computational problems. You might even give the "opposition" the problem instance that conceals your message. To decode the message, they must solve the instance, which might take a hundred years on the fastest computer.

The other field of computer science that studies codes is called coding and information theory. The codes in question are not meant to protect sensitive data from prying eyes, rather they are used to prevent its bitwise destruction during transmission. Electrical interference can destroy or alter a signal, whether it travels through wires, air, or empty space.

The field was started by Claude Shannon, a computer science pioneer who worked as a research scientist at AT&T Bell Laboratories in the 1940s and 1950s. Shannon's concern was the safeguarding of communications from errors. Messages that were transmitted in bits, for example, might be corrupted by electronic noise in the transmission channel, whatever it might be. One of the bits might get changed from a 0 to a 1 or vice versa. Shannon and his successors in the field have constructed many clever *error-correcting codes* that use redundant bits to allow the receiver of a message to recover from such errors. Some of these codes have been used by the National Aeronautics and Space Administration for years. Most space probes, for example, transmit their pictures in bits, but only after translating them into an error-correcting code.

Here is a very simple example of a code that cannot correct errors but can detect them. The receiver can only determine that something went wrong with the message during transmission. Let's say that you're going to transmit a single bit to a friend, but you're afraid that it might get spoiled during its transmission. One way around this problem is to transmit this bit along with another, identical bit. If a single error alters the message as it speeds along a wire or crosses empty space, the receiver will know an error has occurred by detecting the fact that the two bits no longer match. For example, if you want to transmit a 1, you would add

NASA sends a photo by encoded signals

another 1 and transmit the message 11. A single error will convert this message into either 01 or 10. The receiver will know that an error has occurred when it detects the mismatched pair. A code that is able to detect errors like this is called an *error-detecting code.*

Unfortunately, the receiver will not be able to reconstruct the one-bit message from the two bits that arrived. If the message 01 arrives, for example, the receiver won't know whether you sent 00 and the second bit was corrupted or whether you sent 11 and the first bit was spoiled. Is it possible to devise a code that will also tell the receiver *which* bit got changed during transmission?

To devise an error-correcting code for the one-bit messages, I am going to shift the discussion to geometry and examine a cube. But, you say, what do cubes have to do with codes? Read on.

The cube shown in the next figure represents all possible three-bit binary numbers from 000 to 111. Only the corners and edges of the cube are shown, because these are the only parts relevant to codes. Next to each corner of the cube I have placed one of the three-bit numbers. I have placed them so that numbers on adjacent corners differ in just one bit. In fact, this is a crucial property of the placement.

Imagine now that you are a fly wandering along one of the edges of the cube. Every time you traverse an entire edge, traveling from one corner to another, you have moved a *Hamming distance* of 1. Traverse two consecutive edges and you have traversed a Hamming distance of 2. As you can see by examining the cube, the greatest Hamming distance between any two corners is 3.

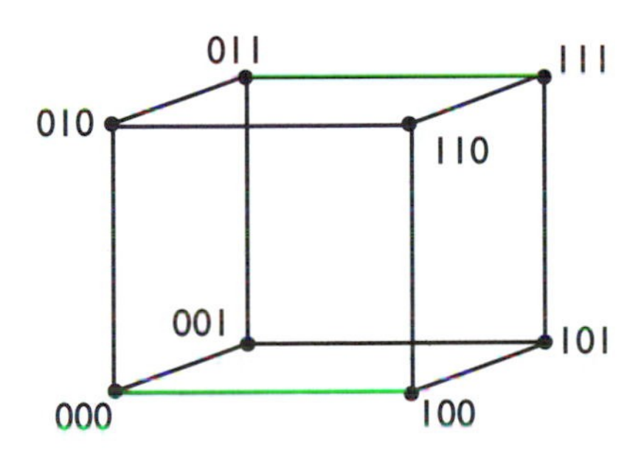

A cube and some codes

Now, instead of being a fly, imagine you're a three-bit number winging through space. Simultaneously, you inhabit one of the corners of the cube. If one of your bits gets changed, however, you move from that corner to an adjacent one with a label that matches your new bits. You have been changed. How will the receiver know what message you were carrying?

Consider two three-bit numbers that appear at opposite corners of the cube. If these numbers were adopted as a code, you and the person you intend to send messages to would share the following table:

Message bit	*Transmitted code word*
0	010
1	101

These code numbers have a Hamming distance of 3 from each other. If one of these numbers were transmitted to someone else and an error occurred, the receiver could still reconstruct the number you originally sent. For, with just one error in it, the corrupted message would still be closer to the original code number than to the other. The receiver, who also possesses the code, would know that this was the intended message.

Suppose you sent the 0-word, 010. If an error struck one of these bits, the receiver could end up getting any one of three numbers:

110, 000, or 011

Now these all differ from 010 in just one bit. On the other hand, they differ from the other code word, 101, in two bits. If you locate these numbers on the cube illustration on page 275, you will see that they are closer to the corner labeled 010 than to 101. The receiver would know that the intended message was 010 or "0." Of course, most messages consist of more than one bit. To transmit a multibit message such as 010110, each bit must first be encoded in the appropriate code word before transmission: 010 101 010 101 101 010.

By using higher dimensional cubes, in effect, one can construct codes that will detect and correct more than one error. The code used by space probes, for example, consists of 32 words, each 32 bits long. Used to transmit images of a distant planet to Earth, for example, each word of the code could carry any one of 32 possible gray-level values for an individual pixel. The code is so robust that up to seven errors can occur in a word as it crosses space, and the receiving station on Earth will still know what word must originally have been transmitted.

If you want to think about this space probe code in terms of geometrial figures, you must work with a 32-dimensional cube, which has 2^{32} corners. This is quite a lot. From these, a coding theorist would select the 32 corners that form the code. They are all separated from one another by a Hamming distance of 15. This is what gives the code its remarkable ability to correct up to seven errors.

Coding and information theory has many other applications to computing. For example, text with a certain amount of redundancy (common in most human languages) can be compressed by being appropriately encoded, sometimes with savings of up to half the memory space that the message might otherwise occupy.

SUMMARY

Now that you are among the character processing cognoscente, you have the ability to write a huge variety of programs that use or manipulate characters. In the last chapter of this book, you will even find a project that involves writing part of a word processor! The key to it all is a table called the ASCII code, along with the ORD and CHR functions that manage the translation back and forth between characters and their code numbers.

You also learned something about encryption with the creation of an encryption program called *CodeMaker*. If this exercise did not make you too paranoid, you will even be able to remember how to use some of the new Turbo Pascal tools, such as the CASE statement, modular division with MOD, and a new type of formal parameter that carries information in only one direction.

The cloak-and-dagger approach to programming culminated in the creation of a file-based version of *CodeMaker* that introduced you to all the main file processing statements such as ASSIGN, RESET, REWRITE, and CLOSE, and to the special forms of reading from and writing to files. Here, you had to remember to include the filename within the parentheses that accompany such statements.

The computer science excursion took a different view of codes, namely, how to protect binary messages from interference. While no amount of computer science can shield an actual message, it has a lot to tell you about how to structure such messages so that the receiver of a message can detect errors and even recover from them, as well.

EXPLORATIONS

1 Using the simple Caesar cipher outlined at the beginning of this chapter, try encoding the message, BARBARIANS INVADING FROM NORTH. Use a shift value of 8.

2 Now, using the polyalphabetic cipher with key (8, 13, 3), encode the message, "aliens invading from space." Use the ASCII table for this purpose. You won't have to translate between characters and numbers the way *CodeMaker* did, because you can simply examine the table and count the appropriate number of characters down its columns.

3 Suppose someone sends you a message that was encrypted by a polyalphabetic cipher such as (6, 2, 38). Can you decrypt the file? If you think about it, you can readily alter the *CodeMaker* program to do just this. It's a matter of changing the program key into a new one that was derived from (6, 2, 38). Can you come up with a general recipe, formula, or algorithm that will convert any coding key value into a decoding value?

4 Write down the values of the following functions. Consult the ASCII table, if necessary:

a ORD('K')
b CHR(85)
c ORD('%')
d CHR(33)

5 Modify the *CodeMaker* program by enabling the user to specify the three key values at the beginning of the program. Use this version of the program to test your answer to Exploration 3.

6 Modify the *CodeMaker* program to remove the restriction that the user can enter only one line of message. One way to do this is to include an additional test in the program for the Carriage Return signal (ASCII code 13). When the program recognizes this signal, it simply skips to the next, following character.

7 Suppose you want to write a program that constructs a histogram for the number of workers with 1, 2, 3, or 4 years of seniority. As part of this program, you will need a statement that processes the value of the variable *Senior*, which contains the seniority of a sequence of employees. Depending on the value, the program must increment an array called *Histogram* at the index value 1, 2, 3, or 4, as appropriate. Write a single CASE statement that will do all this and allow for the possibility of values outside the range from 1 to 4. For these values, you want to increment a single variable called *Safe*.

8 Without looking at the answer that appears at the end of these Explorations, (a) write your own header and declarations for the *CodeMaker* program, and (b) do the same for *CodeMaker2*.

9 Change the first and last modules in *CodeMaker* into procedures. The resulting program will then consist essentially of a procedure call, the encryption module as it presently stands, and another procedure call.

10 Here is a program that processes characters entered by the user. Explain the nature of the process once you have analyzed the program.

```
PROGRAM Echoes;

VAR Position, Index: INTEGER;
VAR NewChar: CHAR;
TYPE Charray = ARRAY[1..100] OF CHAR;
VAR Stuff: Charray;

BEGIN
WRITE('Please begin typing: ');
Position := 0;
REPEAT
   Position := Position + 1;
   READ(NewChar);
   Stuff[Position] := NewChar;
UNTIL ORD(NewChar) = 32;
WRITELN;
FOR Index := 1 TO Position DO
   WRITE(Stuff[Index]);
END.
```

11 Write a program that converts all lowercase letters in a file to uppercase letters. It should leave all other characters just as they are and replace the original file by the processed one.

12 Using information provided in this chapter, write a program that enables a user to enter a message text (in plain English) into a file for use by the *CodeMaker2* program. Design the program by writing an algorithm, refining it, then translating it into Pascal code.

13 Polyalphabetic ciphers, such as the type employed in this chapter, are very easy to break. Even more sophisticated encryption systems, such as public key encryption, have certain weaknesses. Only one encryption system is probably immune from a deciphering attack, the *one-time pad*. This system also employs shifts, but the key consists of an extremely long list of numbers. To obtain such a list, take any long text, even the one in SECRETS.TXT, and use the ordinal value of successive characters in the text as shift numbers for encrypting some other, entirely unrelated text. The text that provides the shift values is called a one-time pad because it can only be used once without fear of decryption. Write a Turbo Pascal program that uses one file, in this manner, to encrypt another.

14 Write a program that will convert an arbitrary, eight-bit binary number into the corresponding decimal number. Begin by designing an algorithm, then translating it into a program. Your program should accept the eight bits from the user one bit at a time. It should also include helpful prompts and screen messages.

15 Here is a simple code for transmitting the bits 0 and 1:

```
0: 000
1: 111
```

How many errors will this code detect? How many errors will it correct? Does it have any relationship to the three-bit code described in the last section?

16 Here are the first five words from a code similar to that used for space probes like *Mariner 7*. For each pair of words in this "code," determine the Hamming distance between them and place the distances in a 5×5 table. What error-detecting and error-correcting capabilities would the code consisting of these five words alone have?

0000000000000000
0101010101010101
0011001100110011
0110011001100110
0000111100001111

17 Write a Turbo Pascal program that decodes (possibly) corrupted messages by comparing them with 010 (representing 0) and 101 (representing 1). It will choose whichever of the two words is closest to the user-entered three-bit message, then it will inform the user whether a 0 or a 1 was transmitted.

Answer to Exploration 8a

```
PROGRAM CodeMaker;
{This program accepts a line of text from the user,}
{stores an encrypted version of the text in an array,}
{and outputs the array at the end of the session.}

VAR Index, K, Count: INTEGER
VAR Letter: CHAR;
TYPE Message = ARRAY[1 . . 80] OF CHAR;
VAR Plain, Crypt: Message;

PROGRAM CodeMaker2;
{This program reads text from a file, encrypts it,}
{stores the encrypted version in another file, and}
{then reads it to check the encryption process.}

{declarations module}
VAR K, Count: INTEGER;
VAR Letter: CHAR;
VAR Plain, Crypt: TEXT;
```

The Tortoise and the Hare

Searching and Time Complexity

You have reached an important point in this introductory journey into computer science. Up to now, the demands of learning a programming language have crowded these pages with programming advice and programs that illustrated the advice. It has been difficult, given these demands, to absorb much theory.

You are now in a position to blend theory and practice by exploring two key fields of computer science, algorithmic analysis and complexity theory. The setting will be a race between two programs, a slow one called *Tortoise* and a fast one called *Hare*. But don't expect any upsets. *Hare* will be very fast indeed.

Algorithmic analysis involves just what you'd expect, analyzing algorithms. What for? To see whether the programs that are based on them will run quickly or not. In particular, you will look at the problem of searching an array. How quickly can a program search an array for a particular item? The answer depends, in part, on how the items are organized. Algorithmic analysis leads the way by comparing two algorithms, one for a slow searching program called *Tortoise* and one for a fast searching algorithm called *Hare*. Strange as it may sound, you can "run" an algorithm without even writing a program.

Complexity theory focuses on individual problems (such as searching) and seeks to discover algorithms that solve the problem in the shortest possible time. The theory has established that some problems can be solved very quickly, whereas others may take the lifetime of the universe to solve. Still others cannot be solved at all!

You will apply algorithmic analysis to the *Tortoise* program and to *Hare* to prove that *Hare* is faster. Then you will watch an actual race to see the theory borne out.

The Racetrack

Imagine a very long array, filled with integers. If you want to search this array for a specific number, you might scan it from left to right. This could be called the tortoise approach, methodically moving from one entry to the next until you locate the item sought. If the item is not even in the array, you would plod on to the end before reporting that the item is not there.

3	9	14	24	25	41	47	64	73	75

The racetrack

Another way to search the array is to hop all around like a hare until you find the item sought (or discover that it's missing). The hare approach, however, requires a special order for the items. The figure above shows an array in which the integers are arranged in ascending order from left to right. Suppose you want to discover (by computer) whether the number 47 happens to be in this array. The *Tortoise* (if I may call the first method that) goes through the array from left to right, comparing each new number it encounters with the number 47. By the time it has visited seven elements, it discovers the 47. The *Hare*, on the other hand, would hop to the very middle of the array and compare the number there with 47. If the number there was larger than 47, then the Hare would "know" that it had gone too far. It would therefore hop back to the middle of the left half of the array. However, the number stored there is less than 47,

The tortoise and the hare

in this case. The *Hare* would thus make another hop forward to the middle of the right half of the array. The *Hare* would be using the fact that the data were already sorted into ascending order. By the time it found 47, it would have inspected a mere four elements.

I haven't told you everything about the *Hare's* method yet, but I will. In the meantime, in case it strikes you as odd that someone would be concerned about searching speeds, think for a moment about how often data must be searched in our computerized world.

Computers and Time

Computers first became popular because they helped to solve certain problems very quickly. Back in the 1950s, when computers could be found only in large businesses, universities, and government institutions, the problems they solved were pretty mundane. They computed payrolls, tracked inventory, or managed large files, such as customer accounts or social security numbers. It became immediately apparent, however, that the more computers were used, the more problems people continued to find for them to solve. And the size of problems that computers were expected to tackle also increased. It was one thing for an insurance company to search a file of several thousand accounts a few dozen times a day. It was quite another for a large bank to search a file of several million names thousands of times a day.

A high premium came to be placed on programs that ran as quickly as possible on the problems they were expected to solve. At the same time, hardware was getting faster. Programs that took several minutes to run on an earlier generation of machines now ran in seconds. But the improvements in speed only encouraged folks to tackle even larger problems.

Early on, computer scientists recognized the importance of applications and began the search for programs that would run quickly. However, they also recognized that it made sense to analyze running times in a general way. Rather than analyze specific programs running on specific computers, they found that it was possible to analyze the underlying algorithms much more conveniently and in a more meaningful way. They devised techniques that established how long it would take a program (or algorithm) to run, based on an order-of-magnitude scheme. For example, program A might be able to sort a file of n names in a time that was proportional to n^3, whereas program B could do the same job in a time that was proportional to n^2. Which program would you rather run?

The n^2 one, of course, because this number is much smaller, when n is large, than the other number.

Among the more useful techniques employed by computer scientists was the one called "divide-and-conquer." You may recall one application of the technique to quad trees at the end of Chapter 4. In general, the technique solves a problem by dividing it into two subproblems, then conquering them separately. If necessary, a problem may have to be subdivided more than once before any conquering is possible. Well, the divide-and-conquer technique resurfaces here, giving legs to the *Hare*.

A Tale of Two Algorithms

Although I have just spoken of the need to search large files, Turbo Pascal files cannot be searched as conveniently as arrays. That is why I will search "files" in the form of arrays. Moreover, because all files are essentially numbers anyway, I will strip everything down to essentials and work with numbers alone. The arrays considered will contain nothing but integers and, to be definite, they will have ten entries. Later, I will increase that number substantially. Here, without further ado, is the first algorithm. It searches an array called *NumFile*, sequentially:

Tortoise Algorithm

```
input a number as This
set Found to false
set Place to 1
while (Found = false) and (Place <= 10)
   set That to Numfile[Place]
   if This = That
      then set Found to true
      else increment Place
if Found = true
   then output: This, "found at", Place
   else output: This, "not found"
```

After a number called *This* has been input, the algorithm initializes the Boolean variable *Found* to false. It then enters a search loop in which hopefully, it will find the sought-after item and set *Found* to true. The counting variable *Place*, which is set to 1 before the loop starts, increases by 1 at the end of each iteration. If and when the algorithm finds the item, the value of *Place* will give its position in the array *NumFile*.

Some thought had to go into the loop, the first decision being whether to make it a FOR-loop or whether to make it a WHILE- or REPEAT-loop. If I weren't so eager for this algorithm to run as quickly as possible, I would be content with a FOR-loop. After all, I know exactly how big the array is and a FOR-loop need only index its way through the entire array. But, if the algorithm happens to find *This* early in the array, why should it waste time iterating, fruitlessly searching the rest of the file? The *Tortoise* program will need all the time-saving help it can get.

A WHILE-loop will certainly provide the early-exit facility, but there are now two ways that it can end: It may find the item, as already mentioned, or it may not find it. In the latter case, it will work its way through the entire array. There are two ways the algorithm can exit from the loop:

1. *Found* becomes true,
2. *Index* reaches 10, the size of the array *NumFile*.

Within the loop, the algorithm simply assigns numbers, one at a time, from *NumFile* into the variable *That*. It tests the truth of the expression

This = *That*

that is, whether the number sought happens to equal the one currently read in from the array. If the expression is true, the IF-statement sets *Found* equal to TRUE. When the computer has finished executing the loop, it reports its success or lack of it to the user, depending on the value of *Found*.

I have, of course, prejudged the race between the algorithms by calling the first one *Tortoise* and the second one *Hare*. If you glance at the *Hare* algorithm below for a moment and compare it to *Tortoise*, you will notice immediately that the second algorithm is somewhat longer and more complicated than the first, even though it solves exactly the same problem. This phenomenon often occurs when a programmer attempts to develop faster algorithms (and programs) to do the same job. The new program may run faster, even many times faster than the earlier one, but it almost always gets longer and more complicated.

The complication of the longer program may bring new disadvantages, but the running metaphor enters the picture again. The general phenomenon of large, fast programs versus small, slow ones, reminds one of muscle and speed. Faster runners often have bigger, better developed leg muscles. In any event, the idea that to get something (speed) you must give up something (simplicity) is called a *trade-off*, and trade-offs are very common in computer programming.

The *Hare* algorithm searches an array by using the divide-and-conquer technique. The actual process, called *binary search*, will only work on files that have been sorted, like a phone book, into a special order—in this case, ascending. The binary search technique divides the file to be searched into two equal, smaller segments, hence the word *binary*, meaning "two." It then decides which of the two segments must contain the sought-after item and confines further searching to that segment. It then divides *that* segment into two equal, smaller segments, decides which of the two must contain the sought-after item, and confines further searching to one of the smaller segments. . . .

If I sound as though I'm repeating myself, it's because I am: After all, I was describing the same process repeated on a new, smaller segment. But you get the picture. The process goes on dividing until it conquers, so to speak. If the item is there, binary search will find it. Here, without further ado, is the algorithm for the *Hare* program.

Hare Algorithm

```
input a number as This
set Found to false
while (Found = false) and (segment size > 0)
   set Place to middle of Segment
   set That to NumFile[Place]
   if This = That
      then set Found to true
      else if This > That
         then set Segment to upper half of Segment
         else set Segment to lower half of Segment
if Found = true
   then output This, "found at", Place
   else output This, "not found"
```

The "segments" referred to by the algorithm are simply sections of the array. At first, the whole array is one segment. A key step in the algorithm divides the current segment in two and replaces it by one of the halves, depending on the results of the comparison of *This* with *That*. The next diagram illustrates the process. The row of ten boxes represents the array *NumFile*. In its first iteration, the algorithm goes to the middle of the segment (the whole array). The array has an even number of entries, so, in picking a middle element, the algorithm must choose one of the two middle elements—say, the one on the left. This element has index value 5, and the *Hare* algorithm assigns this value to *Place*. It assigns the value stored in *NumFile*(5), namely, 25, to the variable *That*, then compares the latter value with the number sought, 47, stored in *This*.

If the two variables happen to have the same value, then the number sought has been found. The variable *Found* would consequently be set equal to TRUE and the algorithm exits from the loop. But if the variables *That* and *This* are not equal, the number sought must be either to the right or to the left of the array element at *Place*. Because the elements of the array are sorted into ascending order, the choice made by the IF–THEN statement will always be the correct one: If *This* is greater than *That*, the number sought must be to the right of the current array position, in the upper half of the current segment (if it is there at all). Otherwise, it must lie to the left, in the lower half.

The *Hare* algorithm begins and ends much the way *Tortoise* did. The only remaining question will be "How can Turbo Pascal accommodate this apparently new data structure called a segment?" It doesn't. In other words, I can easily define a segment as simply two variables, say, *Low* and *High*. The first variable will contain the index value of the array element

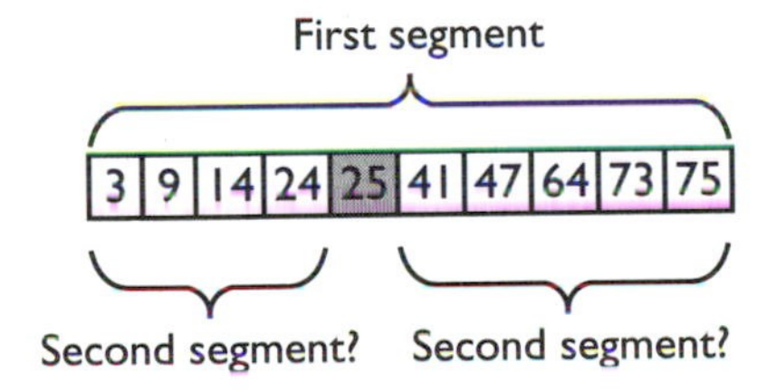

Dividing and conquering array segments

at the low end of the segment, while the second variable will contain the index value for the high end. In the preceding diagram, for example, the two variables would take on the following initial values:

Low = 1 High = 10

In its first iteration, the algorithm will locate the middle of this segment, namely, position 5 in the array. After deciding that the element sought lies above this position, the algorithm will form a new segment defined by a new value for one of the defining variables:

Low = 6 High = 10

On the next iteration, the *Hare* algorithm examines the number stored at the middle of the new segment, namely, 64, in the eighth position. The number sought, 47, is less than 64 and so must lie to the left of it. The new segment should then be defined by new values:

Low = 6 High = 7

At each iteration, either variable can change its value. The size of the segment will shrink to one-half its previous value, or less. Here, the power of the divide-and-conquer technique becomes apparent. At each iteration, the algorithm will divide the current segment (the one that must contain the sought-for element if it is there at all) in half. How many iterations will it take before the number is found or the array is exhausted?

To calculate the "middle" of a segment is a little tricky. If *Low* and *High* were the end points of a line segment, the midpoint would simply be the average:

(Low + High)/2

Unfortunately, the resulting number would have to be of type REAL, not a suitable value for an array index. The next section introduces a new Turbo Pascal operator, companion of the MOD operator covered in the previous chapter.

The DIV Operator

The operator called DIV, or *integer divide*, works like your grade school exercises in long division. Given one number to divide into the other, you dutifully produced a dividend and a remainder. For example, in dividing 89 by 7, you would get 12, with a remainder of 5. As you already know, Turbo Pascal calculates the remainder of the division with the MOD operator. It produces the quotient with DIV:

```
89 DIV 7 = 12

89 MOD 7 = 5
```

When assigning the results of these operations to variables, you could write:

```
Quotient := 89 DIV 7;

Remainder := 89 MOD 7;
```

Of course, you are not confined to integers as participants in the DIV and MOD operations. But if you use variables or expressions, instead, you must ensure that they have the type INTEGER. This was true of the way MOD was used in the *CodeMaker* program of Chapter 8:

```
K := Count MOD 3;
```

It will also be true when I use the DIV operator in the upcoming program:

```
Place := (Low + High) DIV 2;
```

If *Low* equals 3 and *High* equals 8, for example, then 11 DIV 2 would be 5.

The Refined Algorithm

The refinement differs slightly from the earlier algorithm. I have only installed refinements on the calculations that involve segments:

Hare Algorithm

input a number as *This*
set *Found* to false
set *Low* to 1, *High* to 10

```
while (Found = false) and (Low <= High)
   set Place to (Low + High) DIV 2
   set That to NumFile[Place]
   if This = That
      then set Found to true
      else if This > That
         then set Low to Place + 1
         else set High to Place −1
if Found = true
   then output This, "found at", Place
   else output This, "not found"
```

One of the most useful features of algorithmic refinement is the opportunity to find logic errors. I uncovered one while refining *Hare*. If you examine the second relation in the WHILE-loop of the previous algorithm, you will find the following inequality:

```
segment size > 0
```

The test allows the loop to continue as long as the two boundary markers for the segment are not equal. Translated into a relation between *Low* and *High*, the algorithm above would have used the following test:

```
Low < High
```

In some cases, this would have prevented *Hare* from completing the search. If the two variables had the same value, the segment would consist of a single element. If this element were the sought-after number, *Hare* would never discover it because the loop would exit at that point. By widening the test slightly, permitting *Low* to equal *High*, I have allowed the WHILE-loop to go through the one extra iteration it might need to find the sought-for number.

Analyzing the Algorithms

I am now ready to analyze these algorithms and to discover, *without even running the corresponding programs*, which will be faster.

The ultimate concern for anyone using a program that takes a significant amount of time to run is exactly how long it will take. Because many programs will run with a variety of inputs, it also becomes important to know how long the program will take for different inputs. For example, the two searching programs will not only run on a great variety of arrays of ten elements, but they will also run, when suitably modified, on arrays of any size. How then can you compare two programs over an infinite number of possible inputs? The answer will come in a moment, but first I must be a little more explicit about what I mean by "how long?"

When a program runs on a computer, it absorbs CPU time. As you may recall, CPU is the acronym for the "central processing unit." How much of the CPU's time (in seconds) is actually spent on running the program? There are three kinds of *run times* for a program that the algorithmic analyst must be aware of

1. The *actual run time* in CPU seconds of the program for a particular input
2. The *average run time* in CPU seconds, over all inputs of a given size
3. The maximum run time, or *worst-case run time*, in CPU seconds, over all inputs of a given size

For example, a program might take 1.31 CPU seconds to search an array of a million items. It might, nevertheless, have an average run time on all possible arrays of a million items of 0.82 CPU seconds. It might even be that, of all these million-number arrays, the one I started this example with took the longest. That array would then be called the worst case, and the run time of 1.31 CPU seconds would be the worst-case run time.

Do you think me crazy because I spoke of the run time of an algorithm? Because they are not programs, algorithms cannot "run" on computers, of course, but they have a run time of sorts. In an algorithmic context, computer scientists call this sort of run time the *complexity* of the algorithm. I will explain this term fully in a moment. First, however, you should know that the three kinds of run times for a program correspond to three kinds of complexities for an algorithm.

You might not be surprised to learn that the average run time of a program will turn out to be closely related to the average time complexity of the underlying algorithm. The same sort of thing is true for the worst-case complexity. But all of this merely brings me back to the question, "What is the complexity of an algorithm?" The short answer is, "The number of steps the algorithm must take in coming up with an answer."

Enter a number
Input a number as This
set Found to False
set Place to 1
while (Found = false) and
set That to
if This = Tha

Programs run in computers, algorithms run in heads

Connecting the Dots

I will illustrate the concepts of average and worst-case complexities on the *Tortoise* algorithm. It is reproduced in the following figures, and I have added, beside each line, some empty circles that I will call "dots." The dots are arranged in columns. Each dot stands for the potential execution of the algorithmic step beside it. The columns represent iterations of a loop. How many steps must the algorithm go through to complete its task?

To make life easy for *Tortoise*, let's search for the third element of the array, namely, 14:

3	9	14	24	25	41	47	64	73	75

How many steps will the algorithm take to discover 14 in the array? Make a copy of the page containing the algorithm and the dots, if you like, and follow along.

As noted earlier, each column represents one iteration of the algorithm's loop. Fill in the dot at the top of the first column to signify that the first step (reading in the number 14) has been completed. The next two steps must, in any case, be executed, so fill in both of the corresponding dots. Now connect the first filled dot to the second and the second

***Tortoise* algorithm**

input a number as *This*	O	O	O	O
set *Found* to *false*	O	O	O	O
set *Place* to 1	O	O	O	O
while (*Found* = false) and (*Place* <= 10)	O	O	O	O
set *That* to *NumFile*[*Place*]	O	O	O	O
if *This* = *That*	O	O	O	O
then set *Found* to true	O	O	O	O
else increment *Place*	O	O	O	O
if *Found* = true	O	O	O	O
then output *This,* "found at", *Place*	O	O	O	O
else output *This,* "not found"	O	O	O	O

to the third. These connections signify the "flow of control" of the algorithmic process, so to speak. I am pretending that an actual program is being executed.

The next step,

while (*Found* = false) and (*Place* <= 10)

requires that I decide whether both these variables satisfy their respective relations. Because I have just set *Found* equal to false and *Place* equal to 1, they do. This means that the flow of control will pass on immediately to the next step within the loop. Fill in the dot for the WHILE-step and connect it to the previous filled dot. Within the loop, you find the following steps:

set *That* to *NumFile*[*Place*]
if *This* = *That*
then set *Found* to true
else increment *Place*

Tracing Programs

The process of going through an algorithm or program in a step-by-step fashion is called *tracing*. This technique can be used, not only to determine the complexity of a program or algorithm, but also to discover faults. Operating in the latter mode, make a table of the program's variables and, each time a variable changes, record the new value in the table. If you choose the right input and the program contains a fault, you should discover it by comparing the values of the program's variables with what they should be.

The program below will serve as an example for the tracing process. You will see this program later in the chapter. It uses the binary search technique to search the special array [1, 2, 3, . . .]. The variable *Size* limits the search and the variable *This* takes a value that is one greater than *Size*. (This arrangement guarantees worst-case performance by the program.)

In the trace below, *Size* is assumed to have the value 3, so *This* will have the value 4. Such small values are frequently sufficient to bring out a fault, and they produce shorter traces as well.

I have stripped the program *Does It Work* of comments and statements that need not be subjected to the tracing process. You may trace through the program and, on each iteration of the main loop, note the values of the main variables, as in the table on the right.

```
PROGRAM DoesItWork;
{declarations missing}
BEGIN
READLN(Size);
This := Size + 1;
Found := FALSE;
```

	Place	*Low*	*High*	*That*
initial value		1	3	
iteration #1	2	2	3	2
iteration #2	2	2	3	2
iteration #3	2	2	3	2

Fill in the dots, connecting them as you go (noting what each one means) until you come to the "if *This* = *That*" step. You must fill in this dot also, and connect it with the preceding dot. But, because *This* = 14 and *That* = 3, the two variables are not equal. Consequently, you do not fill in the next dot below it, but the one after it, where the variable *Place* is incremented. The line connecting the two dots should make a detour around the empty one. This iteration of the WHILE-loop is now finished.

```
Low := 1;
High := Size;
WHILE (Found = FALSE) AND (Low <= High) DO
   BEGIN
   Place := (Low + High) DIV 2;
   That := NumFile[Place];
   IF This = That
      THEN Found := TRUE
      ELSE IF This > That
         THEN Low := Place
         ELSE High := Place;
   END;
END.
```

By keeping track of the variables as the program "executes," you can sometimes spot an error very quickly. This program, even with the simple input of 3 for *Size*, reveals one of the most fundamental flaws a program can have. It does not terminate! The values of key variables do not appear to be changing, from one iteration to the next. You might run such a program, then wonder why it's taking so long. Next day, you might still be sitting there.

When you examine the program more closely to discover the reason why it does not terminate, you should notice that when the segment size is just 2, the DIV operator always chooses the leftmost element of the segment as *Place*. But this is the value that *Place* had on the previous iteration. To fix the fault, you should change the offending instruction to the following:

```
Low := Place + 1;
```

Presumably the program now works. Or does it? (See Exploration 8.)

To continue the analysis, join the dot for the ELSE step to the dot in the *second* column that is aligned with the WHILE-loop. Returning to this step, decide whether *Found* is still true and *Place* is still <= 10. Not surprisingly, the two variables continue to satisfy these relations, so the loop will go through at least one more iteration. Fill in the dot for the WHILE step and continue as before, working your way down to the IF step.

At this stage, your connect-the-dots diagram should look like the second connect-the-dots diagram below. Once again, you will arrive at the IF step by following an unbroken chain of connected dots. And again, because the second number in the array, 9, does not equal 14, you skip to the ELSE step and join it both to its predecessor and to the dot in the third column directly aligned with the WHILE-loop. You now repeat the same analysis as in the previous two iterations. This time things are different when you get to the IF step. *This* and *That* both equal 14. Fill in the IF step dot and the THEN step, joining dots up as you go. The THEN step sets *Found* to true.

When you move up to the head of the WHILE-loop for the fourth time, things are different. *Found* is no longer false and, because the logical connective is "and," it makes no difference what value *Place* has. The relation as a whole is false and no steps inside the loop will be executed. Fill in the dot for the WHILE-loop one last time and now run the connecting line down the outside of the fourth column to the dot directly opposite the "if Found = true" step.

Tortoise algorithm

input a number as *This*
set *Found* to false
set *Place* to 1
while (*Found* = false) and (*Place* <= 10)
    set *That* to *NumFile*[*Place*]
    if *This* = *That*
        then set *Found* to true
        else increment *Place*
if *Found* = true
    then output: *This*, "found at", *Place*
    else output: *This*, "not found"

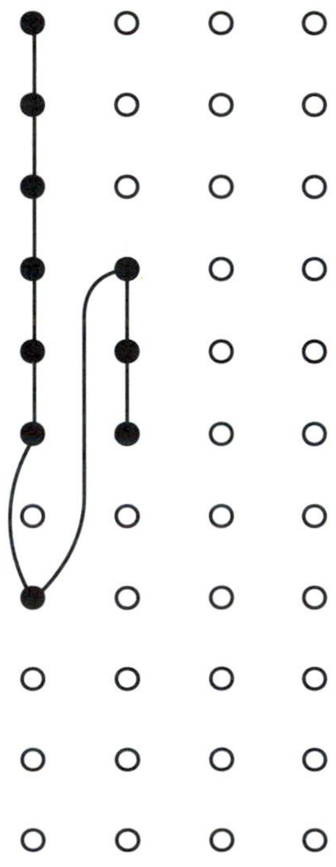

Because *Found* is now true, you must move on to the last step you will process, namely,

then output: *This*, "found at", *Place*

The trail of dots ends here because the next step will not be executed and there is nothing else for the algorithm to do. It has found *This* in the array and it terminates. The third connect-the-dots figure shows the completed diagram. How many dots did you fill in? You can count them in the last diagram—18. The initial segment of the algorithm used three dots, and the three times through the loop used four dots each. The final iteration used three dots, one for the test at the head of the WHILE-loop and two for the final IF step in the algorithm.

It is useful to break the numbers down like this, because in a moment I'll be developing a formula. In the meantime, merely notice that to search the array in this particular example, the algorithm executed a total of 18 steps. This number represents the complexity of the algorithm for this particular problem instance.

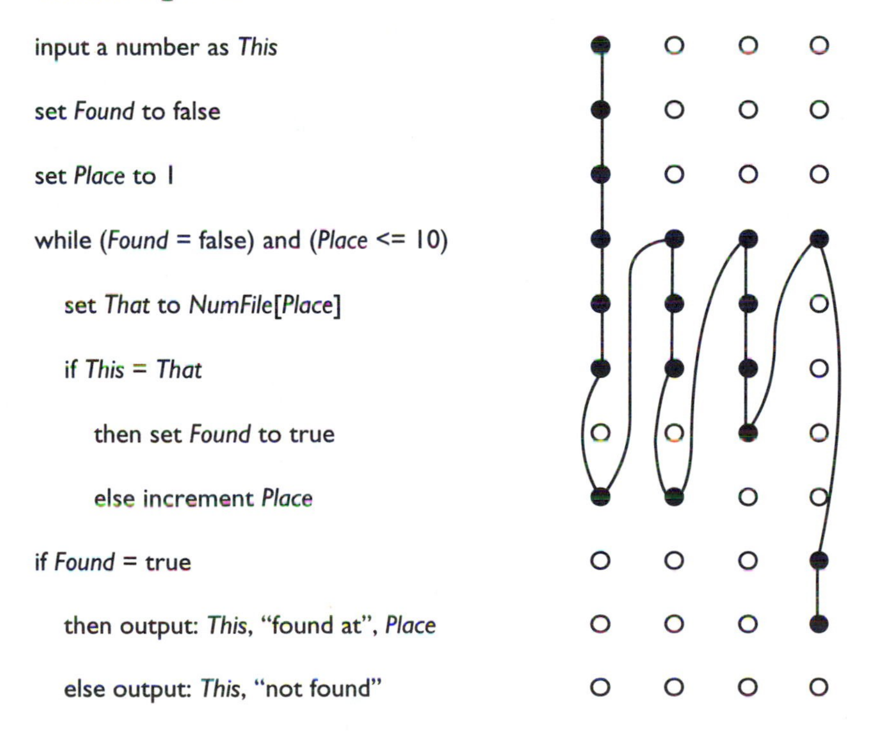
***Tortoise* algorithm**
input a number as *This*
set *Found* to false
set *Place* to 1
while (*Found* = false) and (*Place* <= 10)
set *That* to *NumFile*[*Place*]
if *This* = *That*
then set *Found* to true
else increment *Place*
if *Found* = true
then output: *This*, "found at", *Place*
else output: *This*, "not found"

You might ask how long the algorithm would take on the average array of ten elements or even how long it would take in the worst case. However, if you know a certain formula first, this whole exercise becomes much simpler.

A Useful Formula

Whatever array of numbers the *Tortoise* algorithm faces, it will always execute the first three steps. And for every iteration of the main loop, whether or not a match is found, the algorithm executes four steps. If there are n such iterations, the number of steps taken so far is given by the formula:

$$3 + 4n$$

By adding the three additional steps the algorithm takes to terminate, I get the final formula:

$$3 + 4n + 3, \quad \text{or} \quad 4n + 6$$

In an array of size 10, the worst case occurs when the element sought lies in the last position. Substituting 10 for n in the formula, I get 46 as the number of steps taken. In a more general setting of an array having n elements, the worst case formula is already staring you in the face (above).

Computer scientists call the *Tortoise* algorithm a *linear-time algorithm* because the complexity function, $4n + 6$, is a linear function. If you don't happen to know what a linear function is, you should read the next section. Even if you do know what a linear function is, you might want to brush up on functions generally. It's a good way to appreciate the relative speed of the two searching programs, the *Tortoise* and the *Hare*.

How Slow Does Your Function Grow?

Mathematicians make a broad distinction between functions on the basis of the size and growth rates of their principal terms. A *polynomial function* consists of one or more terms all added together. For example, $4n + 6$ is a polynomial in n, as are the following functions:

$$6n^2 + 2n - 15$$

$$4n^3 - 258n^2 + 23n - 1$$

and so on. Each term consists of a constant multiplied by a power of some variable such as n. Such functions are classified by the size of the highest power that occurs in any of the terms. This power is called the *degree* of the polynomial. The names of a few such polynomials are:

n	linear	first-degree polynomial
n^2	quadratic	second-degree polynomial
n^3	cubic	third-degree polynomial

I won't bore you with an extended list. The important thing to notice is that the degree of a polynomial determines the speed with which it grows, as n gets larger and larger. As the variable n gets large (on the right-hand side of the horizontal axis in the accompanying figure), each of the three functions increases. The linear function increases moderately, the quadratic function increases much faster, and the cubic function increases fastest of all. You may compare the three functions for any problem size, by drawing a vertical line from that size through all three functions.

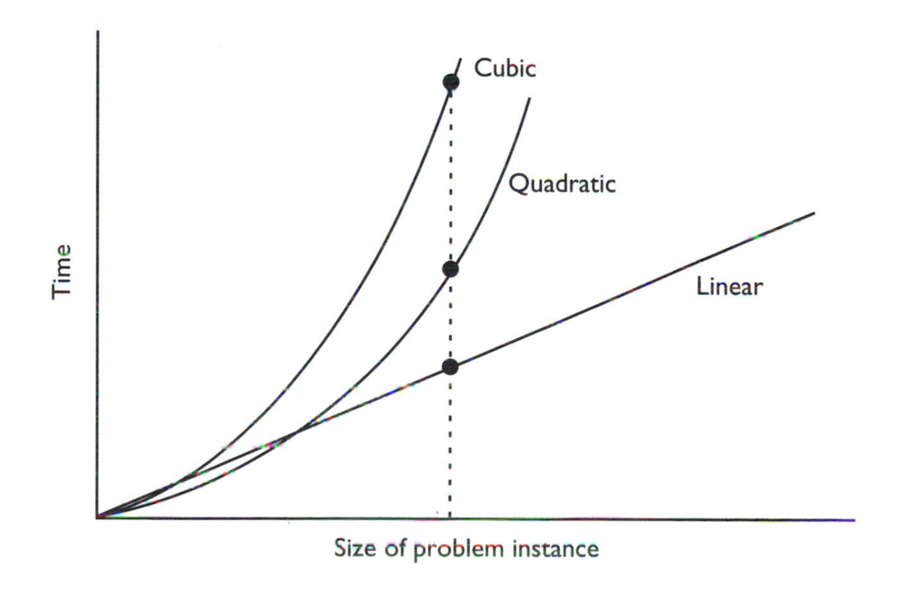

Linear, quadratic, and cubic polynomials

Of course, programmers want algorithms with complexity functions that grow as slowly as possible, so they have a special interest in low-order polynomials. From this point of view, the *Tortoise* program will be faster than search algorithms that took a quadratic or cubic number of steps.

But not all functions are polynomials. Another function that crops up very frequently in complexity analysis is the logarithmic function, a function that grows very slowly indeed. For my current purposes, the logarithm of a number is the power to which 2 must be raised to equal the number. There are other kinds of logarithms, based on the powers of constants other than 2, but my earlier definition describes the sort of logarithm that computer scientists use most frequently. In computer science, as you have already begun to appreciate, many things come in twos.

According to my definition, the logarithm of 32 is the power to which 2 must be raised to reach 32, namely, 5. In other words, $2^5 = 2 \times 2 \times 2 \times 2 \times 2 = 32$. I therefore write $\log(32) = 5$. There is also a logarithm of 33, which happens to be 5.044, given to three decimal places. In this case, I write $\log(33) = 5.044$. (To see how you can compute such logarithms with a hand calculator, see Exploration 3 at the end of this chapter.)

As you can see from the next graph, the logarithmic function (in black) grows much more slowly than the three polynomial functions that I discussed earlier. If you were ever to discover an algorithm with logarithmic worst-case complexity, that might be the best of all, because it would beat any of the polynomials. Or would it? Can you think of a function that grows more slowly than a logarithm?

Back to Complexity

You may be a little confused by talk of fast-growing functions and fast algorithms. But, as you have already seen, the last thing you want in a fast algorithm is a worst-case complexity function that itself grows fast. In other words, the faster the complexity function grows, the slower the algorithm. Let's take an example.

Imagine a search algorithm that had worst-case complexity that was a second-degree polynomial, a quadratic—say, $3n^2 + 3n - 8$. I will call this hypothetical algorithm *Snail*. Let's compare this polynomial with the one for the *Tortoise* algorithm. Recall that for $n = 10$, the worst-case complexity of the *Tortoise* algorithm is

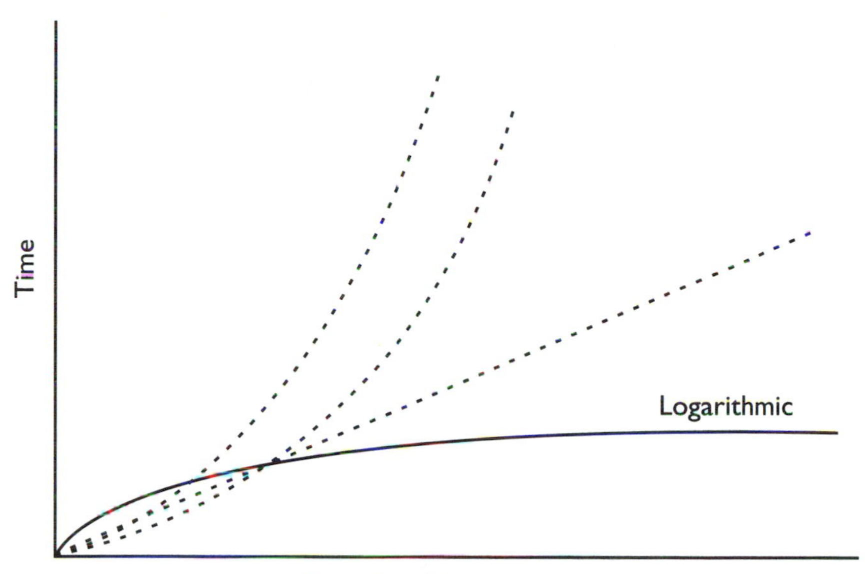

The logarithmic function grows more slowly

$$4n + 6 = (4 \times 10) + 6$$
$$= 46$$

The *Snail* algorithm, however, has a faster growing complexity function and is much larger at $n = 10$, namely,

$$3n^2 + 3n - 8 = (3 \times 100) + (3 \times 10) - 8$$
$$= 300 + 30 - 8$$
$$= 322$$

which is much larger than 46. In other words, *Snail* could take as many as 322 steps to solve the searching problem that *Tortoise* could always solve in 46 or fewer steps. I might as well state all this in the form of a principle:

The faster the worst-case complexity function of an algorithm grows, the slower the algorithm runs in the worst case. The more slowly the worst-case complexity function grows, the faster the algorithm is in the worst case.

Of course, worst-case complexity is just one way to analyze the speed of an algorithm. Another important measure is the average time complexity. Unfortunately, it is often very difficult to figure out the average-case run times for most algorithms. As it happens, it is relatively easy to figure out with the *Tortoise* and *Hare* algorithms, but I have decided to concentrate on worst-case complexity instead. Suffice it to say that the average-case complexity for both algorithms would be something like half the worst-case complexity.

The formulas for the worst-case and average-case run times for *Tortoise* have one thing in common. They are both *linear*. If you plot the time taken against the size of input, you will find that the graph of the function is a straight line. As I have already explained, algorithms may have worst-case run times that are logarithmic, linear, quadratic, or worse.

Speed of an Algorithmic Hare

The time has now come to analyze the algorithm called *Hare*. I have laid it out with columns of dots in exactly the same way as I did for the *Tortoise* algorithm. To test yourself on the method of analysis, make a copy of this page, as you did previously with the *Tortoise* algorithm. Before reading on, play connect-the-dots with the *Hare* algorithm, using the same example as you did previously. Let *Hare* search for the number 14 in the array

3	9	14	24	25	41	47	64	73	75

To develop a general formula for how long *Hare* will take on any input, I observe, for starters, that the algorithm always takes three steps before entering the main loop. Within the loop, *Hare* always takes six steps if it cannot match *This* and *That*. A successful match, however, requires only five steps in the main loop. Finally, the algorithm will always require three steps to finish, namely, one for the test at the top of the loop and two more steps for the IF steps at the end of the algorithm. If the main loop is iterated m times, the total number of steps required can be calculated as

$$3 + 6(m - 1) + 5 + 3 \text{ steps for a successful search}$$

$$3 + 6m + 3 \text{ steps for an unsuccessful search}$$

***Hare* algorithm**

input a number as *This*	○	○	○	○
set *Found* to false	○	○	○	○
set *Low* to 1, *High* to 10	○	○	○	○
while (*Found* = false) and (*Low* <= High)	○	○	○	○
set *Place* to (*Low* + *High*) DIV 2	○	○	○	○
set *Place* to *NumFile*[*Place*]	○	○	○	○
if *This* = *That*	○	○	○	○
then set *Found* to true	○	○	○	○
else if *This* > *That*	○	○	○	○
then set *Low* to *Place* + 1	○	○	○	○
else set *High* to *Place* – 1	○	○	○	○
if *Found*=true	○	○	○	○
then output: *This*, "found at", *Place*	○	○	○	○
else output: *This*, "not found"	○	○	○	○

After the algebraic dust settles, I discover that *Hare* will take 6m + 5 steps for a successful search and 6m + 6 steps for an unsuccessful one. I can check the validity of these formulas by applying them to the ten-element array that I have been using as a demonstration of the connect-the-dots method. For this example, it would take three iterations of the main loop to produce a segment that consists of a single element. If *Hare* were searching for the number 14, it would find it; and the complexity, according to the formula above, would be $6 \times 3 + 5 = 23$ steps. This is the answer you should have obtained when analyzing the *Hare* algorithm in this case.

If you compare this complexity with that of the *Tortoise* algorithm on the same input, you may receive a bit of a shock. *Tortoise* took only 19 steps to complete the search! What went wrong? Nothing. The fact is that *Tortoise* is slightly faster on small arrays. It remains to be seen how the two algorithms will compare on larger ones.

You can complete the analysis of the *Hare* algorithm as soon as you know how to make a mathematical link between m, the number of iterations of the main loop, and n, the size of the array. You can already see that the complexity for an unsuccessful search will be slightly greater than that for a successful one. Because the *Tortoise* algorithm takes the same number of steps for either kind of search, it seems fair to run the race for a number that neither will find in the array.

In the worst case, m counts the number of times that the segments are halved until the segment size becomes 1. When this happens, the element being sought will either lie in that one-element segment or it will not be in the array at all. How many times is that? Try going in reverse. How many times must you double 1 until you first exceed the size n of the original array? The answer must be 2^m. As I stated earlier, I will define the logarithm of n to be that power:

$$\log(n) = m$$

Now, m is always an integer and log(n) is not necessarily an integer, so the inequality isn't quite true as it stands. But let's understand it to mean that m either equals log(n) or equals the integer just above log(n). This understanding happens not only to reflect the actual situation, but also makes the notation much simpler. When it comes to such broad comparisons, I do not bother to distinguish between a real number and an adjacent integer.

Because the number m happens to be log(n), the worst-case complexity of the *Hare* algorithm turns out to be logarithmic:

$$6m + 6 = 6 \log(n) + 6$$

The dominant term in the expression representing worst-case complexity of *Hare* is a logarithm. In other words, the amount of time it takes in the worst case to search an array of size n is on the order of log(n). Because this is worst-case complexity, you can immediately infer that the *Hare* program performs this well or better on *all* problem instances of size n. A quick glance at the curves in the illustration on page 303 should convince you that the logarithmic function grows much more slowly than the linear function as n gets larger and larger. In other words, a logarithmic algorithm has a worst-case run time that is ultimately much shorter than that of its linear colleagues like *Tortoise*, not to mention algorithms that take quadratic time or worse.

Fast Algorithms = Fast Programs

The complexity of an algorithm is always reflected in the complexity of any program based on it. The reason for this is soon found. Think about the process by which you refine an algorithm to become a program. Each of the steps of the algorithm is expanded into a fixed number of program statements. The greater the number of steps an algorithm must take to solve a particular problem instance, the more program statements the computer must execute. In fact you can usually come up with some constant K, one that depends on the algorithm and program in question, that enables you to relate the program's running speed directly to the complexity of its underlying algorithm.

Let's use the symbol T to stand for the time the program takes on a problem instance of size n and the symbol S to stand for the number of steps the algorithm takes on the same instance. Then the expression

$$T = KS$$

is close enough to the truth to be usable. In other words, the time taken by the program is just a constant times the number of steps taken by the algorithm on each problem instance. As the size of the problem grows, the number of steps taken by the algorithm may also grow, but the run time of the program will definitely grow in the same way. Almost exactly.

The only thing standing in the way of writing the equality with complete confidence is the fact that the actual run times or complexities may each have an additional but different constant term. These may cause the complexities to differ somewhat, but the difference itself will be a constant. Moreover, the difference will become insignificant for very large problem instances.

Before writing the actual programs and comparing them, I must lay down the ground rules for a fair contest.

Rules of the Race

Both *Tortoise* and *Hare* have worst-case complexity when asked to search for a number that is *not* in the test array. So what arrays will I test the two programs on? If I test them on arrays of 1000 entries, who will have the patience to enter all those numbers? As it turns out, there is a nice way out of this dilemma. A bit of theory puts me on the road to sound practice.

To be perfectly fair, both *Tortoise* and *Hare* will be given the same arrays to search and the same items to search for. As it happens, both algorithms will take the longest possible time on a given array if the item sought is greater than any number in the array. Because the numbers in the arrays are presorted in ascending order, it makes no difference at all *what* the numbers are as long as it's possible to to put either algorithm through exactly the same paces. As the following example shows, it's not necessary to test arrays with arbitrary numbers in them.

problem instance 1: Find the number 501 in the array
[12, 16, 23, 33, 39, 103, 387, 389, 450, 455]

problem instance 2: Find the number 11 in the array
[1, 2, 3, 4, 5, 6, 7, 8, 9, 10]

Tortoise would require exactly the same number of steps searching the array of instance 1 as it would on the array of instance 2. The same thing is true of *Hare*.

Arrays that consist of nothing more elaborate than the integers 1, 2, 3, and so on can readily be generated within a program. The following code will generate an array of any *Size* up to a declared maximum of, say, 1000 positions. Because I have decided that the number to search for will be one larger than the largest element of the array, this code also sets the variable *This*.

```
FOR Index := 1 TO Size DO
   NumFile[Index] := Index;
This := Size + 1;
```

The test arrays will consist of consecutive integers, and the time that each algorithm takes will be recorded and, later, plotted.

The Programs

The algorithmic contestants in the array-searching race can now be clothed in the flesh of Turbo Pascal and placed on a series of array racetracks. Following the previous order, I will start with the *Tortoise*:

```
PROGRAM Tortoise;
{Tortoise uses the sequential search method}
{on arrays of up to 1000 entries.}

{declarations module}
VAR This, That, Index, Size, Place: INTEGER;
VAR Found: BOOLEAN;
TYPE RaceTrack = ARRAY[1 . . 1000] OF INTEGER;
VAR NumFile: RaceTrack;

BEGIN

{input module}
WRITE('Please enter the size of the array: ');
READLN(Size);

{initializing module}
FOR Index := 1 TO Size DO
   NumFile[Index] := Index;
This := Size + 1;
Found := FALSE;
Place := 1;

{search module and main loop}
WHILE (Found = FALSE) AND (Place <= Size) DO
   BEGIN
   That := NumFile[Place];
   IF This = That
      THEN Found := TRUE
      ELSE Place := Place + 1;
   END;

{reporting module}
IF Found = TRUE
   THEN WRITELN('The item ', This, ' was found in position ', Place, '.')
   ELSE WRITELN('The item ', This, ' was not found.');
WRITELN;

END.
```

How to Time a Program

Turbo Pascal comes equipped with a procedure called GETTIME, which returns the current time of day in hours, minutes, seconds, and hundredths of a second. To time a program, you can easily install two timing modules, one right after the BEGIN, the other just before the END. In the first module, the values returned by GETTIME can be assembled into clock time in hundredths of a second, as follows:

```
{timing module}
GETTIME(THour, TMinute, TSecond, TSec100);
Start := TMinute*6000 + TSecond*100 + TSec100;
```

The actual parameters are simply my names for the standard VAR parameters used by the procedure

```
(Hour, Minute, Second, Sec100)
```

the latter parameter indicating hundredths of a second.

The second module looks almost the same as the first, except the variable *Finish* replaces the variable *Start*.

The actual parameters must be declared as a data type called WORD, essentially a 16-bit unsigned (positive or zero) integer. You may add such numbers together and assign them to an integer

You will note that I have replaced the input section proposed in the algorithm by a new one. I no longer expect the user to input the number sought. For the purpose of the race, it has been replaced by a prompt for the *Size* of array to run the program on. A new assignment statement sets the variable *This* to the value of *Size* + 1. The array *NumFile*, declared to be of type *RaceTrack*, has 1000 positions reserved for it by the computer, according to the TYPE declaration. However, the program does not have to use all the positions. If the user enters a value of 500 for *Size*, for example, the array *NumFile* will consist of the first 500 consecutive integers and this will be the array that *Tortoise* searches.

variable. In a program to be timed in this manner, you must include the declaration for these variables:

```
VAR THour, TMinute, TSecond, TSec100: WORD;
```

The GETTIME procedure is part of the DOS unit, so you must add the

```
USES DOS;
```

statement just below the program header.

When I attempted to time the *Tortoise* and *Hare* on my computer in this manner, I found that even hundredths of a second were far too coarse to catch the tiny times the programs took. The final expedient was to enclose the main part of each program in a loop of 1000 iterations. The time this new, magnified program took to run fell easily within the ambit of the timing variables. But even then, *Tortoise* took only a few seconds of real time!

After wrapping the programs I wanted to measure in a master loop, it was a simple matter to divide the reported running time by 1000 to get the time for a single run. This number had then to be converted to milliseconds, or thousandths of a second. To get even better numbers, I changed the maximum size of the test array to 10,000 and tested both *Tortoise* and *Hare* on arrays of size 1000, 2000, and so on up to 10,000.

If you read the *Tortoise* program over carefully, you will find that it reflects the algorithm in all other important respects. You should have no trouble understanding the code.

The *Hare* program uses the same input module as *Tortoise* does, and it also follows the earlier recipe very closely:

```
PROGRAM Hare;
{Hare uses the binary search method}
{on arrays of up to 1000 entries.}

{declarations module}
VAR This, That, Index, Size, Low, High, Place: INTEGER;
VAR Found: BOOLEAN;
```

```
TYPE RaceTrack = ARRAY[1 . . 1000] OF INTEGER;
VAR NumFile: RaceTrack;

BEGIN

{input module}
WRITE('Please enter the size of the array: ');
READLN(Size);
WRITELN;

{initializing module}
FOR Index := 1 TO Size DO
   NumFile[Index] := Index;
This := Size + 1;
Found := FALSE;
Low := 1;
High := Size;

{search module and main loop}
WHILE (Found = FALSE) AND (Low <= High) DO
   BEGIN
   Place := (Low + High) DIV 2;
   That := NumFile[Place];
   IF This = That
      THEN Found := TRUE
      ELSE IF This > That
         THEN Low := Place + 1
         ELSE High := Place - 1;
   END;

{reporting module}
IF Found = TRUE
   THEN WRITELN('The item ', This, ' was found in position ', Place, '.')
   ELSE WRITELN('The item ', This, ' was not found.');
WRITELN;

END.
```

It would be most convenient if I could have a race between *Tortoise* and *Hare* by simply running the programs on arrays of size 100, 200, 300, and so on, up to 1000, and timing them at each run. Unfortunately, a stopwatch would be useless. On an array of size 1000, *Tortoise* is still blindingly fast on my machine and probably on yours, as well.

How, then, will I time the programs? The box on pages 310 and 311 gives the details of the answer to this question. For my tests, I installed two timing modules in both programs. The first module, inserted right after the array-generating loop, stored the starting time in a variable called *Start*. The second timing module, inserted right after the end of the main loop, stored the finishing time in a variable called *Finish*. It was then a simple matter to subtract one variable from the other to get the elapsed time.

The race was finally run between the array-searching contestants on arrays of size 1000, 2000, and so on up to 10,000. (See the box on pages 310 and 311 for an explanation.) The accompanying chart shows the results. The *Tortoise* program complexity plods steadily upward along the expected straight line with only minor variations that resulted from the changing size of numbers the program encountered. The *Hare* program complexity follows the expected logarithmic path except for occasional plateaus caused by the extreme efficiency of the binary search method.

It looks as though *Hare* is slower than *Tortoise* near the 1000 array-size mark. At least, it looks this way until I tell you that I had to multiply the run times of *Hare* by 100 just to get them to show up on the chart. In other

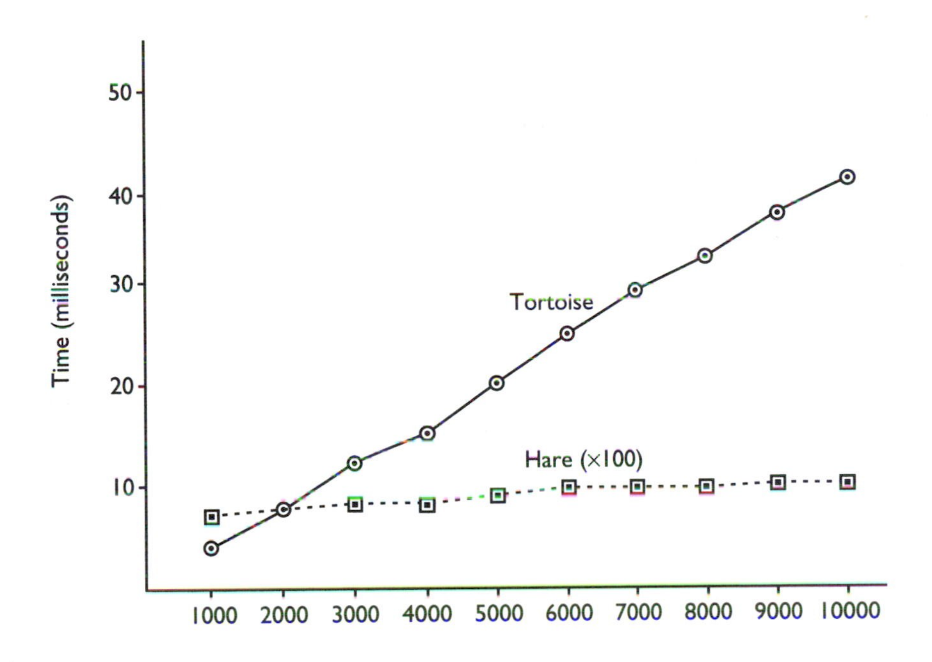

Array size

words, to appreciate the true complexity of *Hare*, you must lower its trend line to one-hundredth of the height value shown! *Hare* is fast, there's no doubt about it. Only for the smallest arrays does *Tortoise* beat *Hare*.

SUMMARY

This chapter has featured a blend of problem solving, computer science, and programming that illustrates the synergy between these areas better and more accurately than any previous chapter could have done. People who solve problems for a living, whether programmers or computer scientists, benefit greatly from the interplay of programming skill on the one hand and knowledge of computer science on the other.

Some computer scientists spend more time analyzing algorithms than they do programming. They do not have to run elaborate experiments to see which of two algorithms is faster. By analyzing the algorithm and developing a complexity function that describes an algorithm's performance on all problem instances of any size, they already know which of two algorithms is faster. In the long run, any program based on a faster algorithm will run more quickly than any program based on a slower one.

Now you can appreciate, as never before, the real power of the divide-and-conquer problem-solving strategy.

EXPLORATIONS

1 Can you think of a function that grows more slowly than a logarithm? Please don't say "half a logarithm." Technically, you'd be right, but I'm looking for something that differs from a logarithm by more than a constant factor.

2 Use the binary search strategy employed by *Hare* to determine how many iterations of its main loop would be required to locate each of the numbers stored in the array [1, 2, 3, 4, 5, 6, 7, 8, 9, 10].

3 Use a hand calculator to figure out the logarithms of the following numbers:

a 16
b 33
c 23.82

For you to be able to do this problem, your calculator must have the ability to raise any number to any power, usually symbolized by the power key with a formula something like x^y on it.

You can solve part (a) without a calculator, of course, but give the power function a workout by raising 2 to the appropriate power to get 16. For the other numbers, you will have to be a bit cleverer. You may, of course, use trial and error, but what about binary search?

4 Complete the analysis of the *Hare* algorithm by duplicating the dot diagram on page 305, then putting the algorithm to work on the same problem instance that you used with the *Tortoise* algorithm.

5 Run the *Tortoise* program on an array of size 1000. It should finish very quickly. Next, change the declaration of the *RaceTrack* TYPE to allow arrays of size up to 10,000. Run it anew with sizes of 5000 and 10,000. Do you see much difference? Try to time the algorithm in the following manner. Insert a master loop of 1000 iterations around the program as described in the box on pages 310 and 311. Now run the program on arrays of size 5000 and 10,000, timing the runs as accurately as you can with a stopwatch or wristwatch. Divide the result (in seconds) by 1000. The time that *Tortoise* takes on the array of 5000 integers should be about half the time it takes on the array of 10,000 integers. (*Note:* You may have to re-declare the timing variables as TYPE LONGINT.)

6 Rewrite *Hare* as a program that searches an array of characters. You can generate the array by using characters 32 to 126 in the ASCII table as shown in Chapter 8. To determine which of two characters is the "greater," you can simply compare them as you would two integers. The program should prompt the user to input a character that lies in the array.

7 The following program fulfills a need that certain people have to be mystified by computers. First, fill in the declarations for the variables you find in the program. Next, analyze the program. It's easy to guess what it does, but how does it do it? Finally, does the program work in all cases? Trace it by the technique outlined in the box on page 296. If the program is broken, fix it.

```
PROGRAM SevenGuesses;

BEGIN

WRITELN('I can tell your age in seven steps.');
WRITELN('Each time I guess, tell me whether I am');
WRITELN('too high [enter H] or too low [enter L].');
WRITELN('If I guess correctly, enter a Y.');

Guess := 26;
Range := 26;
Correct := FALSE;
WRITELN('My first guess is 25.');

WHILE NOT Correct DO
   BEGIN
   READLN(Response);
   IF Response = 'Y'
      THEN Correct := TRUE
      ELSE BEGIN
         Range := Range DIV 2;
         IF Response = 'H'
            THEN Guess := Guess - Range;
            ELSE Guess := Guess + Range;
         WRITELN('My next guess is ', Guess);
         END;
   END;

WRITELN('What did I tell you?');

END.
```

8 Trace through the program in the box on page 296 after it has been repaired in the manner suggested there. Does it work on the test input? What about other values of *Size*?

9 Use the divide-and-conquer strategy to solve the following problem. An array consists of 0's and 1's. First there are some 0's, then the rest are all 1's. Your program, based on the *Hare* algorithm, must find the index value for the last 0 in the array.

10 Using the graphics facility in either DOS- or Windows-based Turbo Pascal, make a plot of the logarithmic function, the linear function, the quadratic function, and the exponential function. Use a variable X that runs from 1 to 100 and plot the points on the screen at horizontal coordinates that run from 50 to 150. To make the plots show up for most of their range, use the following functions:

logarithmic: use the built-in function LN(X)
linear: use X/2
quadratic: use X*X/10
exponential: use the built-in function EXP(X)

The first and last Turbo Pascal functions are based on the number *e*, (approximately 2.718) instead of 2, but they have the same growth properties.

11 What would you do if the SQRT function suddenly disappeared from Turbo Pascal? You'd have to write a new function. Do this, incorporating what you learned about functions in Chapter 7. Your function (don't call it SQRT or you will get an error) should take any positive real number as input and output the square root of that number. For your function to work as quickly as possible, it should employ a binary search inside a loop. Let the function guess an initial value and test it by squaring. Thereafter, employ a variable called Squeeze that falls to half its previous value on each iteration. If the function's guess overshoots, it should decrease the current guess by the amount Squeeze. If it undershoots the given value, it should increase the guess by the value of Squeeze.

10 The Daily Planet

Sorting and Editing Files

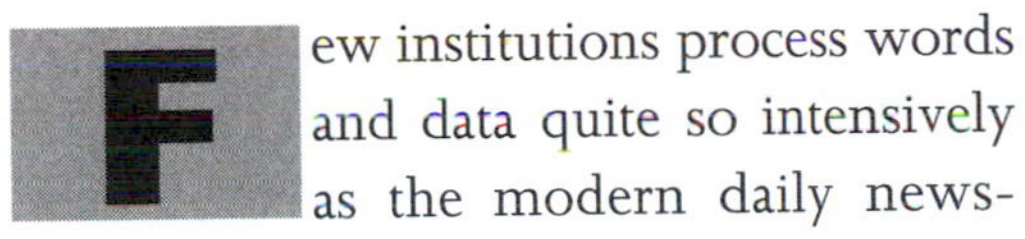

Few institutions process words and data quite so intensively as the modern daily newspaper. From the stock pages to the editorial section, words and numbers are arranged and massaged right up to the last moment before press time, when the files that hold the pages disgorge their contents into the print computer.

I will implement two modest processing operations as a focus for Turbo Pascal features, both old and new. The first project puts the stock page in order by sorting the records of daily stock market prices by company. The second project will imitate an important word processor function. It will enable an editor to search a text file for any word and to replace each occurrence of that word by a new one.

In the process of writing the sorting program, I will introduce strings and talk about how to work with a file of records. The project will also round off what you learned in the previous chapter about searching. I will analyze a bare-bones version of the sorting algorithm to discover its complexity.

One function of word processing will illustrate the principles of software engineering, a key field in a world that demands fault-free programs that are easy to understand and maintain.

The Business Pages

Perry White, retired editor of *The Daily Planet*, fondly recalls the old days when Clark Kent and Lois Lane would beat the streets for stories, then spend several hours pounding on their Underwoods to get out the news. Nowadays, they would tap the stories into word processors capable of massaging the prose faster than Superman could type. And when the stock prices had to be reorganized, how fast could Superman have sorted the entries by company name? Not any faster than my sorting program.

A glance at a typical stock page shows the behavior of prices during the day's trading on major exchanges like the New York Stock Exchange and NASDAQ. The business editor receives stock prices by wire at the end of a day's trading. However, the records arrive in an order based on ticker symbols, and readers prefer to read a stock page on which the stocks are sorted by company name. To keep the project of sorting a file within reasonable bounds, I have decided to restrict it to three items: the company name, the ticker symbol, and the closing price.

Sorting Numbers

To begin, I will design a program that merely sorts numbers in an array; then I will analyze the program to follow up on the complexity lessons of the previous chapter. I will then adapt the program to the present purpose by converting it to a file-sorting program.

As programmers start to consider the problem of sorting numbers, they become fascinated, almost obsessed. They think, "How do I sort a

The Daily Planet				**July 3 1997**
Company name	Ticker symbol	Closing price	High	Low
Aardvaark	ADV	2.12	2.25	2.00
Abco	AB	4.50	4.60	4.45
Armbruster Ind.	ARM	12.25	12.50	12.00
Armenian Ent.	ARE	22.12	23.50	21.50
Baalbek	BLK	5.75	5.87	5.75
Bright's	BRI	34.95	37.50	34.60
etc.				

Stock page

bunch of numbers? How, for that matter, do I sort just ten numbers?" They could make a separate project out of that problem alone. In fact, it is very common, either when they talk to each other or when they talk to themselves, for programmers to imagine they *are* programs. This mental habit is not as serious as it sounds and rarely leads to other problems. It seems to be rooted deep in the human psyche and actually leads to useful behavior. Consider, for example, the question above: "How do I sort a bunch of numbers?" The answer to the question, part of the fantasy of programmers, might begin with an informal idea involving the exchange of just two numbers:

> "If I just keep exchanging consecutive pairs of numbers that are out of order, sooner or later, I'll end up with a sequence that is entirely in order."

One way to do this is to scan through the array, one element at a time, exchanging pairs that are out of order as you go. The scan would obviously involve a loop. The question that remains is how many times would you have to scan the array in this manner to ensure that all the numbers are arranged in increasing order? In the worst case, you might have to do this as many times as there are numbers.

A programmer who thinks he is a program

The *BubbleSort* Algorithm

Consider the following case, where the numbers are in the worst possible order, that is, in descending order:

```
[83 81 74 55 38 35 29 24 11 6]
```

I am going to pretend that I am a program that scans the array from left to right. Each time I come to a new pair of out-of-order numbers, I will reverse their order. After one pass through the array, it should have the following appearance:

```
[81 74 55 38 35 29 24 11 6 83]
```

What happened? First, I compared 83 and 81. Finding 83 to be the larger of the two, I swapped their positions. But then I found myself comparing the next two numbers, 83 and 74. Again, I switched the numbers. In this way, the number 83 made its way from the bottom of the array to the top, like a bubble working its way through water. In fact, this sorting technique is called a *bubble sort* for this very reason.

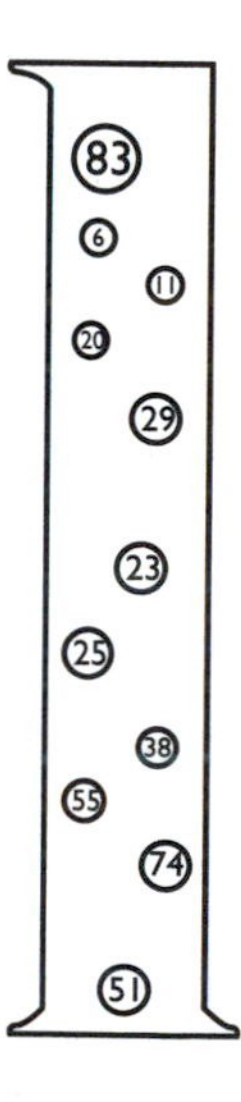

Bubbles suggest a sorting algorithm

A second pass through the array will produce a new one in which the second element, 81, has also worked its way to the end:

```
[74 55 38 35 29 24 11 6 81 83]
```

After seven more passes, the number 6 will occupy the first position of the array. A final pass will be unnecessary because 6 will already be less than all the other elements. In total, then, nine iterations of the scan-and-exchange operation will be necessary. This result suggests a second, outer loop, in the manner of the following algorithm called BubbleSort:

```
for Outer running from 1 to 9
   for Inner running from 1 to 9
      if Num[Inner] > Num[Inner+1]
         then Swap(Num[Inner], Num[Inner+1])
```

The array Num carries the ten numbers to be sorted, and the indices Outer and Inner scan through the array positions. Only the index Inner plays any role in the swapping process, however. The outer loop simply counts through the values of Outer to ensure that the inner, scanning loop runs enough times to sort the array in the worst case. It should be clear that this algorithm involves a degree of overkill for all easier arrays.

The body of the inner loop consists, essentially, of a single step. If the current element of the array Num is greater than the next one, then "you" want to swap the numbers in those positions. This sounds like an ideal job for a procedure. But how will it swap the numbers?

How to Swap

As you will soon see, swapping the values of two variables is just a bit trickier than it sounds. But here's a scenario that might help: Imagine you're wearing trousers or slacks and that you have a nickel in your right pocket and a dime in your left pocket. The right pocket represents one variable (with value 5) and the left pocket represents the other variable (with value 10). Considered as variables, your pockets can only store one coin at a time. How then, would you exchange the coins in your two pockets if you weren't allowed to have two coins in the same pocket at the same time?

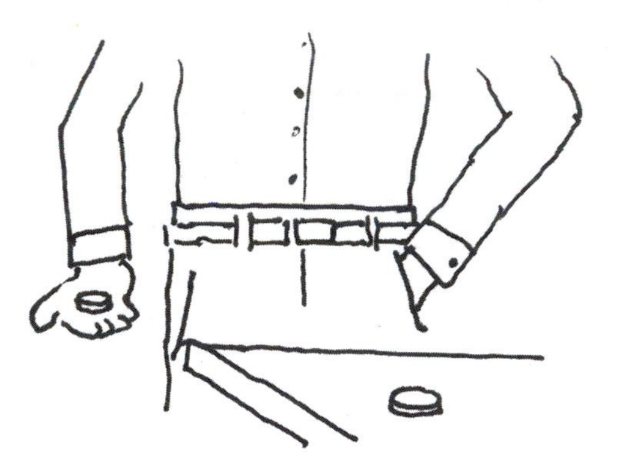

Exchanging coins suggests a procedure

There seems to be no alternative to the following sequence of steps:

1. Take the coin from one pocket and put it on a table.
2. Take the coin from the second pocket and put it in the first pocket.
3. Take the coin from the table and put it in the second pocket.

It seems like you need an extra variable (the table) to hold one of the values temporarily while you move the coin from one pocket into the empty one. The extra variable shows up in the swapping procedure below, where it is called *Temp* (for temporary).

procedure: *Swap(This, That)*
set *Temp* to *This*
set *This* to *That*
set *That* to *Temp*

Whatever values *This* and *That* happen to have, this procedure will exchange their values. When incorporated into a Turbo Pascal procedure, *This* and *That* will have to be VAR parameters, because they must pass their newly swapped values back to the main program.

Here is the complete algorithm laid out in a manner that anticipates the program to come. I have omitted the input module, because that will involve reading from a file, an operation that has no impact on the complexity of the *BubbleSort* algorithm:

```
procedure: Swap(This, That)
set Temp to This
set This to That
set That to Temp

input the array Num

for Outer running from 1 to 9    ← start analysis here
   for Inner running from 1 to 9
      if Num[Inner] > Num[Inner+1]
         then Swap(Num[Inner], Num[Inner+1])
```

The Complexity of *BubbleSort*

This algorithm can be analyzed in much the same way I analyzed the search algorithms in the previous chapter. Imitating the way a computer would execute a corresponding program, I start at the outer loop and work my way in.

The outer loop would set the index variable Outer to 1. Execution would then pass to the inner loop, which would set the index variable Inner to 1. The computer would then execute the main body of the loop. The comparison of the values stored in Num at the positions Inner and Inner + 1 would count as one step. The procedure (if executed) would require one step to call and three steps to execute. As part of the worst-case approach, I will assume that the procedure gets executed with every iteration of the inner loop body.

Each iteration of the inner loop, in other words, will eat up five steps. These five steps will be executed once for each of the inner loop index values, and I must add a step for the increment in the variable Inner. So far, then, the complexity count stands at

$$9 \times (5 + 1) \text{ steps}$$

But these steps will all be executed over again when the value of Outer changes from 1 to 2. And again, when it changes from 2 to 3. Adding the one step that changes the value of Outer, I multiply by 9 to get a final figure for the complexity of the BubbleSort algorithm:

$$9 \times (1 + 9 \times (5 + 1)) \text{ steps}$$

I have not simplified the formula above because I want to generalize it immediately to the case of an array with n entries. Simply replace the number "9" by "n – 1," the number of times both loops would need to be iterated:

$$(n-1)(1+(n-1)(6)) = (n-1)(6n-5)$$

With a little algebra, this expression simplifies considerably. I multiply through by n, then subtract the result of multiplying through by –1:

$$\text{complexity} = 6n^2 - 5n - 6n + 5$$

$$= 6n^2 - 11n + 5$$

Do you recognize the complexity indicated by this expression? I called it "quadratic" in the previous chapter. In other words, the number of steps taken by the *BubbleSort* algorithm will go up as the square of the size of the array. This is not a very efficient algorithm, but it will do for my purposes, because the editor of the business page will not be running the sorting program continually.

There are sorting algorithms that require on the order of n log n steps to sort an array of size n in the worst case, but they lie beyond the scope of this book. Nevertheless, you can compare the efficiency of an order n log n algorithm with an order n^2 algorithm by recognizing that the latter takes

$$n/\log n$$

times as many steps. With a value for n as small as 128, for example, the ratio becomes 128/7, or about 18 times as long to run the order n^2 algorithm.

The *BubbleSort* Program

Because the algorithmic outline above is already very close to being a Turbo Pascal program, I might chance it and translate the algorithm directly into a program, then run it.

```
PROGRAM BubbleSort;
{sorts an array of ten integers into ascending order}
```

```
{declarations module}
TYPE Numbers = ARRAY[1 . . 10] OF INTEGER;
VAR Num: Numbers;
VAR Inner, Outer: INTEGER;

{This procedure swaps the value of two variables.}
PROCEDURE Swap(VAR This, That: INTEGER);
VAR Temp: INTEGER;
BEGIN
Temp := This;
This := That;
That := Temp;
END;

BEGIN {main program}

{Input module}
{TO COME}

{bubble sort module}
FOR Outer := 1 TO 9 DO
   FOR Inner := 1 TO 9 DO
      {If numbers out of position, swap them.}
      IF Num[Inner] > Num[Inner+1]
         THEN Swap(Num[Inner], Num[Inner+1]);

{display module}
WRITE('The sorted array is: ');
FOR Inner := 1 TO 10 DO
   WRITE(Num[Inner], ' ');

{output module}
{TO COME}

END. {of main program}
```

I have omitted the module in which the program reads in the array *Num* from a file. I have also omitted the module that writes the sorted array back into the file. I will produce these modules after I have explained a new kind of file in Turbo Pascal.

The *BubbleSort* program reflects the algorithm very closely, so there is little need to explain it. However, it illustrates the use of procedures, particularly the manner in which parameter values get passed back and forth between a procedure and the places in the program that call it. The program calls the *Swap* procedure from only one place, namely, the THEN part of the conditional statement that tests whether or not two consecutive array elements are in the correct positions. If they are not, the THEN portion of the conditional statement is triggered and the procedure is called by the simple expedient of naming it along with its parameters:

```
THEN Swap(Num[Inner], Num[Inner+1]);
```

In this case, the array elements Num[Inner] and Num[Inner+1] serve as the actual parameters. Whenever the procedure is called, these two variables will contain the values of two adjacent numbers in the array. Suppose the numbers are 23 and 5, respectively. The two values of the actual parameters Num[Inner] and Num[Inner+1] get passed to the formal parameters, *This* and *That*, in the *Swap* procedure itself. In other words, the parameters *This* and *That* end up with the values of 23 and 5, respectively. When the procedure has done its thing with these values, namely, swapped them, the formal parameters will have the values 5 and 23, respectively.

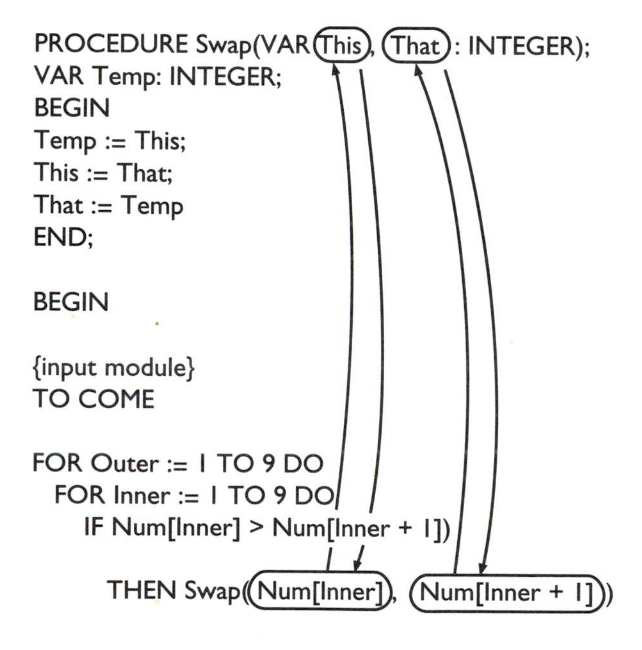

Parameter passing in the *BubbleSort* program

Because *This* and *That* are declared to be VAR parameters, however, the story does not end there. The two values now get passed back to the original actual parameters, Num[Inner] and Num[Inner+1], but now they are in the opposite order, namely, 5 and 23, respectively.

Strings and Records

You will recall that the original aim of the sorting program was to sort, not numbers, but words (or acronyms). In order to refurbish *BubbleSort* as a program that handles a mixed file of numbers and words, I introduce a new type of file, one that employs the Turbo Pascal RECORD type.

Think for a moment about *The Daily Planet* stock page. The simplified format that I will adopt consists of a company name, a short acronym or stock trading symbol, and a closing price. In terms of Turbo Pascal types, the first two items would be strings, while the third would be a real number. A *string* is essentially an array of type CHAR. Turbo Pascal allows you to treat a string as an independent data type with its own declarations. When printed or displayed, strings consist of sequences of characters. English words are strings, but so is "hrsmlpwsitns" or even "1k9a&<fDE#&." In other words, a string is any sequence of characters enclosed in single quotes.

You have already seen plenty of strings in action. Every time you used a WRITELN statement with a message in it, the message was surrounded by single quotes. This was a string, too.

A *string variable* is like any other kind of variable, except that it takes strings as values. To declare a string variable, you must use the usual declaration syntax with the word STRING instead of another type. When you declare a string variable in this manner, the computer will set aside 255 bytes or character-sized memory slots to hold the characters that might make up the string. To keep the memory requirements modest, however, you can set limits to the size of strings allowed as values for a string variable by adding a number inside square brackets right after the key word STRING.

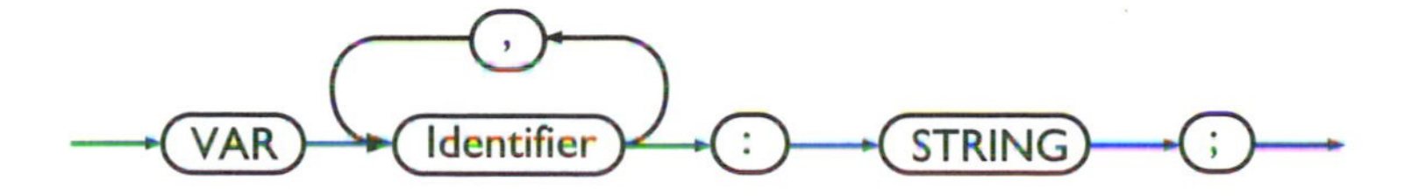

Syntax diagram for a string declaration

You could declare a string variable called *Person* that was to contain names no longer than, say, 100 characters. (Do you know anyone with a name that long?)

```
VAR Person: STRING[100];
```

I will use two string variables—say, *Company* and *Symbol*—to represent the company name and stock ticker symbol in the sorting project. I could make assignments to these variables, as follows:

```
Company := 'Aardvaark';
Symbol  := 'ADV';
```

A Turbo Pascal program can assign values from one string variable to another, provided the assigned string has a declared length that is no larger than the string being assigned to. A program can also assign a single character to a string variable, but it cannot assign a string to a character variable.

To discover the length of a string, that is, the number of characters currently stored in the array, you can use the Pascal LENGTH function. It returns the actual number of characters present. For example, if the assignment of the string 'Aardvaark' were actually made to the string variable company, the LENGTH function would return the following value:

```
LENGTH(Company) = 9
```

You can even compare two strings or string variables with the usual relational operators like <, >, >=, and so on. Just as characters are ordinal types, so are strings. You can think of a telephone book as a very long list of strings, all in alphabetical order. Thus, when you compare two strings such as 'ADV' and 'ARM', you may get a true or a false expression, depending on what relation you use:

```
ARM <= ADV   ARM <> ADV   ARM > ADV
```

Of these three relations, the first is FALSE because ARM does not precede ADV in alphabetical order, the second is TRUE because the strings are not equal, and the third is TRUE because ARM comes after ADV in alphabetical order. As you go through the phone book from a Turbo Pascal point of view, the strings become "greater and greater" in the alphabetic sense.

The Stock File

Up to this point, the only kind of file you have used in a Turbo Pascal program is a text file. While perfect for a multitude of applications, including word processors, text files have their limitations. What if you want to store several different kinds of data in the same file? A *record* consists of one or more *fields*, each occupied by a specific variable that can be of any type. The file for the stock pages contains several types of information. In my cut-down version of the file, there are company names, trading symbols, and prices. This is an ideal application for the Turbo Pascal RECORD type.

You have become familiar with no less than six Turbo Pascal types, namely, INTEGER, REAL, CHAR, BOOLEAN, TEXT, and (just a minute ago) STRING. Imagine a new type of variable that could consist of one or several of these types simultaneously. A Turbo Pascal RECORD variable can consist of a single variable or several of various types. The declaration for a record must begin with the key word TYPE, just as the declaration for arrays did. The rest of the syntax is shown in the adjacent figure.

I will plunge immediately into an example by declaring a record that the stock-sorting program can use:

```
TYPE StockItem = RECORD
   Company: STRING[MaxLength];
   Symbol: STRING[MaxLength];
   Price: REAL;
END;
```

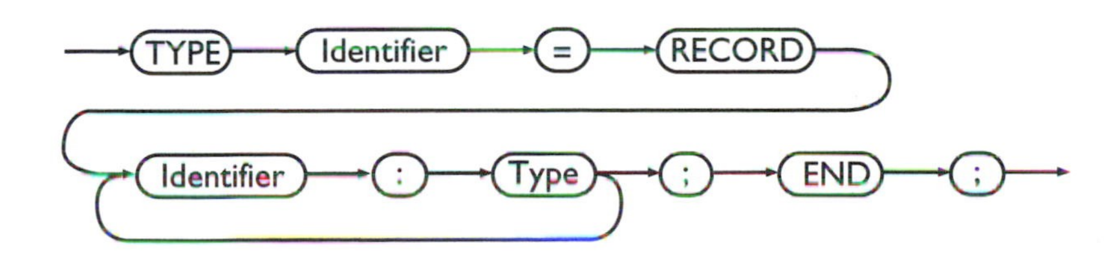

Syntax for a RECORD type declaration

The first statement declares a RECORD type called *StockItem*. The three fields correspond to three separate variables. The variable *Company* will hold a company name, a string with up to *MaxLength* characters in it. The variable called *Symbol*, also a string, will also hold up to *MaxLength* characters. Just prior to this record declaration, I will later declare the CONSTant *MaxLength* equal to 20. This allows up to 20 characters in a company name and up to 20 characters in the trading symbol, although normally only three are used. The third field in each record will be occupied by a stock price, embodied in the REAL variable called *Price*.

One of the beauties of the RECORD data type lies in the flexibility with which a Turbo Pascal program can manipulate such records. For example, you can make an assignment of an entire record into a variable that has been declared to be of this type. With a declaration like

```
VAR OneItem, AnotherItem: StockItem;
```

you can make the following assignment:

```
OneItem := AnotherItem;
```

To access individual fields of a RECORD data type, a program must use a special dot notation. The name of a record variable followed by a dot and the name of the field variable will serve to isolate the datum. The following expression, for example, isolates the stock symbol that occupies the current record stored under the name *OneItem*:

```
OneItem.Symbol
```

If you wanted to assign this value to a string variable called, say, *Ticker*, you could use the following statement:

```
Ticker := OneItem.Symbol;
```

The same kind of notation applies equally well to array variables. In the program that you will see shortly, the array *StockRec* will hold the records we have been discussing. The dot notation will serve to extract the *Symbol* component of these records, as well.

The flexibility allowed by the Turbo Pascal RECORD type has no better illustration than its use in procedures. I can adapt the *Swap* procedure in the *BubbleSort* program by simply redeclaring the formal parameters to be of type *StockItem*.

```
PROCEDURE Swap(VAR This, That: StockItem);
VAR Temp: StockItem;
BEGIN
Temp := This;
This := That;
That := Temp;
END;
```

The new parameters, along with the internally declared record variable, *Temp*, will act just like other variables when the procedure makes its three assignments. The string or number occupying each field will be assigned to its corresponding field in the record to the left of the assignment operator. If the variable *This* consisted of the values 'Alcan', 'AL', and 31.50, for example, these values would occupy their respective fields in the record variable *Temp* as soon as the first assignment statement was executed.

Refurbished in this manner, the procedure *Swap* will exchange values with all its previous aplomb. For the stock file to be read in the first place, however, the program will need a handle for the file of records it must sort. Let's call it *StockFile*. Like an array declaration, a file declaration uses a TYPE statement:

```
TYPE StkFileTp = FILE OF StockItem;
VAR StockFile: StkFileTp;
```

The *BubbleStock* Program

In the main program, I must also do a wholesale replacement of INTEGER variables by RECORD variables. Notice that I have changed the name of the program to reflect its new mission in life.

```
PROGRAM BubbleStock;
{sorts a file of stock data into alphabetical}
{order by company name}

{declarations module}
VAR Inner, Outer, Count: INTEGER;
```

```
CONST MaxLength = 20;
TYPE StockItem = RECORD
                    Company: STRING[MaxLength];
                    Symbol: STRING[MaxLength];
                    Price: REAL;
                 END;
TYPE StkFileTp = FILE OF StockItem;
VAR StockFile: StkFileTp;
TYPE StkArrayTp = ARRAY[1 . . 100] OF StockItem;
VAR StockRec: StkArrayTp;

{This procedure swaps two records.}
PROCEDURE Swap(VAR This, That: StockItem);
VAR Temp: StockItem;
BEGIN
Temp := This;
This := That;
That := Temp;
END;

BEGIN {main program}

{set up file to read}
ASSIGN(StockFile, 'STKDTA.DAT');
RESET(StockFile);

{file-reading module}
Count := 0
WHILE NOT EOF(StockFile) DO
   BEGIN
   Count := Count + 1;
   READ(StockFile, StockRec[Count]);
   END;

{bubble sort module}
FOR Outer := 1 TO Count DO
   FOR Inner := 1 TO Count - 1 DO
      IF StockRec[Inner].Company > StockRec[Inner+1].Company
         THEN Swap(StockRec[Inner], StockRec[Inner+1]);

{change gears}
CLOSE(StockFile);
REWRITE(StockFile);

{display module}
WRITELN('The sorted records follow: ');
```

```
FOR Inner := 1 TO Count DO
   BEGIN
   WRITE(StockRec[Inner].Company, ' ');
   WRITE(StockRec[Inner].Symbol, ' ');
   WRITE(StockRec[Inner].Price);
   WRITELN;
   END;

{output module}
FOR Inner := 1 TO Count DO
   WRITELN(StockFile, StockRec[Ind]);

{close the file}
CLOSE(StockFile);

END. {of program}
```

The program *BubbleStock* sorts a file of records that each consist of three fields: company name, ticker symbol, and price. Initially, records in the file called *StockFile* are arranged in alphabetical order by ticker symbol. The program sorts the file into a new order, alphabetical by company name.

In the declarations module you will recognize the variables used in the earlier *BubbleSort* program. A new integer variable called *Count* has been added. It keeps track of the number of records in the file, and the program uses this variable as a limit in two FOR-loops, one that displays the newly sorted records and another that stores the records back in *StockFile*.

Furthermore, I have defined the type *StockItem* and then applied it to the definition of two other types, *StkFileTp* and *StkArrayTp*. The latter two, in turn, enable me to define a file called *StockFile* and an array called *StockArray*. The program uses the array to hold the records of the file both before and after sorting.

The name *StockFile* must be ASSIGNed to a file in the system, namely, 'STKDTA.DAT'. Files with the DAT extension include most of the nontext files you will ever want to store data in. Once the program has informed the computer what external file the name *StockFile* refers to, it RESETS the file. This statement opens it for reading, the operation to be performed by the very next program module.

The program module that reads *StockFile* into the array *StockArray* uses the NOT EOF condition to control iteration of the WHILE loop. It is usually a good idea to add the name of the file being used as a parameter for the EOF function, even though the filename is not a required part of the syntax of the EOF function. For data files, you must always use a READ statement because the concept of a line (as in READLN) is absent from such files. Within this loop, the READ statement transfers the data, one record at a time, from StockFile to the array StockArray. By the time the reading process reaches the end of the file and the EOF function becomes TRUE, the variable Count holds the total number of records.

The bubble sort module looks just like it did in the BubbleSort program, except it has been retooled to handle records instead of integers. The Boolean expression that follows the IF uses the dot notation to specify just one field of the record contained in StockArray[Inner]. The name Company ensures that the comparison is based only on company names and not on the ticker symbol or the price. Looking at this for a moment, you might realize that you could replace the notation ".Company" by ".Symbol" to sort the file by ticker symbol. You could even replace it by ".Price" in order to sort the records by price. (See Exploration 9.) Except for the slightly complicated notation induced by record-handling requirements, this module is identical to its previous incarnation and works exactly the same way.

Once the bubble sort module has done its thing, the records in the array have all been sorted into alphabetical order by company names. It is then time to change gears, closing StockFile to further reading and reopening it to writing.

The display module now uses the value of Count to control the process of writing the individual fields of each record to the screen. Notice once again how the dot notation enables the program to access the individual fields of records stored in StockArray. Three WRITE statements take the display across a line of the screen and the WRITELN takes the cursor down to the next line for the next three values. After displaying the records stored in StockArray, the program uses the same kind of loop to store them back in StockFile, this time in sorted order. The program then closes the file and ENDs.

Your tour of the design and construction of the BubbleStock program is now over. You have discovered that once the elements of the Turbo Pascal RECORD type are mastered, sorting files is no more difficult than sorting integers. It might interest you to know, meanwhile, that the complexity of this version of the sorting program is unchanged from the earlier version. It will still take on the order of n^2 steps to sort a file of n records.

Sony SNE 54.75
Sprint FON 40.12
SterlElec SEC 17.00
Sun Co SUN 27.50
Tandy TAN 46.75
Tektronix TEK 54.50
Texaco TX 75.87
Timken TRV 40.37
Travelers TRV 62.37
Tribune TRB 65.87
Tyco Toys TTI 5.00
US Air U 12.75
US Inds USN 17.50

The last few lines of the display

No News Is Bad News

Back in the newsroom of *The Daily Planet*, reporters are furiously entering their stories. One reporter, who has been consistently misspelling the name of a surprise witness in a murder case, suddenly discovers this. It might drive him crazy, given his deadline, to work through the entire story and change the spelling. Luckily, he is using a word processing program that has this capability, among many others.

I will ask you to imitate this particular portion of a word processing program for three reasons:

1. It makes a great project.
2. It gives you insight into the structure of word processing software.
3. It permits me to introduce the last computer science topic of this book.

Software Engineering

The amazing developments in computing over the last few decades have depended on the appearance of a succession of increasingly better computers, each faster and having more memory than the one before. But it has depended even more, in a sense, on the development of increasingly sophisticated programs that would be useless without the high speed and large memories of modern machines.

Applications programs form the very crux of the computer revolution, driving it forward by making computers increasingly indispensible at home and in the workplace and by creating a demand, in turn, for even faster computers with even larger memories. Applications programs, whether spreadsheets or word processors, inventory controllers or airline schedulers, modem software or computer games, typically involve hundreds of thousands of lines of code—in some cases, millions. It can even be argued that such programs are more complicated than the computers they run on!

As a result of this complexity, applications programs are written, not by a single programmer, but by a team of programmers and managers that must coordinate its activities to a very high degree. The field called *software engineering* has emerged as a result of a recognition that, without the discipline imposed by the designing process and team management, the writing of large software packages would degenerate into unmanageable chaos.

Software engineering recognizes that all large programming projects pass through a set of characteristic phases called the *software cycle*. You may even participate in the cycle if you become involved in a team of classmates to build the word processor software called *WordChange*.

The Software Cycle

Applications programs, typically developed by a software firm for public or corporate use, undergo a life cycle that reminds me of the life of a human being, from conception to death.

Conception Phase. The cycle begins when a client approaches a software developer with an idea for something he thinks a computer might be able to do, something his firm will pay to have done, if possible. There follows a series of meetings about the idea until, with the client's help, the developer produces a list of requirements that the program must meet. The requirements might be revised through a series of further meetings but eventually the process moves on to the . . .

Specification phase. In this phase, the development team must decide what the program is to do in as much detail as possible. In other words, it must specify how the computer is to behave from the user's point of view. How, precisely, will it interact with the user? What form

Bugs and Faults

Software engineers prefer not to use the term "bugs" in referring to logical and other errors in the code produced by a programming team. The reason is psychological. The term "bug" encourages a passive, nonresponsible attitude on the part of programmers: "A bug crept into my program!"

Not all faults are bugs in the sense that I have been using that term. Sometimes a software team produces a piece of code that meets all specifications, only to discover that they misinterpreted the specifications or that they were not what the client wanted in the first place. From the client's point of view, the software contains a fault even though, from the programmer's point of view, it *was* bug-free.

will the output take? How fast must the response be? These and a host of other questions about the proposed package must all be answered by the development team.

Strange as it may sound, most software faults are generated in the specification phase. (See the box on this page.) Faults occur not only because someone specified the wrong form of interaction. The specifications may have contradictory requirements or may be incomplete by failing to anticipate a situation that neither the client nor the developer thought of.

Design Phase. If the specification phase is about what the program is to do, the design phase is about how the program must do it. The development team must decide how the program will carry out its mission by first setting up an algorithmic outline, which can then be divided into modules. The team leader assigns modules to different programmers, exploiting their strengths and allowing for their weaknesses.

Each module is then designed by the team or by individual programmers. At this stage, variable names can be assigned and data structures such as files or arrays are determined and named. The input and output properties of each module are also defined at this stage. Module A may use input that is provided as output by Module B. It follows that the programmers responsible for these modules must be aware of what form the input and output must take.

During this and all other phases, all decisions, algorithms, and minutes of design meetings are documented. Programming in the dark, without communication and documentation, is a recipe for disaster.

Implementation Phase. At some point during development of the new program, the team takes a collective breath and launches the implementation phase. Now, the algorithms for various modules making up the program must all be coded, that is, translated into whatever language the team happens to be using and tested thoroughly on a large variety of inputs that exercise the modules in every conceivable way.

Integration Phase. When all the modules are ready, the main program is written and the modules incorporated, sometimes individually, sometimes all at once. The composite program is assembled. Now is when the team must do its level best to detect faults in the program.

The client might be invited in at this point to exercise the program in various ways that he believes are typical or desirable. Many faults are located, but some, inevitably, remain.

Software engineering is not like mechanical engineering. If a bridge fails, you have to build (and design) another. But if a large piece of software (like an operating system) fails, it makes no sense to scrap the whole thing. The developer must locate and fix the fault, if possible.

Maintenance Phase. Once the client has officially accepted the software, the developer's job is not done. In fact, over half the costs of new software are incurred during this phase. The developer, after all, normally

A software failure?

has a contractual obligation to maintain the software. This agreement means not only continuing the relentless pursuit of faults in the program, but also considering feedback from the client who, as the program's main user, now has many suggestions for "improvements." "We think that our customers should be able to change the database themselves," announces the sales manager for the client company one day. Now the development team, or some part of it, will modify the program to make this possible.

Here, as much as anywhere during the software life cycle, the advantages of well-structured and documented programs becomes fully apparent. With relative ease, programmers find their way back into the program, refamiliarizing themselves with the modules that will need changing, reading the code for those modules without undue puzzlement.

Retirement. At last the program, after many years of use, hopefully, is ready to be retired. The new program to be developed for the client is simply too different to make refurbishing of the old program worthwhile. At this point, the team's responsibilities for that particular program come to an end. When the new program is ready, it replaces the old on many disk drives and main memories. Software dies a quiet death.

The *WordChange* Project

I will now bring these phases to life, to the degree possible under the present conditions, by setting up a programming team and assigning modules to individuals in the team. Your lecturer can act as team manager, or one of you might take on that task.

I will take you just beyond the specification phase, far enough to lay out the modules. Beyond a bit of programming advice for each of the modules, I will then leave you to finish the project yourselves.

The Specification. The *WordChange* program must take two words entered by the user as input. The program must search a text file for the first word and, every time it encounters that word, replace it with the second word. When the program has finished, all instances of the first word in the file must have been replaced by the second word.

As a sample text for this word processing program to work on, a file called NEWS.TXT has been provided. This file contains a number of mistakes that must be corrected. After analyzing these specifications sufficiently to allow the writing of a preliminary algorithmic design, I will make specific suggestions for dividing the work of the project among individual students.

What steps must such a program go through to change a word in a file? It must first of all accept two words from the user, the word that needs to be changed and a word that will replace it. The program must then read through the file, one word at a time. Each word it reads in must be compared to the target word; if it matches, the program must write the substitute word into the file, replacing the target word. You will encounter some subtleties as you work your way into this project, but without even trying, I have already come up with a bare-bones outline for the algorithm.

```
get the word to be changed
and its replacement from the user

while processing the file
  assemble characters into a word
  if the word does not match the word to be changed
    then write the word in a temporary file
    else write replacement word in the temporary file

replace the original file by the temporary one
```

You can probably already imagine how you might divide the work of this project among individuals. However, you might also be fooled by the brevity of this description. For example, the following step would constitute a major module of the program:

```
assemble characters into a word
```

How will the program know when a complete word has been read from the file? Obviously it will have to watch for blanks, among other things.

The Programming Team. Here is one way to divide up the work among three students. In a normal university class, there will be more than three students. Why not count off three-student teams until all the students have been assigned to a team. If the number of students is not divisible by three, the lecturer might create one or two teams with just two people in them, perhaps some of the more adventurous and eager students.

The following division of programming labor represents just one way to carve up the algorithm:

programmer 1: user interface and file management
programmer 2: main loop
programmer 3: word recognition

I will explain each of these subprojects in enough detail to get the team started.

Programmer 1: (user interface and file management) As the first member of the team, you will be responsible for code that reads in words as strings input by a user. You may find it handy to use the LENGTH function to provide programmer 2 with a measure of both the word to be changed and its replacement. The measures would be stored in variables that programmer 2 might employ.

You will also be responsible for setting up files for reading or writing and for closing them later. You will name all the text files, including a temporary file to hold the results of the word processing until the entire input file has been scanned. You must also write code that displays the corrected file on the screen before the original file is replaced by the new one.

Programmer 2: (the main loop) The main loop will almost certainly want to begin as follows:

```
WHILE NOT EOF( . . . ) DO
```

The blank filename is for programmer 1 to fill in. The main loop must compare the word supplied to it by the recognition module (see programmer 3) with the target word. If you happen to be programmer 2, you may want to proceed with the comparison by first comparing the sizes of the recognized word and the target word. If they do not match, there is no need to proceed with a character-by-character comparison. It may even be that you become lazy and decide to bypass such a comparison, letting the string equality test do it all:

```
Target = Found (?)
```

Programmer 3: (word recognition) As programmer 3, you will write the software that reads the input file character by character. You must store these characters in a string one character at a time by using your string variable in array mode. If your variable happens to be called *NewWord*, for example, your code might keep track of the length (*Len*, say) of this variable in order to add a new character:

```
NewWord[Len+1] := NewChar;
```

A key part of your module will be the procedure by which you distinguish between characters that could be part of English words from blanks and other word terminators such as commas and periods. This part will exploit some characteristics of the ASCII code rather heavily. Along the way, you will enjoy figuring out how to handle the case of the apostrophe or single quote.

Nota Bene

Each team must also select one of its members to act as records officer. This person will write the program header and all declarations (except, possibly, for procedures). The records officer will therefore gather the names of all variables from other team members and make a list in which each variable is defined, both as to type and meaning within the program.

My only fear in leaving you like this is that the class may become obsessed and refuse to stop programming until it has produced an entire word processor!

SUMMARY

Thanks to you, *The Daily Planet* continues to run smoothly. The stock page has all its companies in order and editors can replace any word they want in a news file by any other word.

Along the way, you have become familiar with two very important Turbo Pascal data types, STRING and RECORD. A *string* variable is just an array of characters that you can assign individual characters to by using array notation. You can also assign a whole string to a *string* variable in one go. The RECORD type brings the symphony of types to a climax (for now) by allowing a variable that embraces all variables. A record, after all, may consist of several fields, each accessed by its own variable.

These types became very useful in dealing with stock market data. There, each record consisted of a company name, a stock symbol, and a price. Strings will play no less crucial a role in the word processing program.

EXPLORATIONS

1 Just for fun, turn back to Chapter 2, where we wrote the *AddTutor* program. Pretend you are a program and describe how you work with the student, statement by statement.

2 Here is an array of five numbers. Sort them by using a bubble sort, producing a new array at each step:

$$[7 \quad 9 \quad 3 \quad 1 \quad 5]$$

3 Devise a five-element array that will tie up the *BubbleSort* algorithm as long as possible. This will be the worst case that will absorb on the order of all n^2 steps.

4 There are algorithms that can sort an array of n entries in the order of n log n steps. Argue that this complexity is better than the complexity of the bubblesort algorithm by a factor of (log n)/n. Make the argument on purely algebraic grounds. This means comparing the two complexities by making a ratio of them and then canceling terms.

5 (For the puzzle-minded) Show that to swap the values of two real variables, you don't *really* have to use an additional variable. Instead you can use a combination of multiplication and division and the two variables alone!

6 Write a program that takes an array of integers as input and determines the median number as output. This is an array entry for which half the entries are larger and half smaller. One way to tackle the problem, perhaps the simplest way, is to adapt the sorting program *BubbleSort* to this enterprise. Applied to an array, the program will produce a sorted array. An additional statement or two will suffice to count halfway along the array and reproduce the entry there.

7 Declare *Driver* to be a string variable of length not exceeding 100 characters. Make an assignment statement in which this variable receives the value 'Mary Worth'. Finally, define a new character variable and assign the third character of the string *Driver* to this variable.

8 The state licensing bureau keeps a file of all drivers under its jurisdiction. The file consists of records that contain nine fields:

driver's name
license number
age
sex
violation points
street address
city
state
zip code

Declare a Turbo Pascal RECORD type that has these fields, each with its own name. Declare a record variable called *Driver* that has this type. In a program that uses the file mentioned earlier, what statement would assign the license number of the driver in *Driver* to the string variable *License*?

9 Enter the *BubbleStock* program by hand or from a disk. Run the program on the file provided and report on the results. Were any of the stocks not listed in order of company name? Now alter the program so that it sorts, not on the basis of company name but on the basis of the ticker symbol. Resort the file and report on what the program displayed. Finally, alter the program so that it sorts on the basis of price. Report on the median stock price for the whole data set. (See Exploration 6.)

10 Write the word recognition module that programmer 3 was challenged with in the section on software engineering.

11 What does the following program do?

```
PROGRAM LCRider;
```

```
VAR Letter: CHAR
TYPE LetterType = FILE OF TEXT;
VAR LetterFile, NewFile: LetterType;

BEGIN

ASSIGN(LetterFile, 'LETTERS.TXT');
ASSIGN(NewFile, 'NEWLET.TXT');
RESET(LetterFile);
REWRITE(NewFile);

WHILE NOT EOF(LetterFile) DO
   BEGIN
   READ(LetterFile, Letter);
   IF (Letter >= 'A') AND (Letter <= 'Z')
      THEN Letter := CHR(ORD(Letter) + 32);
   WRITE(NewFile, Letter);
   END;

CLOSE(LetterFile);
CLOSE(NewFile);

END.
```

12 Design and write another miniature word processing function. This one must read a text file (use the one provided for the *BubbleSort* program) and scan it for individual characters. The program counts the characters and reports on the total size of the file in bytes.

Appendix
Turbo Pascal Advisory

This advisory can help you in two ways. First, it provides syntax, semantics, and operational descriptions for the major statement types covered in Chapters 1–3. (The syntax and semantics of the statement types covered in Chapter 4 on are provided in full in the relevant chapters.) At the same time, for each statement type covered in this book, this advisory gives important items of information that will help you take full advantage of Turbo Pascal. It will help you extend your programming abilities, complete Explorations, and bring projects to a successful conclusion.

Statement types are covered in alphabetical order under the following headings:

- Assignment statements
- Conditional statements
  - IF-THEN
  - IF-THEN-ELSE
  - CASE
- Data structures and declarations
  - Variables
  - Arrays
  - Strings
  - Text files
  - Files of records
  - Objects
- Input/output statements
  - READLN and READ
  - WRITELN and WRITE
- Loops
  - FOR-loops
  - WHILE-loops
  - REPEAT-loops
- Statements in general
  - Simple statements
  - Compound statements
- Subprograms
  - Functions
  - Procedures

Assignment Statements

The main vehicle for numerical calculation and information transfer in Turbo Pascal is the assignment statement. As you may recall from the examples in the first two chapters, the assignment statement consists of a calculation and a variable name or identifier separated by the assignment operator :=.

The syntax diagram governing assignment statements includes only arithmetic expressions:

The linear diagram is deceptively simple. An arithmetic expression begins with an identifier followed by the := operator followed by an expression followed by a semicolon. The term "expression," however, includes not only arithmetic expressions but Boolean expressions, either of which can be quite complicated.

What does an assignment statement mean? The meaning is computational. For every variable in an arithmetic expression, for example, the computer looks up the value, then incorporates the value into an ongoing calculation of a value for the expression as a whole. In carrying out this evaluation, the computer works from the left side of the expression to the right. As it goes, it also works out the values of expressions inside parentheses first. In the case of nested parentheses, it starts on the innermost expressions.

```
Target := Previous + ((1 + Tremble/Widget)*Windage) - Allowance);
```

A computer would evaluate this arithmetic expression, for example, from left to right, but it cannot add the value of *Preview* to the expression inside parentheses until it has evaluated it. And the computer cannot do that until it has evaluated the innermost expression:

```
1 + Tremble/Widget
```

Here it must first divide the current value of *Tremble* by the current value of *Widget*, then add the result to 1. With the expression in the innermost parentheses evaluated, the computer may then multiply this value by the value of *Windage*. Only then may it add the result to *Previous* and subtract the value of *Allowance*.

Turbo Pascal does not generally allow assignment statements in which one kind of variable is assigned to another (it makes no sense to assign a CHAR value to a REAL variable, for example), but it does allow some mixed assignments. For example, you may assign an INTEGER-valued expression to a LONGINT variable but not the converse. You may also assign a CHAR-valued expression to a STRING variable but not the other way around. Such assignments make sense because a long integer may take ordinary integer values, just as a character is a special case of a string.

Conditional Statements

Conditional statements are of three types:

IF-THEN
IF-THEN-ELSE (Chapter 5)
CASE (Chapter 8)

The syntax of the IF-THEN statement follows:

A simple conditional statement of this type consists of the word IF followed by a Boolean expression followed by the Pascal word THEN followed by a statement.

Conditional statements are a principal means of directing the flow of computation within a program in a way that depends on the computation itself. You are already familiar with how the three types of conditional statements operate. In general, the statement that follows an IF, a THEN or even a case can be any executable Turbo Pascal statement.

No semicolon appears after the THEN component of an IF-THEN-ELSE statement. If you want the program to execute a compound statement following either a THEN or an ELSE, you must follow the normal rules for forming compound statements (see the section on statements on page 359), placing a BEGIN before and an END after the statements that make up the compound statement.

Unlike the IF conditional statements, the CASE statement may employ any number of cases and therefore of statements within it. When the computer executes a CASE statement, it executes only one of the component statements, whether simple or compound.

Data Structures and Declarations

The general variable declaration looks like this:

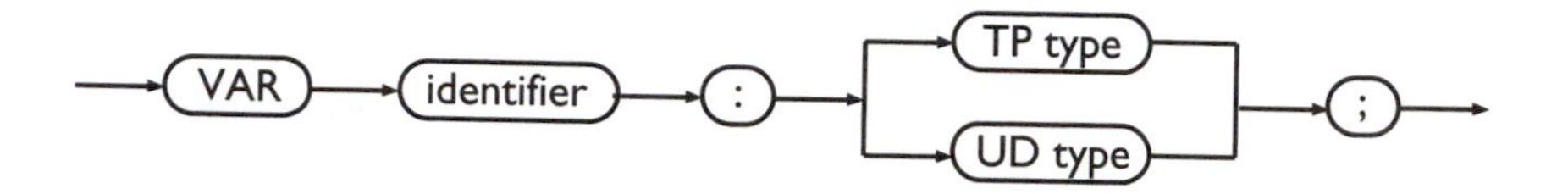

The term "TP type" refers to Turbo Pascal types such as REAL, INTEGER, CHAR, BOOLEAN, STRING, and TEXT. The term "UD type" refers to user-defined types such as arrays and records. The diagram is general enough to embrace all variable declarations that contain a single VAR.

Syntax diagrams for array declarations appear in Chapter 6, for text file declarations in Chapter 8, and for record declarations in Chapter 10. In those chapters you will also find the type declarations that go with data structures like arrays and records.

The idea of a variable in Turbo Pascal is fluid. It includes not only the variables of the first four types studied in this book (REAL, INTEGER, BOOLEAN, and CHAR) but more complex data types, as well. The latter could be characterized as variables with more than one part.

You have used arrays frequently in this book and you already know a lot about them. You may not know that you can assign one array to another, holus-bolus, without the need for a loop. The two arrays should be of the same type and dimension (number of components). The statement

```
BArray := CArray;
```

assigns every element of the array *CArray* to its corresponding element in the array *BArray*.

Turbo Pascal functions, whether built-in or user-defined, cannot return an array as a value. Procedures, on the other hand, are allowed to return arrays as values provided that the arrays in question are declared within the procedure's parameter list as VAR parameters.

Arrays may be declared of any size, but when you use an array in a program, you are under no obligation to ensure that the array is filled. For example, you could declare an array type

```
TYPE Arraytype = ARRAY[1 . . 1000] OF REAL;
```

yet the program might use only the first 50 values of this array through input statements, output statements, or assignment statements.

You are not confined to a single index when using arrays. A two-dimensional array has two indices and both must be specified to access elements of the array. The following declaration specifies a two-dimensional array called *Map*:

```
TYPE MapArray = ARRAY[1..25, 1..56] OF REAL;
Map: MapArray;
```

With index variables, say *Lat* and *Long*, a program could access individual array elements, as in the statement

```
Color := Map[Lat, Long];

Color := Map[14, Long];

Color := Map[Lat, 24] + 0.5;
```

In short, as long as you specify both indices, a program may use a two-dimensional array in exactly the same way it uses one-dimensional arrays, the ones you've been using up to now.

Strings, as you know, are essentially arrays of type CHAR. Strings are defined and declared in Chapter 10, but you've been staring at strings ever since Chapter 1. Every group of characters enclosed in single quotation marks is a string. Typically, such strings appear in WRITE and WRITELN statements. Such strings amount to constants, when it comes to string variables. A variable of type STRING[100], for example, might have taken any of these string constants as values.

Instead of making you declare an array whenever you want to use a string, Turbo Pascal lets you declare strings directly, as shown in Chapter 10. Like arrays, strings do not have to be filled. If you declare a string to hold 100 characters, as in the previous paragraph, you can use it to hold a single letter, if you like! If you declare a string without the square bracket notation, the computer will set aside 255 places for characters in the string.

Text files, the subject of Chapter 8, brought with them a host of special statement types, such as ASSIGN, RESET, REWRITE, and CLOSE. A program must always CLOSE any file that it has read from or written to before doing any other file processing. If the program is not going to write to a file it has already opened before accessing another file, it must CLOSE the file.

The most important fact about text files is that they are normally organized into lines. A *line* consists of a group of consecutive characters followed by a special character called an *end-of-line marker*. Lines in a file can be of any length. It all depends on the program that created them. For example, one file might consist of 10 characters per line while another file might have a variable number of characters per line.

The end-of-line marker can be accessed through the Turbo Pascal function EOLN. As with the end-of-file function, EOF, the end-of-line function can be used effectively in WHILE-loops, as in the following fragment:

```
WHILE NOT EOLN
   BEGIN
   READ(TextFile, Symbol);
   next statement, etc.
```

The computer will read the elements of the file, one character at a time, until it encounters the end-of-line marker. At this point the function EOLN will automatically become true and the WHILE-loop will exit.

If you tried to use READLN in place of READ in the above fragment, the computer would read a single character, then skip to the next line of the file. READLN comes into its own with text files whenever you want to read just one or a few characters (as many as there are variables in the

READLN statement) from each line. It may happen that the lines of the file consist of only a few characters each. The statement

```
READLN(TextFile, Symbol1, Symbol2, Symbol3);
```

might be just the thing for a text file in which every line has three characters, for example. It would read these characters into the variables *Symbol1*, *Symbol2*, and *Symbol3* before going on to read the next line.

Text files can be parameters in procedures, just as arrays can. As with arrays, text files must be declared as VAR parameters.

Files of records have a very different organization than that of text files. First, record files have no lines. As a result, you should not use READLN with record files. READ is the statement of choice. By the same token, you use WRITE, not WRITELN, with record files. Although files of records have no end-of-line markers, they do have end-of-file markers, just as text files do. Consequently, you must use the EOF function (in a WHILE- or REPEAT-loop) when attempting to read a complete file of records.

Objects, covered in Chapter 7, extend the idea of program modularization by packaging procedures and data together into a single OBJECT type. A variable of this type, called an *instance*, can be assigned, read, written, and manipulated in most of the ways Turbo Pascal allows with any other kind of variable.

To what I have already said about objects, let me add one piece of advice for avoiding the cumbersome dot notation. Suppose you had an object variable called *Recipe*. This object contains a procedure called *Cook* and an array called *Cookies*. If the program is going to make frequent references to either the method, as in

```
Recipe.Cook
```

or the data, as in

```
Recipe.Cookies
```

you may employ a WITH-statement. Before executing the statements in question, your computer should have encountered the statement

```
WITH Recipe DO
```

The statements involving *Cook* and *Cookies,* when placed between a subsequent BEGIN/END pair, may all be simplified by referring to the procedure or the array as

```
Cook
```

and

```
Cookies
```

Input and Output Statements

The syntax diagrams for READLN and WRITELN follow. If you substitute READ and WRITE for READLN and WRITELN, respectively, you have the syntax diagrams for the latter types of statements, as well.

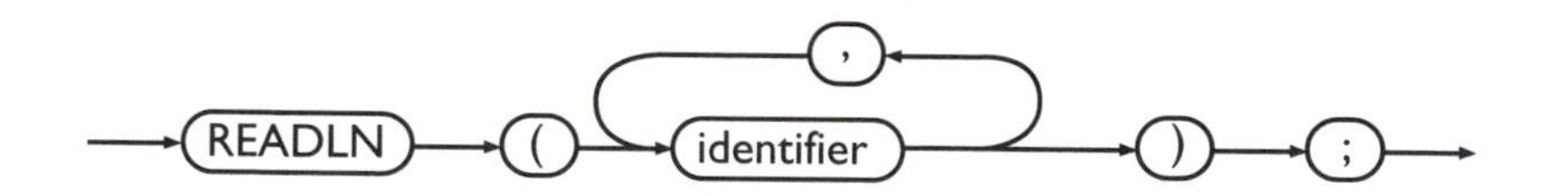

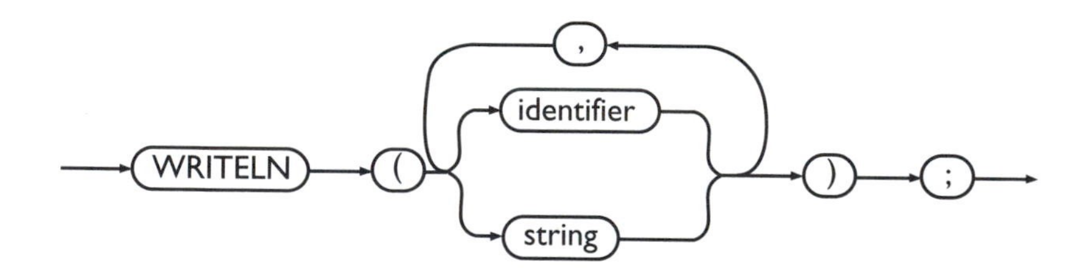

The READLN statement consists of the Pascal word READLN followed by a left parenthesis followed by any number of identifiers separated by commas followed by a right parenthesis and the usual semicolon.

The WRITELN statement begins with the Pascal word WRITELN followed by a left parenthesis followed by a choice of identifier or message. The term "string" refers to any string constant, that is, a sequence of characters enclosed by single quotes. Naturally, none of the characters may be a single quote. As the back-arrow indicates, the identifiers and messages (which may occur in any order you like) must be separated by commas, just like the identifiers in a READLN statement. After the last identifier or message comes a right parenthesis and a semicolon.

When the computer executes a READLN statement, it waits for input from the keyboard and, when the ENTER key is pressed, reads in the number the user has entered. What does this mean? The computer stores the number entered by the user under the name that appears within the READLN statement's parentheses. In fact, no matter how many variable identifiers appear in the READLN statement, the computer patiently awaits the user's input for each variable and stores the number in its memory.

When the computer executes a WRITELN statement, however, data flows in the opposite direction. The computer separately processes the identifiers and messages that make up a WRITELN statement. Each time it comes to an identifier, it looks up the current value stored under that variable name and displays it on the screen. Each time it comes to a message enclosed in single quotes, it repeats the message, verbatim, on the screen.

Throughout this book, you have used all four kinds of input or output statements in a variety of contexts. Little further advice can be given except to stress the differences between READ and READLN and between WRITE and WRITELN.

When the computer executes a READLN statement, it accepts the input for each variable in the READLN variable list. If the user, who enters the values separated by blanks, attempts to enter another value, the computer ignores it, since the READLN has already jumped to the beginning of the next line in a figurative sense. When the computer executes a READ statement or multiple READ statements, on the other hand, it keeps accepting input on the current line and, if necessary, beyond it. This means that subsequent values may be entered on the next line.

When entering characters for a string variable, you must use the READLN statement because a READ will not be able to distinguish the last character of a given input string from the blank that separates input values.

Turbo Pascal has a habit of returning you to the edit screen as soon as your program has executed. This annoys many people. To get around this problem, you may add the following statement at the end of your program:

```
READLN;
```

When no variable is specified as input, the computer simply pauses when it encounters this statement during its execution. The pause gives you time to inspect the display on the screen and enjoy the effect of your program. As soon as you press any key (I prefer the spacebar), the program finishes executing the READLN, then terminates.

Loops

The syntax diagram for FOR-loops reveals a feature of FOR-loops that many programmers find handy:

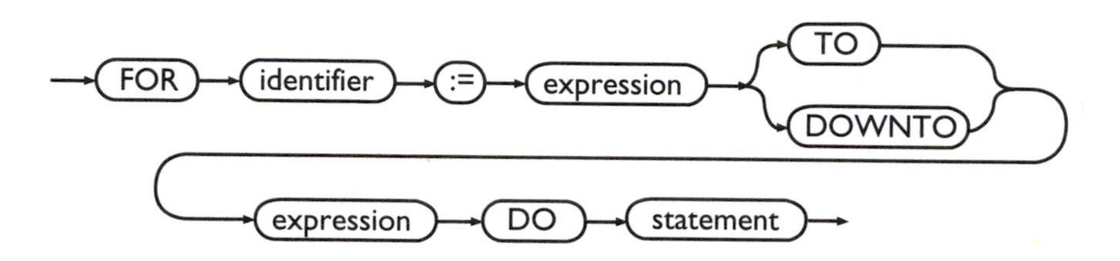

The "identifier" must be a variable of type INTEGER, as must the expressions that provide the intial and final values of the variable. You are already familiar with FOR-loops that employ the TO option. If the initial expression has a value that is greater than the value of the final expression, the FOR-loop will not execute. In such cases, you may want to use the DOWNTO option. This enables a FOR-loop to count down from any initial value to any terminal value that is less than the initial one. This feature is useful when you want to process an array in reverse order, for example.

Finally, you should know that whether you use a TO or a DOWNTO in a FOR-loop, the intial expression does not have to evaluate to a positive value. For example, the following FOR-statement control part is perfectly valid:

```
FOR Index := -7 TO 15 DO
```

This loop will be executed for values –7, –6, –5, . . . , 15 of *Index*.

Your experience with WHILE- and REPEAT-loops makes further advice unnecessary. In using WHILE-loops, however, I would remind you to ensure that the Boolean expression in the control part can be evaluated. Every variable that participates in the Boolean expression must already have a value. This does not need to be true of a REPEAT-loop, as long as the participating variables all have values by the time execution reaches the control part at the end of the REPEAT-loop.

Sometimes a student is astonished because a program he or she runs just refuses to quit. Nonterminating programs may suffer from infinite loops. A FOR-loop can never be infinite, but WHILE- and REPEAT-loops frequently catch this disease. A WHILE-loop with the following control part will never terminate:

```
WHILE 2 = 2 DO
```

It would be strange for someone to use such an expression to control a WHILE-loop, but sometimes we do the equivalent thing by using an expression that, under some circumstances, can never be false.

Statements in General

The syntax diagram for a simple statement consists of a single arrow branching into seven arrows, each going to a different name for a statement type or group of types:

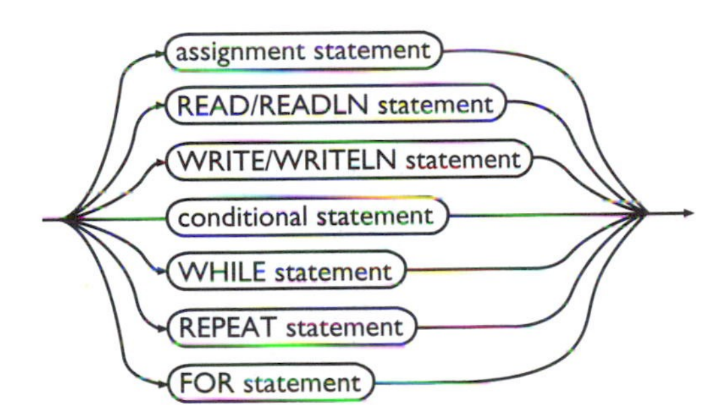

In general, the word "statement" refers not to simple statements alone but to compound statements as well. To define this more general type, I add the category "compound statements" to the list in the figure. I can now define a compound statement with the following simple syntax diagram:

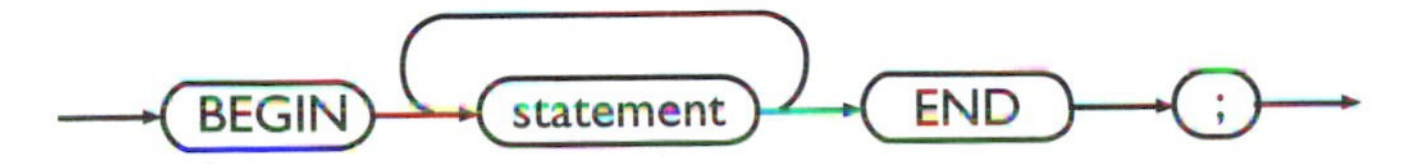

It might interest you to know that an entire Turbo Pascal program can be defined as a special type of statement that consists of a header, declarations, Turbo Pascal words, and other statements, all following a precise syntax. In Chapter 2, in the section on syntax and automata, I pointed out that the computer contains various automata that process the statements of a Turbo Pascal program. A somewhat complicated form of automaton actually "accepts" Turbo Pascal programs (or not) in the way an ordinary automaton accepts the words of its language. In fact, the Turbo Pascal progam-accepting automaton has its own language: It consists of all valid Turbo Pascal programs. It is a frightening but inspiring thought that *all* the Turbo Pascal programs ever written do not amount to even the tiniest fraction of all the Turbo Pascal programs that a modern computer might accept!

Subprograms

Functions, whether built-in or user-defined, always carry their value in the function name. Although in some respects a function name is like a variable, you cannot use it with quite the same abandon as you would a variable. For example, a user-defined function must have at least one assignment statement in which the function name appears as the assigned-to variable. But the function name can never appear on the right-hand side of an assignment inside the function itself.

Some other built-in functions that you may find useful are ROUND, EXP, and LN. The ROUND function works under the same circumstances as TRUNC, except it rounds the argument up to the next integer if its fractional part exceeds 0.5; otherwise it rounds down.

The EXP function, of type REAL, raises the number e (= 2.71828) to the power given by its parameter. The function EXP(2.3), for example, is equivalent to the expression

$$e^{2.3}$$

The built-in function LN calculates the natural logarithm of its parameter.

Procedures may use either VAR parameters, value parameters, or both. When declaring a procedure, you must separate parameters by commas if they share the same type identifier. Otherwise the parameters must be separated by semicolons.

It is extremely important to get the order of parameters right. If your program declares a procedure with the formal parameters First, Second, and Third, you must avoid calling this procedure with actual parameters that reflect a different order, such as FirstNum, ThirdNum, and SecondNum.

Finally, I remind you that when you call a procedure from within a program, you cannot pass a constant value to a VAR parameter. After all, how will the computer pass the computed value to this parameter back to a constant?

Reserved Words in Turbo Pascal

The following words always appear in capitals in the programming style of this book because they are *reserved words*, referred to in the text as "Turbo Pascal words." A programmer cannot use these words for any purpose outside of their intended missions—to frame the syntax of Turbo Pascal statements. Using them as variable names in a Turbo Pascal program will cause an error message and failure of the program to execute.

You will not recognize some of these words because the book does not cover the statements that use them. That does not change the fact that they are reserved, however. Beside each word, where applicable, I have included the statement or expression type that uses them.

Word	*Statement type*
AND	Boolean expression
ASM	
ARRAY	array declaration
BEGIN	statement delimiter
CASE	CASE statement
CONST	constant declaration
CONSTRUCTOR	
DESTRUCTOR	
DIV	integer division operator
DO	FOR- and WHILE-statements
DOWNTO	FOR statement
ELSE	IF-THEN-ELSE-statement
END	statement delimiter
FILE	file declaration
Word	*Statement type*
FOR	FOR-statement
FUNCTION	function declaration
GOTO	
IF	conditional statements
IMPLEMENTATION	

IN	
INLINE	
INTERFACE	
LABEL	
MOD	integer remainder operator
NIL	
NOT	Boolean expression
OBJECT	object declaration
OF	CASE statement
OR	Boolean expression
PACKED	
PROCEDURE	procedure declaration
PROGRAM	program header
RECORD	record declaration
REPEAT	REPEAT statement
SET	
SHL	
SHR	
STRING	string declaration
THEN	conditional statements
TO	FOR-statement
TYPE	user-defined TYPE declaration
UNIT	
UNTIL	REPEAT-statement
USES	USES statement
VAR	declaration statement
WHILE	WHILE statement
WITH	WITH statement
XOR	

In addition, you are urged not to use the following words as variables or other names:

ABSOLUTE	INTERRUPT
ASSEMBLER	NEAR
EXTERNAL	PRIVATE
FAR	VIRTUAL
FORWARD	

(cont.)

(cont.)